ARCHAEOLOGICAL
COMMENTARY
ON THE BIBLE

ARCHAEOLOGICAL COMMENTARY ON THE BIBLE

Gonzalo Báez-Camargo

Doubleday & Company, Inc.
Garden City, New York
1984

Library of Congress Cataloging in Publication Data
Gringoire, Pedro, 1899–1983
Archaeological commentary on the Bible.
Translation of: Comentario arqueológico de la Biblia.
Includes bibliographical references and index.
1. Bible—Antiquities. 2. Bible—Commentaries.
I. Title.
BS621.G6913 1984   220.9'3   82-45473
ISBN 0-385-17968-5

Dedicated
to the Five Great Ones
of Biblical Archaeology

Sir Flinders Petrie
William Foxwell Albright
Nelson Glueck
Roland de Vaux, O.P.
Kathleen Kenyon

IN MEMORIAM

CONTENTS

FOREWORD by Eugene A. Nida xi
PREFACE TO THE ENGLISH EDITION xiii
INTRODUCTION: ARCHAEOLOGY AND BIBLICAL STUDIES xv
LIST OF ILLUSTRATIONS xxvi
LIST OF ABBREVIATIONS xxviii
   BIBLIOGRAPHIC REFERENCES xxviii
   BOOKS OF THE BIBLE xxxiv
      In alphabetical order xxxiv
      In biblical order xxxvi

THE OLD TESTAMENT 1
   GENESIS 3
   EXODUS 31
   LEVITICUS 46
   NUMBERS 49
   DEUTERONOMY 53
   JOSHUA 58
   JUDGES 72
   RUTH 77
   THE FIRST BOOK OF SAMUEL 78
   THE SECOND BOOK OF SAMUEL 83
   THE FIRST BOOK OF THE KINGS 88

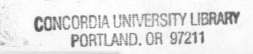

THE SECOND BOOK OF THE KINGS 102
THE FIRST BOOK OF THE CHRONICLES 121
THE SECOND BOOK OF THE CHRONICLES 123
EZRA 128
NEHEMIAH 131
ESTHER 135
JOB 138
THE PSALMS 141
THE PROVERBS 146
ECCLESIASTES 152
SONG OF SONGS (THE SONG OF SOLOMON) 156
ISAIAH 159
JEREMIAH 167
LAMENTATIONS 174
EZEKIEL 175
DANIEL 180
HOSEA 181
AMOS 182
JONAH 184
MICAH 186
NAHUM 187
HABAKKUK 188
ZEPHANIAH 190
ZECHARIAH 191
MALACHI 192

THE NEW TESTAMENT 193
MATTHEW 195
MARK 213
LUKE 218
JOHN 226
THE ACTS OF THE APOSTLES 236
THE LETTER OF PAUL TO THE ROMANS 248
THE FIRST LETTER OF PAUL TO THE CORINTHIANS 250

The Second Letter of Paul to the Corinthians   251
The Letter of Paul to the Galatians   252
The Letter of Paul to the Ephesians   253
The Letter of Paul to the Philippians   254
The Letter of Paul to the Colossians   256
The First Letter of Paul to the Thessalonians   257
The Second Letter of Paul to Timothy   258
The Letter of Paul to Philemon   259
The Letter of Jude   260
The Revelation to John (The Apocalypse)   262
A Selected Additional Bibliography   266
Index   269

FOREWORD

This book on biblical archaeology is remarkable in several respects. First, the author, Dr. Gonzalo Báez-Camargo, until his death in 1983, was a distinguished journalist, lecturer, biblical scholar, member of the Mexican Academy for the Spanish Language, and the author of twenty-two books, twelve of which are on biblical themes. He lectured on biblical and literary subjects in twenty-seven countries (in Latin America, Europe, and Asia) and personally visited almost all the important areas of the biblical world. Through the years he followed closely the work and publications of all leading biblical archaeologists and developed close links to several key Israeli archaeologists now engaged in important excavations.

Second, this volume makes no attempt to argue for or against any one "line" of evidence—so typical of technical discussions of scholarly controversies. Rather, it succinctly summarizes the evidence and scholarly opinions. Where there are significant differences concerning the interpretation of archaeological evidence these are, of course, mentioned.

Third, the information concerning archaeological evidence is arranged in biblical order, from Genesis to Revelation and by chapter and verse, with helpful cross-referencing and a valuable index. Bibliographical references are constantly given so that the reader may follow up any leads which seem to be especially important.

Fourth, this book maintains a positive approach to the biblical record and presents a strong confirmation of the biblical account. At the same time, there is no attempt to gloss over or avoid some of the continuing problems posed by archaeological evidence.

Fifth, though a number of books on biblical life and times have been translated from English into Spanish, this is evidently the first case of a book which has been widely acclaimed in the Spanish-speaking world and which has then been published in English. This volume is not, however, merely a translation of the Spanish text, published in 1979, but has been adapted and updated to make the information as accurate and timely as possible.

I was personally so impressed by the content and manner of presentation of the Spanish text that I immediately thought of the many Bible translators, now working in more than eight hundred languages, who would be greatly helped in their work by having such valuable information. The first suggestion was to translate the book into English and to put it out as a special publication for Bible translators, but it soon became evident that this exceptional contribution to the understanding and appreciation of the Bible deserved a much larger audience. Thousands of readers can now be grateful to Doubleday for making this available to the English-speaking world.

Eugene A. Nida
August 1982

PREFACE

TO THE ENGLISH EDITION

This book was originally written and published in Spanish with a modest end in view. As a Bible teacher for many years, I came to realize what a great help an elementary knowledge of biblical archaeology could be for the average student of the Bible. Most of the information, however, is to be found only in journals and books available in languages other than Spanish. Therefore, it seemed imperative to provide, in a condensed, systematic way, basic archaeological data which would throw light on specific verses, passages, or subjects in the Bible.

That was the purpose of this book in its original edition in Spanish. I had not even the slightest idea that it might be useful outside the Spanish-speaking world. To my great surprise, Dr. Eugene A. Nida, a well-known authority in linguistics and Bible translation, suggested the desirability of having the book translated and published in English.

Since there already exists in English an amazing amount of information on biblical archaeology, this book does not aim to present new discoveries. As the reader will note, most of its sources are in English. But the way the material is presented, selected, and organized by chapter and verse in a single volume makes the book particularly useful for the ordinary student of the Bible who has neither the time nor the means to delve into the imposing bibliography on the subject.

Like all other sciences, biblical archaeology is in a constant state of development. Explorations are taking place and new discoveries are being made every summer at many sites in the world of the Bible. Accordingly, an effort has been made to bring this English edition up to date. The data in the original Spanish edition have been thoroughly revised by a number of corrections, expansions, and additions.

To Dr. Nida I desire to express my gratitude for his personal endeavor to make the publication of this book possible, and both to him and to Mr. Paul C. Clarke for the editing of the English manuscript. To the Reverend Harold P. Scanlin I owe very special recognition for the great amount of time he invested in a careful checking of references and other technical matters. I am indebted also to Dr. Harold W. Fehderau, Coordinator of the United Bible Societies' Translations Department for the Americas, for the facilities extended to me in the preparation of the present translation. And I wish to thank my good friend and colleague Dr. William L. Wonderly for his invaluable assistance at the early stages of the preparation of the English text.

Gonzalo Báez-Camargo
July 1982

INTRODUCTION
ARCHAEOLOGY AND BIBLICAL STUDIES

The science of archaeology is relatively modern. To be sure, for a long while there had occurred in various parts of the world explorations, excavations, and discoveries having archaeological significance. But for the most part such finds were almost haphazard, accidental, without carefully planned procedures, in what Mortimer Wheeler has called "picnic-party excavations."[1] This same author states that "the first scientific exploration in the history of archaeology" was that which was made in one of the tumuli, or funeral mounds, of Virginia by Thomas Jefferson, who later became president of the United States.

It was only in the first half of the nineteenth century A.D. that archaeologists, as yet mostly bungling amateurs and laboring at the cost of much trial and error, began to create what may now truly be called the science of archaeology. At the same time, there began to appear that special application of the science which we now refer to as biblical archaeology. As W. F. Albright, the patriarch of biblical archaeology, has said, "from the chaos of prehistory the Bible projected as though it were a monstrous fossil, with no contemporary evidence to demonstrate its authenticity and its origin in a human world like ours."[2]

Indeed, the world of the Bible seemed to be a world quite different from our own. "Sacred history," as it had been taught for centuries, seemed almost to have unfolded on another planet and at a stage completely unrelated to the history of the peoples of this earth. It was true that many places mentioned in the Bible could be identified, but the biblical events themselves seemed to have taken place as in a dream. For all practical purposes there appeared to be no difference between the stories of the Bible and those of Greek and Roman mythology.

But biblical archaeology has now completely changed such an image of biblical history. This history no longer appears like something wrapped in a nebula—full, indeed, of light, yet imprecise and distant. The personages of the Bible have ceased to be ghostly figures, imposing in their way, yet alienated from this earth of ours. They have come to life as real beings of flesh and blood, moving in a geographic milieu that we can visit today. They left behind them relics of their activities and customs that we can now inspect in the museums. These are the material traces of their transit through this world. This branch of archaeology has given us, above all, a strong sense of the historical reality of the events and the persons that we read about in the Bible. "By the aid of archaeology," says Millar Burrows, "the study of the Bible ceases to be, as it were, suspended in the air, and gets its feet upon the ground."[3]

The story of biblical archaeology, from its uncertain beginnings to its development in present explorations, is truly a fascinating one. Today this science makes use of numerous instructive experiences, and it freely draws from the resources of practically all the other sciences. Our purpose in this introduction is simply to give a very brief synopsis of that story.

By biblical archaeology we mean that branch of the science that has to do with Bible lands, that geographical area extending from Mesopotamia to Egypt and from Asia Minor to the Red Sea, and reaching as far west as the Italian peninsula. Biblical archaeology, however, is not restricted to sites expressly mentioned in the Bible. Excavations of other sites in the same general region have shed a good deal of light on biblical history in matters such as customs in general and particularly in the field of languages.

For many centuries ancient ruins had been known to exist in Bible lands. Palestine in particular is filled with mounds of various dimensions, which the Arabs call tells, and ruins more or less buried under earth and rubble, which they call khirbets. Thus there are many places which are popularly known as Tell- this or Khirbet- that. Rudimentary explorations gave rise to the knowledge, or at least to the suspicion, that the tells contained the remains of ancient population centers. Fortunately for the archaeologist, the people of ancient times had the habit of building their cities on the leveled-off remains of towns that had been destroyed by wars or natural calamities or had simply been abandoned by their inhabitants. Others would build anew on the ground that covered this rubble. Thus a tell would grow layer after layer, sometimes attaining a very considerable volume and height. By digging into these tells, archaeologists have been able to bring to light the remains of cities which disappeared long ago. Their labor has truly been, in the words of the title of one of the books of the eminent archaeologist André Parrot, "the discovery of buried worlds."

At Megiddo, for example, as many as twenty layers or strata have been unearthed, the earliest and lowest dating from the fourth millennium B.C. At Tell es-Sultan, the Jericho of the Old Testament, one of the oldest cities in the world (if not the oldest), archaeologists have been able to discern, in spite of the devastating effects of the erosion of many centuries, a succession of strata or levels of occupation spanning from the eighth to the second millennium B.C. At Hazor twenty-one strata have been discovered. And so it is in various other cases. Particularly valuable for the archaeologist have been the pottery remains found in the rubble. Usually these are pieces of broken pottery called shards or ostraca, but occasionally ceramic objects almost completely intact have been recovered. The comparative study of the characteristic ceramic forms and designs predominating in various epochs at various places has developed into a complete and surprisingly exact science, so that on the basis of the pottery remains found in the different layers it has become possible to determine with reasonable accuracy the chronology of an entire archaeological site. A further help to this dating from pottery remains derives from the habit of ancient peoples to use bits of broken pottery for jottings, much as we use scraps of paper today. A very considerable number of these shards with writing on them have been well preserved, and so they constitute invaluable documentary evidence by which the development of writing can be traced.

More or less systematic exploration of tells and other ruins began in 1838 with Edward Robinson and Eli Smith, the latter a former missionary in Syria. Their work was principally surface exploration, with very little systematic digging. Albright refers to Robinson as "the father of scientific topography in Palestine." Both of these men made important explorations at Jerusalem. Robinson discovered the remains of an arch which now bears his name. This was part of a series of arches which supported a stairway leading from the west to the south portico of the temple and which has been identified as such by the Israeli archaeologist Benjamin Mazar. For a long while it was believed that these arches had supported a bridge which connected the temple esplanade with the upper city situated on the other side of the Central Valley called by Josephus the Tyropoeon.

The first excavations made in proper form were those by Louis Saulcy (1850), followed by Charles Warren (1867) and Charles Clermont-Ganneau (1869). Saulcy excavated the so-called Tomb of the Kings, to the north of the walled city. Later this was identified as the burial place of Queen Helen of Adiabene (a district in the upper Tigris valley), who had converted to Judaism. It was Clermont-Ganneau who rescued from imminent destruction by the Arabs the famous stele of King Mesa of Moab. H. Guthe, a German, began excavation of the "City of David," the eastern hill situated to the south of the Temple Mount. C. R. Conder and H. H. Kitchener (1872) and G. Schumacher (1884) made other surface explorations. Schumacher began the excavation of Megiddo in 1903–5.

Biblical archaeology began to reach a much higher level of sophistication in 1890 with the memorable work of Flinders Petrie, followed in 1891 by F. J. Bliss. Up till that time the organization which sponsored such explorations and excavations was the meritorious Palestine Exploration Fund of Great Britain, founded in 1865. Toward the end of the nineteenth and at the beginning of the twentieth centuries, A.D., however, other important sponsoring agencies were established: the Ecole Biblique de Jérusalem of the Dominicans (1890), the Deutsche Orient-Gesellschaft (1898), the American Schools of Oriental Research (now the Albright Institute; 1900), and the Deutsche-Evangelische Institut für Altertumskunde des Heiligen Landes (1902). Various others have since arisen. Since World War II archaeological explorations in Palestine have enjoyed the valuable patronage of the Department of Antiquities of Jordan, the Hebrew University of Jerusalem, and the Department of Antiquities and Museums of Israel. Universities and cultural and scientific societies of Great Britain, the United States, France, Germany, and other nations have added valuable support to the ongoing work of biblical archaeology.

Perhaps the three most notable discoveries realized in Palestine until the present date (1981) have been the cuneiform tablets of Ras Shamra (Ugarit), the Qumran (Dead Sea) scrolls, and the cuneiform tablets of

Ebla. The first occurred in 1928 and brought to light texts which greatly increased our knowledge of the religion and customs of Canaan before the Israelite conquest and during the earliest stages of the Israelite colonization. The Ugaritic language of the Ras Shamra tablets is similar to Hebrew; both languages have come from the same Semitic base. Consequently, the discovery of those tablets has contributed appreciably to biblical philology. The Qumran scrolls are of two kinds: copies of biblical (Old Testament) books which are older by at least a thousand years than any previously known Hebrew Old Testament manuscripts and nonbiblical texts which afford much valuable information concerning the organization, doctrines, and customs of a Jewish sect known previously only from information provided by contemporary secular sources. These precious documents were discovered in 1947. Finally, the excavation of the ruins of another very ancient city of Canaan, Ebla, lying to the south of present-day Aleppo, brought to light in 1974 tablets which date as early as 2400 B.C. Later, in the excavations of 1975, some 15,000 more tablets were uncovered. Then in 1976 some 600 other fragments were found. These are inscribed with cuneiform characters in another Canaanite dialect related to Ugaritic and Hebrew. They belonged to the archives of the royal palace in Ebla and probably constitute only a small part of the total archives.

Some of the more illustrious names in the field of biblical archaeology from 1890 till the present date are the following: L. H. Vincent and Roland de Vaux, both of the Ecole Biblique de Jérusalem. Vincent undertook important archaeological labors in this city. The results are seen in his monumental work *Jérusalem de l'Ancien Testament*. De Vaux excavated Tirzah and carried on excavations in Qumran. R. A. Parker worked in Jerusalem. G. A. Reisner and C. S. Fisher excavated Samaria; R. A. S. Macalister, Gezer; E. Sellin, J. Garstang, and more recently Kathleen Kenyon, Jericho. Sellin also excavated Taanach. Nelson Glueck made extremely careful explorations of archaeological sites in the Negev and the eastern side of the Jordan, and at Eziongeber he excavated ruins which date from before the time of Solomon. Albright excavated Kiriath-sepher; E. L. Sukenik, Samaria; G. Ernest Wright, Shechem; Yigael Yadin, Hazor; Fisher (mentioned above), A. Rowe, and G. M. Fitzgerald excavated Beth-shean (Beishan). Kenyon also accomplished important work in the City of David in the southeastern hill of Jerusalem. In recent years Mazar has made some important excavations at the foot of the wall of the Temple Mount. Besides those already mentioned, the state of Israel has produced a brilliant generation of biblical archaeologists, such as Ruth Amiran, Nahman Avigad, Yohanan Aharoni, T. Dothan, M. Avi-Yonah, P. Bar Adon, J. Kaplan, Magen Broshi, A. Negev, Avraham Biran, as well as several others.

When a person becomes aware of the discoveries of biblical archaeology, the first question usually is whether these confirm "the truth of the Bible." The answer depends on what is understood by biblical truth. Must biblical history be understood as a detailed and precise chronological arrangement of events and other facts? In many cases archaeological discoveries have indeed confirmed in a remarkable way the historical data of the Bible. But in other cases certain serious problems occur in matters of detail and chronology. These will be dealt with at their proper places in the commentary.

Why do these problems arise? First of all, it is important to realize that the Bible is not a textbook of history in the manner in which we usually think of history. Biblical history is basically "the history of salvation." Strictly speaking, the Bible is not even the history of the people of Israel. The supreme purpose of the Bible is to reveal God's redemptive action in the relationship between God and humanity. This action took place as God intervened in human affairs on the earth in specific historical contexts. It is for this reason, and only for this reason, that the Bible contains history in the general sense of the term. In other words, what the Bible does is to register God's mighty acts, motivated by his redemptive purpose in the course of history.

Sacred historians did not write history in the same manner as Herodotus, Xenophon, or Plutarch wrote history in ancient times, and much less so in the manner of present-day historians. Their business was to show the mighty hand of God at work both in natural phenomena and in human affairs. They were primarily concerned with those aspects of history which served to reveal the redemptive activities of the one true God. Details were of secondary relevance. They set forth in vivid terms God's loving and merciful actions, even when these actions took the form of stern rebuke and terrible punishment. The rest they touched on lightly, summarized, condensed, or even omitted altogether.

From our modern point of view we expect the historian to give us facts, figures, and other data with meticulous accuracy, all within a framework of strict chronological order. What we want is information and, as far as possible, exhaustive information. But the major purpose of biblical historians was not to impart mere information. They were not so much interested in the details as in the *meaning* of events. In all the happenings they recorded they saw the "signs" of divine intervention and reported those happenings in such a manner as to try to uncover their deep moral and religious significance. Therefore they would often compress and even telescope events, and in matters of detail frequently used round and even symbolical numbers instead of precise figures; but they were always careful not to obscure the profound significance of events and things.

When biblical history is focused and understood in this transcendental manner as the history of salvation, as the document of "biblical faith," we can see how pointless it is to expect archaeology to demonstrate or to prove the truth of this faith. This faith is principally and essentially concerned with relationships between Creator and creature, between God and humanity, and it can neither be demonstrated nor refuted by the discoveries of archaeology, whatever they may be.

Eminent Christian and Jewish archaeologists as people of biblical faith agree with Glueck when he says: "Those people are essentially of little faith who seek through archaeological corroboration of historical source materials in the Bible to validate its religious teachings and spiritual insights."[4] And G. W. van Beek writes: "Archaeology does not and cannot prove the Bible. The Bible deals with man's relationship to God, and is, therefore, beyond the proof of archaeology or any other discipline. While archaeology confirms many details of history and lays bare the environment of the Bible, the history and environment with which it deals is human, not divine. It can neither confirm theology nor open the realm of faith."[5]

Archaeological "proof," affirms Wright, "certainly . . . does not extend to the validity of the religious claims the Bible would place upon us, and we must remember that the Bible is not a mine for scientifically grounded certainties about anything. It is instead a literature that places before us one of history's major religious options."[6] What then is the relevancy of the discoveries of archaeology with respect to the Bible? In order to understand the tremendous contribution which archaeology does make to the field of biblical studies, it is necessary to begin, as we have already tried to do, by recognizing its limitations and then to understand the nature of its contribution, all the while keeping in mind what the central purpose of biblical history is. We live in the context of history, and it is in this context that the Bible brings to us the message of salvation. Archaeology likewise is related to history, and accordingly its contributions to the understanding of the Bible are of tremendous importance.

"What archaeology can do for biblical study," Wright goes on to say in the passage cited above, "is to provide a physical context in time and place which was the environment of the people who produced the Bible or are mentioned in it. Inscriptional evidence is of exceptional importance for biblical backgrounds and even for occasional mention of biblical people and places." Another eminent archaeologist and biblical theologian, Burrows, declares, "What we really need, after all, is not to defend the Bible but to understand it. It is here that archaeology makes its greatest contribution."[7]

De Vaux says, "It must be understood that archaeology cannot 'prove' the Bible. The truth of the Bible is of a religious order; it speaks of God and man and their mutual relations. This spiritual truth can neither be proven nor contradicted, nor can it be confirmed or invalidated by the material discoveries of archaeology."[8]

In a word, the contribution of archaeology to the study of the Bible is to cast light on the historical and cultural stage in which occurred those events which revealed the intervention of God in human affairs as he unfolded his plans for the redemption of humanity. Up to the present time archaeology has had two effects upon the historical authenticity of the biblical narrative.

On the one hand, it has with increasing clarity placed this narrative within the framework of general history. No longer do we see two different worlds, one the world of "sacred history" and the other the world of "profane history." All of history is one history, and it is God's history, for God is the God of all history. This was one of the distinctive messages of the great Hebrew prophets, and in this their universalism consisted. By fitting biblical history into general history, archaeology has demonstrated the validity of many biblical references and data. It has cast light, either implicit or explicit, on many of its allusions to the customs and cultures which prevailed at various periods within biblical history, and it has given us insights into the meaning of a number of passages which otherwise would be not only obscure but also puzzling and even disturbing to the ordinary reader.

On the other hand, archaeology has also given rise to some real problems in regard to the relationship between its findings and certain details in the biblical narrative, especially if these details are taken in a strictly literal sense. This volume mentions some of those problems and plausible theories which have been proposed for their solution. In a few cases, perhaps it will never be possible to say the final word. This is due to the considerable time that has elapsed since the events and to other factors that cannot be completely eliminated. There are, for instance, the great differences between the cultures and mentality of the peoples of antiquity and those of today. At any rate, if archaeology has until now not only raised but left unanswered a lot of questions, this nevertheless provides a worthwhile stimulus to further and more thorough research on the part of archaeologists and to a more solid reflection on the part of Bible scholars, hence leading to a sharper discernment between what is fundamental and what is superficial.

One of the valuable services rendered by archaeology has been the certain identification of many places mentioned in the Bible. In some cases attempts to identify places by other means had been so uncertain that not a few persons had come to think that many of those places never really existed. In a number of instances archaeological discoveries have been truly amazing, and attention is called to them in this commentary. In most cases, however, the detailed and precise identification of so-called holy places is still very doubtful. Unfortunately, traditions concerning places associated with the life of Jesus are rarely older than the third century of our era. Some of the traditions are creditable, but by no means all of them. In most cases archaeology provides evidence, not to the authenticity of the places themselves, but simply to the antiquity of the traditions concerning them.

This fact applies even more to those other traditions which have a weaker basis and which sometimes are even in direct contradiction to clear statements in the Bible. Perhaps the most notable example of such is a place called Tabgha on the shore of the Sea of Galilee. A chapel which has stood there since at least the fourth century B.C. has been traditionally identified as the location of the feeding of the five thousand (see the commentary on Mt 14:19). On the matter of the "moving" of holy places for practical reasons, the incident mentioned by Burrows is worth remembering: "A guide in Egypt remarked frankly to a friend of the writer, 'The place where Moses was found in the bulrushes used to be farther up the river, but we moved it down here to make it convenient for the tourists'."[9]

While archaeology has indeed proved to be a valuable aid in the study of the Bible, the Bible itself has proved in some instances to be no less an aid to archaeology. At certain times archaeologists must have said to themselves, "According to the Bible we should find such and such an important site around here." Then they started to dig, and they found it! The experience of Yadin, who directed the excavation of Hazor on the basis of the data he found in the Bible, may have been shared more or less by other archaeologists. In referring to the discovery of the great Solomonic gate in that city, Yadin remarks, "We went about discovering it with Bible in one hand and spade in the other."[10]

"The progress of archaeological investigation will make the Bible stand out more and more brightly against the background of the ancient Orient," wrote Albright,[11] adding that due to archaeology the Bible "no longer appears as an absolutely isolated monument of the past, as a phenomenon without relation to its environment."[12] Parrot, professor in the School of the Louvre and curator in chief of the French National Museums, who headed the mission which excavated Mari, has summed up three principal aspects of the contribution which archaeology has made to our understanding of the Bible. "Firstly, it has confirmed *historical facts*" narrated in the Bible; and even if some inaccuracies of detail were to be discovered in the biblical record, these "do not detract from the 'substantial' truth of the historical [biblical] tradition. . . . Secondly, archaeology has established the exact locations of places. . . . The sites once rediscovered and located on the ground, it seems that the Revelation becomes more tangible. . . . But archaeology has done more than simply confirm secular or sacred history and rediscover its sites. It has restored to us the soul of those vanished peoples itself, by revealing in the documents dug from the soil their way of life. It shows us the God of Revelation at work."[13]

Accordingly, the author hopes that this volume, along with the exegetical and hermeneutical aids available to the reader, will prove to be a valuable additional help toward understanding the biblical text. It is hoped that the reader will become more aware of the reality and authenticity of the eternal message of salvation contained in the Bible.

NOTES

(For a key to the abbreviations used here, see the List of Abbreviations: Bibliographic References, p. xxviii.)

1. *Archaeology from the Earth*, Oxford: Clarendon Press, 1954, p. 8.
2. Cited by G. Ernest Wright, BAW, p. 18.
3. WMTS, p. 115.
4. Cited by G. Ernest Wright, BAR-1, p. 18.
5. *Interpreter's Dictionary of the Bible*, I, 205, article "Archaeology."
6. BA, 34 (1971), p. 73.
7. WMTS, p. 6.
8. NATC, p. 68.
9. WMTS, p. 9.
10. BAR-2, p. 199.
11. APB, p. 177.
12. Ibid., p. 127.
13. DBW, pp. 112, 114–15, 116.

LIST OF ILLUSTRATIONS

following page 82

Ur ziggurat
Ancient Jericho
Dome of the Rock
Siloam inscription from Hezekiah's tunnel
Mosaic of the church at et-Tabgha
Storehouse at Beersheba
Herod's funeral monument
"Moses' seat" inscription
Inscription of Pilate's name
Western (Wailing) Wall

following page 130

"Tomb of Herod's Family"
Alabaster flasks from the Holy Land
An "Upper Room"
Qumran Cave 4
Jericho of Jesus' time
Gerasa, part of the Decapolis
Pool of Siloam
Pool of Bethzatha

The "Holy Thursday Stairway"
"Jacob's Well"
Roman games inscribed in stone
The Antonia

following page 178

Bay of Tabgha
Ruins of ancient Perga
Chapel of the Ascension
Ancient Corinth
Temple of Apollo at Corinth
Statue of Artemis
The great theater at Ephesus
Temple of Artemis in Sardis

LIST OF ABBREVIATIONS

BIBLIOGRAPHIC REFERENCES

AAS   Parrot, André. *The Arts of Assyria*. New York: Golden Press, 1961.

ABB   Cornfeld, Gaalyah. *Archaeology of the Bible: Book by Book*. New York: Harper, 1976.

ADHL   The Archaeological Institute of America, ed. *Archaeological Discoveries in the Holy Land*. New York: Thomas Y. Crowell, 1967.

AEB   Pettinato, Giovanni. *The Archives of Ebla*. Garden City, N.Y.: Doubleday, 1981.

AGA   Avigad, N., and Y. Yadin. *A Genesis Apocryphon*. Jerusalem: Magnes Press, 1956.

AHL   Kenyon, Kathleen M. *Archaeology in the Holy Land*. 4th ed. London and New York: Ernest Benn and W. W. Norton, 1979.

AHT   Parrot, André. *Abraham and His Times*. Philadelphia: Fortress Press, 1968.

ANEP   Pritchard, James B. *The Ancient Near East in Pictures*. Princeton, N.J.: Princeton University Press, 1954.

ANES   Pritchard, James B. *The Ancient Near East, Supplementary*

Texts and Pictures. Princeton, N.J.: Princeton University Press, 1969.

ANET   Pritchard, James B. *Ancient Near Eastern Texts Related to the Old Testament*. 2nd ed. Princeton, N.J.: Princeton University Press, 1955.

AOT   Schiaparelli, G. *Astronomy in the Old Testament*. Oxford: Clarendon Press, 1905.

APB   Albright, William F. *The Archaeology of Palestine and the Bible*. Cambridge, Mass.: American Schools of Oriental Research, 1974.

AR   *Ariel*. A Quarterly Review of the Arts and Sciences in Israel.

BA   *The Biblical Archaeologist*.

BAH   Horn, Siegfried H. *Biblical Archaeology After 30 Years*. Berrien Springs, Mich.: Andrews University Press, 1978.

BAR   Wright, G. Ernest, and David N. Freedman, eds. *The Biblical Archaeologist Reader*, 2 vols. Garden City, N.Y.: Doubleday, 1961–64.

BAW   Wright, G. Ernest. *Biblical Archaeology*. Rev. ed. Philadelphia: Westminster Press, 1962.

BOT   Parrot, André. *Babylon and the Old Testament*. New York: Philosophical Library, 1958.

BRA   Kenyon, Kathleen M. *The Bible and Recent Archaeology*. Atlanta, Ga.: John Knox Press, 1978.

CHB   Ackroyd, P. R., and C. F. Evans, eds. *The Cambridge History of the Bible*. Cambridge: Cambridge University Press, 1970.

CNI   *Christian News from Israel*.

DBW   Parrot, André. *Discovering Buried Worlds*. London: SCM Press, 1955.

DDB   Ausejo, Serafín de, ed. *Diccionario de la Biblia*. Barcelona: Herder, 1963.

DDQ   Lamadrid, Antonio G. *Los descubrimientos de Qumrán.* Madrid: Instituto Español de Estudios Eclesiásticos, 1956.

DEB   Westphal, A., ed. *Dictionnaire encyclopédique de la Bible.* Paris: "Je Sers," 1932.

DOTT   Thomas, D. Winton, ed. *Documents from Old Testament Times.* Edinburgh: Thomas Nelson, 1958.

DSM   Burrows, M., J. C. Trever, and W. H. Brownlee. *The Dead Sea Scrolls of St. Mark's Monastery.* New Haven, Conn.: American Schools of Oriental Research, 1950.

DSS   Burrows, Millar. *The Dead Sea Scrolls.* New York: Viking, 1955.

DSSE   Vermes, G. *The Dead Sea Scrolls in English.* 2nd ed. Baltimore: Penguin, 1975.

EAE   Avi-Yonah, M., ed. *Encyclopedia of Archaeological Excavations in the Holy Land.* 4 vols. Jerusalem: Israel Exploration Society and Massada Press, 1975–78.

EB   *Enciclopedia de la Biblia.* Barcelona: Garriga, 1969.

ETB   Montet, Pierre. *Egypt and the Bible.* Philadelphia: Fortress Press, 1968.

FFB   *Fauna and Flora of the Bible.* Helps for Translators. 2nd ed. London: United Bible Societies, 1980.

FNA   Parrot, André. *The Flood and Noah's Ark.* London: SCM Press, 1955.

GAQ   Fitzmyer, Joseph A. *The Genesis Apocryphon of Qumran Cave 1, A Commentary.* 2nd ed. Rome: Biblical Institute Press, 1971.

GCH   Parrot, André. *Golgotha and the Church of the Holy Sepulchre.* New York: Philosophical Library, 1957.

GNB   Good News Bible.

GTS   Simons, J. *The Geographical and Topographical Texts of the Old Testament.* Leiden: Brill, 1959.

HAZ   Pearlman, Moshé. *Hazor*. Israel: National Parks Authority, n.d.

HYY   Yadin, Yigael. *Hazor: The Rediscovery of a Great Citadel of the Bible*. New York: Random House, 1975.

IDB   *The Interpreter's Dictionary of the Bible*. New York and Nashville, Tenn.: Abingdon, 1962.

IEJ   *Israel Exploration Journal*.

IFJ   Pax, Wolfgang E. *In the Footsteps of Jesus*. Tel Aviv: Nateev Publishing, 1970.

JAT   Vincent, L. H., and A. M. Steve. *Jérusalem de l'Ancien Testament*. Paris: Gabalda, 1954.

JBL   *Journal of Biblical Literature*.

JOT   Simons, J. *Jerusalem in the Old Testament*. Leiden: Brill, 1952.

JPW   *The Jerusalem Post Weekly*.

JR   Mazar, B., et al. *Jerusalem Revealed*. Jerusalem: Israel Exploration Society, 1975.

KJV   King James Version.

LC   Gray, John. *The Legacy of Canaan*. Leiden: Brill, 1957.

LOC   Parrot, André. *Land of Christ*. Philadelphia: Fortress Press, 1968.

LRQ   Gringoire, Pedro [Báez-Camargo, Gonzalo]. *Los Rollos de Qumran*. Mexico: Edamex, 1979.

LTR   *La Table Ronde*, No. 154. Paris: Librairie Plon, October 1960.

MAW   The Haifa Museum of Ancient Art. *Music in the Ancient World*. 2nd ed. Ministry of Education and Culture and Department of Antiquities and Museums, 1979.

MDQ   Moraldi, Luigi. *I Manoscritti di Qumrân*. Turin: Unione Tipografico-Editrice Torinese, 1971.

MLB   Parrot, André. *Le Musée du Louvre et la Bible.* Neuchâtel and Paris: Delachaux et Niestlé, 1957.

MLD   Burrows, Millar. *More Light on the Dead Sea Scrolls.* New York: Viking, 1958.

MMY   Habermann, A. M., ed. *Megiloth Midbar Yehudah.* Jerusalem: Maybaroth Lesifruth, 1959.

MTL   Mazar, Benjamin. *The Mountain of the Lord.* Garden City, N.Y.: Doubleday, 1975.

NAOT   Parrot, André. *Nineveh and the Old Testament.* New York: Philosophical Library, 1955.

NATC   Sanders, James A., ed. *Near Eastern Archaeology in the Twentieth Century.* Garden City, N.Y.: Doubleday, 1970.

NDBA   Freedman, D. N., and J. C. Greenfield, eds. *New Directions in Biblical Archaeology.* Garden City, N.Y.: Doubleday, 1971.

OLB   Avi-Yonah, M., and E. G. Kraeling. *Our Living Bible.* Jerusalem: Biblical Publications, 1962.

OSJ   Glueck, Nelson. *The Other Side of the Jordan.* Rev. ed. Cambridge, Mass.: American Schools of Oriental Research, 1970.

PBE   Cornfeld, Gaalyah, ed. *Pictorial Biblical Encyclopedia.* Tel Aviv: Hamikra Baolam, 1964.

POTA   Franken, H. J., and C. A. Franken-Battershill. *A Primer of Old Testament Archaeology.* Leiden: Brill, 1963.

RQ   *Revue de Qumran.*

RSAT   Jacob, Edmond. *Ras Shamra et l'Ancien Testament.* Neuchâtel and Paris: Delachaux et Niestlé, 1960.

RSV   Revised Standard Version.

SCKI   Parrot, André. *Samaria: The Capital of the Kingdom of Israel.* New York: Philosophical Library, 1958.

SNT Stendhal, Krister, ed. *The Scrolls and the New Testament.* New York: Harper, 1957.

SPA Michaud, Henri. *Sur la pierre et l'argile.* Neuchâtel and Paris: Delachaux et Niestlé, 1958.

SW Wright, G. Ernest. *Shechem.* New York: McGraw-Hill, 1965.

TAL Torrey, C. C. *The Apocryphal Literature.* New Haven, Conn.: Yale University Press, 1945.

TANT Finegan, Jack. *The Archaeology of the New Testament.* Princeton: Princeton University Press, 1969.

TB Parrot, André. *The Tower of Babel.* New York: Philosophical Library, 1955.

TBAR *The Biblical Archaeology Review.*

TCD Shanks, Hershel. *The City of David.* Tel Aviv: Bazak, 1973.

THL Avi-Yonah, M. *The Holy Land.* London: Thames and Hudson, 1972.

THS Birnbaum, S. A. *The Hebrew Scripts.* Leiden: Brill, 1971.

TNT Metzger, Bruce M. *The Text of the New Testament.* 2nd ed. New York and Oxford: Oxford University Press, 1968.

TOJ Parrot, André. *The Temple of Jerusalem.* New York: Philosophical Library, 1955.

TOT Würthwein, Ernst. *The Text of the Old Testament.* Rev. ed. Grand Rapids, Mich.: Eerdmans, 1980.

UAB Schmökel, Hartmut. *Ur, Assur und Babylon; drei Jahrtausende in Zweistromland.* Stuttgart: G. Kilpper, 1955.

UT Gordon, Cyrus H. *Ugaritic Textbook.* Rome: Pontificium Institutum Biblicum, 1965.

UTB Orlinsky, Harry M. *Understanding the Bible Through History and Archaeology.* New York: KTAV, 1972.

WB Avi-Yonah, M., and Abraham Malamat, eds. *The World of the Bible.* New York: Educational Heritage, 1964.

WFJ   Josephus. *The Works of Flavius Josephus*. Hartford, Conn.:
       Scranton, 1902.

WMTS   Burrows, Millar. *What Mean These Stones?* New Haven:
       American Schools of Oriental Research, 1941.

In this book, portions of documents from the Ancient Near East are
frequently quoted. Words and phrases given in these ancient languages
are printed in italics.

When English translations of these ancient texts are given, parentheses, ( ), mark interpolations made by the translator for a better
understanding of the translation. Material enclosed in square brackets,
[ ], supplies words that are missing in the original, generally because
the original text is broken or damaged.

BOOKS OF THE BIBLE

The verse numbers in some places in the Old Testament are different
in the Hebrew Bible and English translations. In such cases the verse
number from the English is given first, followed by the Hebrew verse
number in parentheses: for example, Psalms 49:10(11).

IN ALPHABETICAL ORDER:

Acts	Acts of the Apostles
Amos	Amos
1 Chron	1 Chronicles
2 Chron	2 Chronicles
Col	Colossians
1 Cor	1 Corinthians
2 Cor	2 Corinthians
Dan	Daniel
Deut	Deuteronomy
Eccles	Ecclesiastes
Eph	Ephesians
Esther	Esther
Ex	Exodus

Ezek	Ezekiel
Ezra	Ezra
Gal	Galatians
Gen	Genesis
Hab	Habakkuk
Hag	Haggai
Heb	Hebrews
Hos	Hosea
Is	Isaiah
Jas	James
Jer	Jeremiah
Jn	John
1 Jn	1 John
2 Jn	2 John
3 Jn	3 John
Job	Job
Joel	Joel
Jon	Jonah
Josh	Joshua
Jude	Jude
Judg	Judges
1 Kings	1 Kings
2 Kings	2 Kings
Lam	Lamentations
Lev	Leviticus
Lk	Luke
Mal	Malachi
Mic	Micah
Mk	Mark
Mt	Matthew
Nahum	Nahum
Neh	Nehemiah
Num	Numbers
Obad	Obadiah
1 Pet	1 Peter
2 Pet	2 Peter
Phil	Philippians
Philem	Philemon

Prov	Proverbs
Ps	Psalms
Rev	Revelation
Rom	Romans
Ruth	Ruth
1 Sam	1 Samuel
2 Sam	2 Samuel
Song	Song of Solomon
	(Song of Songs)
1 Thess	1 Thessalonians
2 Thess	2 Thessalonians
1 Tim	1 Timothy
2 Tim	2 Timothy
Tit	Titus
Zech	Zechariah
Zeph	Zephaniah

IN BIBLICAL ORDER:

Old Testament

Gen	Genesis	Eccles	Ecclesiastes
Ex	Exodus	Song	Song of Solomon
Lev	Leviticus		(Song of Songs)
Num	Numbers	Is	Isaiah
Deut	Deuteronomy	Jer	Jeremiah
Josh	Joshua	Lam	Lamentations
Judg	Judges	Ezek	Ezekiel
Ruth	Ruth	Dan	Daniel
1 Sam	1 Samuel	Hos	Hosea
2 Sam	2 Samuel	Joel	Joel
1 Kings	1 Kings	Amos	Amos
2 Kings	2 Kings	Obad	Obadiah
1 Chron	1 Chronicles	Jon	Jonah
2 Chron	2 Chronicles	Mic	Micah
Ezra	Ezra	Nahum	Nahum
Neh	Nehemiah	Hab	Habakkuk
Esther	Esther	Zeph	Zephaniah
Job	Job	Hag	Haggai

Ps	Psalms	Zech	Zechariah
Prov	Proverbs	Mal	Malachi

New Testament

Mt	Matthew	1 Tim	1 Timothy
Mk	Mark	2 Tim	2 Timothy
Lk	Luke	Tit	Titus
Jn	John	Philem	Philemon
Acts	Acts of the Apostles	Heb	Hebrews
Rom	Romans	Jas	James
1 Cor	1 Corinthians	1 Pet	1 Peter
2 Cor	2 Corinthians	2 Pet	2 Peter
Gal	Galatians	1 Jn	1 John
Eph	Ephesians	2 Jn	2 John
Phil	Philippians	3 Jn	3 John
Col	Colossians	Jude	Jude
1 Thess	1 Thessalonians	Rev	Revelation
2 Thess	2 Thessalonians		

THE OLD TESTAMENT

GENESIS

Gen 1:1 —— *In the beginning God created* From Akkadian texts found chiefly in the excavations of Nineveh, Ashur, and Kish, it has been possible to reconstruct the so-called Chaldean Account of Creation, first published in 1876 in a translation by George Smith. This narrative is also called *Enuma Elish* ("When on high . . ."), after its opening words, "When on high the heaven had not been named"—which recalls the fact that the book of Genesis is called in Hebrew *Bereshith*, after its first word, which is literally "In the beginning-of." A comparison of the Chaldean account with that of Genesis shows some parallels and at the same time some substantial differences. The mythological nature of the former is very pronounced, as is also its obvious polytheism. As in other pagan cosmogonies, in the Chaldean story the universe is the product of the union of a divine pair—in this case Apsu, the "begetter" of heaven and earth, and Mummu Tiamat, "she who bore them all," whereas in Genesis the creation is the sole work of the one transcendent God. After allowance is made for this fundamental difference, the two narratives have in common the concept of a primeval chaos from which the ordered universe emerges. In Genesis this is accomplished by the power of the word of God; in the Chaldean narrative it takes place through an actual battle between the creator gods and chaos. The latter is personified as a mythological monster. The Bible contains only distant and sporadic allusions to this monster which will be noted in the comments on the pertinent passages. A similar idea appears in the Ugaritic myth of the victory of Baal over Yam ("the sea"). In the royal archives of Ebla (Tell

Mardikh), Syria, discovered in 1974, three cuneiform tablets were found containing the same hymn to the divinity who created the universe. Brief and general parallels to the Genesis story may be detected in it. It has been possible to translate only some of its lines. The following is the fragmentary translation offered by Giovanni Pettinato, the first epigraphist of the Italian Mission that excavated the site.

> Lord of heaven and earth,
> you had not made the earth exist,
> you created (it);
> you had not established the solar light,
> you created (it);
> you had not (yet) made exist
> the morning light.
> Lord: efficacious word;
> Lord: prosperity;
> Lord: heroism;
> Lord: . . .
> Lord: "independent";
> Lord: divinity;
> Lord who saves;
> Lord: *happy* life.
>   [BA, 43 (1980), 211; ANET, 60–72, 130–34]

Gen 1:5 —— *God called* As God created, he kept giving names to what he had created. In Middle Eastern thought, to name means to recognize or confirm the existence of something; hence naming becomes essentially synonymous with creating. The *Enuma Elish* (see note on 1:1), in saying "the heaven had not been named," means that its creation had not been completed; and the same is expressed by the addition, "Firm ground below had not been called by name." To name also means to establish authority over that which is named. (ANET, 60–61)

Gen 2:7 —— *formed man of dust from the ground* In Hebrew there is a play on the words *adam* ("man") and *adamah* ("ground"). In the Akkadian myth of man's creation, man is created by the mother goddess Ninhursag, also called Nintu, by mixing clay with the flesh and blood of a god who has been slain for that purpose. Thus it is said that Lullu ("the savage, the first man") was "formed out of clay" and "animated with blood." This myth was then developed into a magic formula to make childbirth easier. This contrasts sharply with the Genesis narrative, in which Yahweh God, the one Creator, although forming man from clay, gives him life by breathing into him his own breath. It is interesting that the name *a-da-mu* appears in the Ebla tablets as a personal name. (ANET, 99–100; BA, 43 [1980], 202)

Gen 2:9 —— *the tree of life also in the midst of the garden* The "tree of life" symbol occurs frequently, stylized in various ways but easily identifiable, in the art of Mesopotamia and of the ancient Middle East generally. It sometimes is shown flanked by human figures or by cherubim and appears in relief work, on seals, or carved in bone or ivory. At times the figure is that of a palm tree. In the documents, however, it is not precisely called a "tree," but is named by synonyms such as "plant" or (in Egypt) "wood." It represents full and happy life on earth and, by extension, perpetual life. (EB, I, 686; WB, I, 21, 22)

Gen 2:13 —— *The name of the second river is Gihon* One of the first of the famous scrolls discovered in Cave 1 of Qumran was that known as the *Genesis Apocryphon* (1QapGen), an amplified paraphrase of the book of Genesis. In this document Abraham tells of one of his journeys through Canaan and neighboring regions and says, "And I began my pilgrimage starting from the River Gihon." He then describes his trip toward the east, passing by the "Great Salt Sea" (the Dead Sea), reaching the Euphrates, and continuing eastward "until I arrived at the Red Sea." Then he says he followed the length of the Red Sea until he reached the "Sea of Reeds," whence, he continues, "I turned toward the south until I came to the River Gihon." The Sea of Reeds (so named in Hebrew) is that which traditional versions call the "Red Sea" and which is still called by this name. It refers to the body of water between Africa and the Arabian peninsula. As can be seen, the *Genesis Apocryphon* distinguishes between the Sea of Reeds and that which it calls the "Red Sea." From the context the "Red Sea" would seem to refer to what is today called the Persian Gulf. In any case, the *Genesis Apocryphon* places the River Gihon somewhere in the general region of the Nile Valley and Ethiopia, coinciding in this with the canonical Genesis. (AGA, 38; LRQ, 329; GAQ)

Gen 4:2 —— *keeper of sheep, and . . . tiller of the ground.* Tablets unearthed in Nippur, dating from the first half of the second millennium B.C., contain a Sumerian poem which offers an interesting parallel to the story of Cain and Abel. It speaks of the rivalry between Dumuzi, the shepherd god, and Enkimdu, the farmer god. However, in this case the one preferred by the goddess Inanna is the farmer—a striking contrast with the biblical narrative. While this difference is an important one, both narratives appear to reflect the step, doubtless not without conflict, from a stage of pastoral nomadism to one of agriculture accompanied by more or less stable human settlements. (ANET, 41–42)

Gen 4:22 —— *Tubal-cain; he was the forger of all instruments of bronze and iron.* The Kenites, one branch of which included Heber, are said to have settled in the desert of southern Palestine and to have been descendants of Moses' father-in-law. They seem to have been connected with Cain and his very close descendant Tubal-cain. If this is the case, it is most significant that the discoveries in the area of Timnah in southern Palestine show its inhabitants to have been, in fact, metalworkers. The Hebrew *qayin* (whence English Cain) means "forger" or "metalworker." The excavations in Timnah have revealed primitive installations for the extraction and refining of copper, including rudimentary smelting furnaces, stores of the ore itself, and tools for crushing the ore. (ABB, 10, 11)

Gen 5:5 —— *all the days that Adam lived were nine hundred and thirty years* The List of Sumerian Kings, found in a cuneiform prism, assigns quite fantastic figures to the reign of each one. For example, A-lu-lim reigned 28,800 years; Al-al-gar, 36,000; En-man-lu-anna, 43,200. Since these figures can obviously not be taken literally, there is ground for considering them mystical or symbolic numbers. While such a possibility cannot be ruled out in dealing with the longevity attributed to the patriarchs, the great difference in numbers of years between Genesis and the Sumerian list permits one to believe that our early ancestors may indeed have enjoyed great longevity, even conceding the possibility that the Genesis figures are not to be taken literally. (WB, I, 28)

Gen 6:17 —— *I will bring a flood* Archaeological excavations in Palestine and Syria have not as yet revealed traces of a general flood such as that described in the Bible. At various Mesopotamian sites (Ur, Kish, Fara, Nineveh) evidences have been found of more or less extensive inundations, but these were apparently local and occurred at different periods. Tablets discovered in Nineveh (1849–54) do contain a Chaldean flood narrative. It forms part of *The Epic of Gilgamesh*, fragments of which have also been excavated in Megiddo, Ugarit, and Ebla. This story shows many similarities (and also many differences) with respect to the biblical narrative. The differences are such that the Genesis account cannot be considered a mere copy or adaptation of the Chaldean one, but the similarities can be considered a confirmation of the flood as a historical occurrence. It is a testimony such as that which traditions of other peoples preserve; for example, the Aztecs spoke of one of the "suns," or periods of the world, as having been destroyed by water. Albright says that the *Atrahasis Epic*, another Mesopotamian narrative, is more like the biblical one. However, the document is very poorly preserved and therefore the information obtainable from it cannot be considered certain. "The flood" is also mentioned in the so-called Weld-Blundell clay prism, which gives in eight columns a list of the kings of Sumer. At one place in the first column it says, as a chronological reference, "The Flood swept over (the earth)"; and further along, "After the Flood had swept over (the earth)." It is impossible on the basis of this list to assign even an approximate date to the event, since the figures in the prism are so exaggerated; one of the kings, for example, is said to have ruled for 36,000 years! (See the commentary on 5:5.) (BA, 36 [1973], 24; BAR-1, 33–40; FNA, 13–53; ANET, 42–44, 93–97, 104–6; UTB, 36; ABB, 9)

Gen 6:18 —— *But I will establish my covenant with you* The idea of a covenant between God and humanity is a key concept, central to biblical thought and to the history of salvation, beginning with this first covenant that God established with Noah. We owe to archaeological research the discovery of documents dating from the second millennium B.C. which contain treaties or covenants between a sovereign and a vassal. The study of these covenants, made by G. E. Mendenhall and quoted extensively by Albright, shows that in the textual formulation of the covenant between God and his people there are elements from the forms of expression employed in these covenants. Mendenhall enumerates these elements as:

identification of the sovereign, usually with the introductory formula "Thus says X, the Great King"; a historical statement about the relationship between the sovereign and the vassal; historical proof of the benevolence shown by the sovereign toward the vassal; and a statement that the text of the covenant is to be deposited in the sanctuary of the vassal. Finally, there is a series of blessings for the one who keeps the covenant and a list of curses against the one who violates it. In these secular covenants there are additional elements which do not appear in the formulation of the covenant with Yahweh, such as the calling to witness of the gods of the two contracting parties. This element is lacking in the covenant with Yahweh, due to the rigorous monotheism of the Hebrews and to the fact that the witnesses are those who make up the people of the covenant (see Josh 24). However, the prophets do at times call "heaven" and "earth" to witness (Is 1:2; Hos 2:21, 22; Mic 6:2). Only in Exodus 23:20–33 and Leviticus 26 do we find God doing something similar. In Deuteronomy 27–28 it is Moses who dictates the curses and blessings which the Levites are to pronounce when the people have entered Canaan—the curses to be pronounced from Mount Ebal and the blessings from Mount Gerizim, with six of the tribes on one mountain and six on the other. (BAW, 100–1)

Gen 10:10 —— *Erech* Uruk in the Sumerian and Akkadian languages and Warka in present-day usage, this city in southern Mesopotamia near the Euphrates was explored about the middle of the nineteenth century A.D. and excavated beginning in 1912. Erech goes back to the fourth millennium B.C. and was one of the most important postdiluvian cities. It was attributed to Nimrod and was conquered by Rim-Sin of Larsa and later by Hammurabi. It served as a center for the worship of Anum and of Inanna, the latter being a goddess of love and war. Her sanctuary, named Eanna Tower (a ziggurat), and a palace have been excavated, with the resulting discovery of sculptures and cuneiform tablets. (ANET, 164; EB, VI, 1149–52)

Gen 11:4 —— *and a tower with its top in the heavens* In Mesopotamia there are imposing ruins of enormous structures in the form of stepped towers or pyramids, called ziggurats. The most important of these are the ones of Ur and of Babylon, dating respectively from the end of the third and the beginning of the second millennium B.C. The one in Ur is square, measuring 142 feet wide by some 205 feet long. It has not been possible to calculate its exact height, but it appears to have had seven stages or stories. The Genesis account seems to refer to the ziggurat of Babylon, called *E-temen-an-ki* ("house of the foundation of heaven and earth"). It is now entirely in ruins, having for centuries been plundered for its bricks, which were used in other buildings. Its nucleus was of adobe, covered with brick some 50 feet thick. The platform upon which it was built measured 1,500 feet by 1,360 feet, but the ziggurat itself measured only 300 feet on each side. As in the case of the ziggurat in Ur, it had three flights of steps—two lateral ones 100 feet high and a central one 132 feet high. According to a tablet found in the ruins of the nearby sanctuary of Esagil, it must have had a height of about 300 feet. The Greek historian Herodotus alludes to this ziggurat, mentioning a circular stairway and eight "towers." It is believed to have had seven stages, like the one in Ur, with a shrine at the top, to which access was had partly by a flight of steps and partly by a ramp.

The ancient Akkadian name of Babylon was *Bab-ilu*, meaning "gate of the god [or gods]," whence the Hebrew *Babel*. Due to the similarity of this name to the Hebrew root *balal*, "to confound," the tradition employed by the writer of Genesis related the ziggurat of Babel or Babylon with the confusion of tongues. Even if the identification of this particular structure with the biblical "tower of Babel" should prove not to be historically exact, it can at least give an idea of what the biblical one must have been like. (TB)

Gen 11:26 —— *Abram* This name has not as yet appeared in any of the documents of Ur, but it does occur in other Mesopotamian documents, from the beginning of the second millennium B.C., under the forms *A-ba-ra-ma*, *A-ba-am-ra-ma*, and *A-ba-am-ra-am*. In Akkadian the name may mean "My beloved father," and in western Semitic "Great by his father" or "The father is exalted." In the Ebla tablets unearthed south of Aleppo, Syria, in 1974 and dating from the third millennium B.C., the name is found in the form of *Ab-ra-mu*. Of course, these names do not refer to the biblical patriarch, but to persons of the same name who lived long before him. (AHT, 36; BA, 43 [1980] 202)

Gen 11:27 —— *Nahor, and Haran* These and other biblical names from the patriarchal period appear in the cuneiform tablets uncovered

at Mari (1936–39) by Parrot and dating from the eighteenth century
B.C. They seem to have been rather common in Mesopotamia. (DBW,
110)

Gen 11:28 —— *Ur of the Chaldeans*. Abraham's native city has
usually been identified, with presumed certainty, as the Ur excavated
in 1922 by Leonard Woolley. It is situated 10 miles from the present
course of the Euphrates and 40 miles southeast of Uruk in southern
Mesopotamia, in the region of ancient Sumer and near the Persian
Gulf. This identification has been maintained in spite of the biblical
data and of several historical facts which militate against it. According
to Genesis 24:4, 7, 10, Abraham repeatedly speaks of "my country"
(understood as "native country") and of the home of his "kindred"
as being Aram, which is a region much farther north, between the
Euphrates and the Tigris. Therefore, the city of Ur from which
Terah and his sons went to settle in Haran, along one of the
tributaries of the Euphrates, almost surely must have been in this
northern region. Furthermore, none of the tablets which mention
the Sumerian Ur speak of it as being "of the Chaldeans." These, as
a matter of fact, did not settle there until around the tenth and ninth
centuries B.C., long after Abraham's time. In spite of all this, Woolley
proclaimed the Sumerian Ur as the Ur of Abraham. And this
continued to be taken for granted, even though other scholars, such
as Cyrus H. Gordon in 1958, supported the biblical narrative which
speaks of the "Ur of the Chaldeans" as being somewhere in Aram
and not in southern Mesopotamia, some 1,000 miles from Haran.
The patriarch and his family were Arameans (25:20; Deut 26:5), at
that time a nomadic people. The objections to locating Ur in southern
Mesopotamia were countered by the argument that certain Aramean
groups might well have gone to settle in the Ur of the south, and
also that when the biblical writer called this "of the Chaldeans" he
could have been using an anachronism—such as other anachronisms
which occur in the Bible—with a view to identifying the place at
the time of writing. However, a tablet from Ugarit mentions an Ur
(actually, there were various cities that bore this name) in Hittite
territory, which corresponds generally to the northern region mentioned above. One tablet found in the excavations of Ebla (1974–
76) seems to clarify the matter conclusively, since it mentions an
"Ur in Haran"—a piece of information that coincides with the

biblical narrative. (TBAR, 3, No. 2 [1977], 20; EB, VI, 1141–44; IDB, IV, 735–38; UAB, 30–40)

Gen 11:31 —— *when they came to Haran, they settled there.* According to the tablet mentioned above, the name "Haran" served to designate a whole region, while in this verse a city with the same name is mentioned. This leads to the conclusion that Abraham's family would have gone from Ur, another city in the same region, to settle in Haran. In view of the light shed upon the patriarchal period by the cuneiform tablets from Mari (see commentary on 11:27), Albright says, "The narratives of Genesis dealing with Abram (Abraham) may now be integrated into the life and history of the time in such surprisingly consistent ways that there can be little doubt about their substantial historicity." The Mari tablets contain significant allusions to customs characteristic of the patriarchs as described in Genesis. (BA, 36 [1973], 10)

Gen 12:6 —— *to the* [holy] *place at Shechem* Abraham had his first contact with the inhabitants of Canaan at Shechem, as he journeyed toward the south. This city plays a very important role in biblical history (see commentaries on Josh 24:1; Judg 9:6, 46). It is one of the best-excavated cities of Palestine. It was first identified in 1903, and archaeological expeditions followed in 1913–14, 1926–27, 1928, 1932, 1934, 1956, 1957, 1960, 1962, 1964, and 1966.

The early period of settlement was begun in the first part of the fourth millennium B.C. by seminomadic people. The population became more sedentary at the time of the Hyksos (eighteenth to sixteenth centuries B.C.). Features from the early period of the city include the remains of walls, of a tamped-earth pavement, and of a cistern; and from later periods, ruins of fortifications, streets, houses, and a temple, as well as tombs and the remains of a large gate of the city. The Hyksos extended their empire as far as Egypt, but when the Egyptians freed themselves from them, they drove them from Canaan as well and destroyed the Hyksos city of Shechem. Remains of the following period have also been found, as well as of the Israelite epoch, especially that of the tenth to the eighth centuries B.C. From this period cisterns, granaries, and dwellings were found, with impressive evidences of the destruction caused by the Assyrians in 724 B.C.

The city remained virtually abandoned until the fourth century

B.C., when people from Samaria occupied the site, having left their own city owing to its profanation by Alexander the Great, who converted it into a vacation colony for his veteran soldiers. Excavations have also uncovered the remains of subsequent periods, including those resulting from its total destruction by the Maccabean king John Hyrcanus, and those of the Roman period. At that time it was renamed Neapolis (a name which persists today in the form of Nablus). The original site is now occupied by the small Arab village of Balatah. (ADHL, 119–28; SW)

Gen 12:10 —— *Now there was a famine. . . . So Abram went down to Egypt* Both archaeological evidence and literary sources provide abundant proof that there were frequent periods of scarcity and famine in Palestine, whose agriculture depended upon the variable rainfall, and that Egypt was a generally well stocked granary for the mideastern and even the western world. One Egyptian bas-relief portrays a group of emaciated and hungry Bedouins. Another, from a tomb of Beni Hasan, shows a caravan of Semites presenting themselves before the governor of Oryx in Middle Egypt, with their wives, children, and cattle, obviously asking to be received as immigrants. From their appearance they are not in this case starving people, but rather, as it would seem, people with foresight who are seeking to escape a threatening famine. This situation of hunger in Palestine and of seeking refuge in Egypt is repeated in the Bible, most notably in the case of Jacob and his sons. (ETB, 3–6)

Gen 13:12 —— *the cities of the valley* "The valley" refers to the deep depression (at some points as much as 1,320 feet below sea level) which extends southward from the lower end of the Sea of Galilee as far as the Gulf of Aqaba, including the Jordan Valley and the Dead Sea region. The five cities mentioned in 14:1, 2 (Sodom, Gomorrah, Admah, Zeboiim, and Bela, or Zoar) are thought to be now covered by the shallow southern part of the Dead Sea. To the southeast and south of the sea, five archaeological sites have been located: Bab edh-Dhra, Numeira, Safi, Feifa, and Hanazir. The first was discovered in 1924 by Albright, and was first excavated by Paul W. Lapp in 1965. The American archaeologists W. E. Rast and T. Schaub found Numeira in 1973 and later the other three sites. From 1975 to 1979 they excavated Bab edh-Dhra and its huge cemetery. The cemetery had already been explored by Lapp, who had also examined Numeira. Both cities have been dated from about the middle of the third millennium B.C. The three remaining sites were still unexcavated in 1980. In the celebrated Madaba Map (see commentary on Mt 3:6), Safi is identified as Zoar. Rast and Schaub have suggested that the five sites mentioned above might be the five "cities of the valley" or "cities of the Plain" (as rendered by some versions), including the famous Sodom and Gomorrah. (TBAR, 6, No. 5 [1980], 27–36)

Gen 13:18 —— *the oaks of Mamre* Over tne years three locations have been proposed for this famous place where Abraham camped: Gebel el-Rumeidi, Khirbet Sibtha (where even a supposed "oak of Abraham" is actually pointed out to visitors), and Khirbet Nimrah, some two miles north of Hebron, which is a walled enclosure known as Ramet el-Khalil (in Arabic, "Heights of the Friend" of God). Excavations at the last named site have revealed Herodian ruins, ruins from the times of Hadrian and of Constantine, and some from the Byzantine and Arabian periods. Constantine erected a church at this place, and the oldest tradition identifies this as the most likely site. (EB, IV, 1224–27)

Gen 14:1 —— *Arioch king of Ellasar* Probably the *Arriyuk* mentioned in the Mari tablets.

Gen 14:5 —— *and subdued the Rephaim* The Rephaim were a semi-legendary people of Canaan, who were famous as giants because of their large stature. Some versions translate Rephaim as "giants." They were also known as Emim and Anakim (Deut 2:10, 11). The name would normally mean simply "Descendants of Rapha"; however, all of the persons by this name mentioned in the Bible are of a much later period. The Ugaritic narrative concerning Aqhat mentions a person called Rapha, who could possibly be connected with the Rephaim as an ancestor or an eponym of this people. Another name given to the same person is Danel or Daniel (see commentary on Ezek 14:14). This name appears in the Ebla tablets as *da-ni-lum*. (ANET, 149; BA, 43 [1980], 202)

Gen 14:13 —— *Abram the Hebrew* This is the first occurrence in the Bible of the ethnic name that was later applied to the people of Israel, and later still to the Jews. In the Mari tablets of the eighteenth century B.C. and in the Tell el-Amarna letters of the fourteenth and thirteenth centuries B.C., there is frequent mention of a mysterious nomadic ethnic group of the regions east of Palestine who were called *Habiru*, *Hapiru*, *Hapiri*, or *Apirim*—all variants of the same name. This has given rise to a lively discussion among scholars as to whether these people should be identified with the Hebrews or with the Proto-Hebrews to whom Abram belonged. Etymologically, the name Hebrew may possibly be derived from Eber (or Heber, following the Latin transcription), a descendant of Shem and eponym for a group of peoples, including one of Abram's ancestors. According to archaeological information, the *Habiru* were nomadic shepherds who became so numerous that they were feared because of their incursions into populated areas. Apparently they consisted of a number of groups or tribes who were all given this name. In the above-mentioned discussion, it would seem that the most reasonable position and the one best supported by archaeological data is that taken by Parrot, following de Vaux and H. Cazelles, whom he cites to the effect that "the Hebrews were only one group in the totality that constituted the Hapiru" (de Vaux) and that there is a "strong possibility, not of an identification with the Hebrews but of a relation to them [the Habiru]" (Cazelles). This also is Kenyon's opinion. This conclusion would seem to find good support in the fact that Jacob was called "a wandering Aramean" (Deut 26:5) and in Ezekiel's saying to Jerusalem, "Your father was an Amorite" (Ezek 16:3). Amorites and Arameans inhabited the region between Canaan and the Euphrates, and the Arameans extended even beyond that river. The name Eber probably means "beyond, on the other side of," referring in this case to the Euphrates River. (AHT, 94–97; AHL, 183, 193)

Gen 14:14 —— *he led forth his trained men* The Hebrew word translated "trained men" is *hanikim*, which may also be translated as "trusted men, followers"; that is, those who made up the retinue of a chieftain. "In a cuneiform letter found by Sellin at Taanach in Palestine, and dating from the fifteenth century B.C. or earlier, the same word appears in the form *hanaku*, pointing to a correct vocalization *hanakim* in Genesis. But the word is Egyptian and is used in Egyptian texts dating from about 2000 B.C. for the retainers of Palestinian chieftains. In later times the word became disused." (Albright, APB, 141)

Gen 14:18 —— *Melchizedek king of Salem* One of the Qumran manuscripts, consisting of thirteen fragments found in Cave 11 (11QMelch), mentions Melchizedek as a prototype of the priesthood by speaking of the priestly office as "the heritage of Melchizedek." The passage is related to the Jubilee, whose proclamation was made by the high priest. Given the fact that the Qumran community was made up of priests, the interest which this manuscript shows in Melchizedek as an eschatological figure is easily understood. He is also mentioned in the paraphrase of this passage which occurs in the so-called *Genesis Apocryphon*, found in Cave 1 at Qumran (1QapGen). The city of Salem (Hebrew *Shalem*), of which Melchizedek was king, is generally identified as Jerusalem (compare Ps 76:2). It is so understood by Josephus (*Antiquities*, I, 10, 2), but this identification cannot be affirmed with certainty. In Psalm 76 we may have merely a poetic abbreviation of Jerusalem, without any attempt at historical or geographical identification with the Salem of Genesis. Some authorities have suggested that the latter may have been Shechem or a place near this city, and it is interesting to note that there exists today a nearby village called *Salim*. Shiloh also has been suggested. An Egyptian potsherd from the nineteenth or eighteenth century B.C., of the so-called execration texts, upon which were written the names of enemies and which were then broken to indicate a curse, bears the name of one *Iyqa-ammu*, king of a place named *Aushamem*, that is, Jerusalem. This form of the name is the equivalent of Akkadian *Urushalim*, according to Burrows, or of *Urusalimum*, according to Albright. In the Ebla tablets, dating from about 2400 B.C., it is written *Urusalima*. In the Tell el-Amarna letters (fourteenth century B.C.) it appears as *Urusalim*, and in later Assyrian texts as *Urusalimmu* or *Ursalimmu*. The name *Salem* would appear to indicate some relation to the Canaanite god *Shalem* (or *Shalmanu*), mentioned in the Ugaritic texts of Ras Shamra, but there is no evidence either that ancient Jerusalem was a cultic center for this god or that this was its local deity. Nevertheless, according to the use of the root *yrh* in Job 38:6, the Hebrew name *Yerushalayim* would mean etymologically "Foundation of Shalem." (The translation "City of Peace" is clearly not correct.) Ceramic fragments unearthed near the Gihon Spring in Jerusalem demonstrate that the city was inhabited at least as early as the beginning of the third millennium B.C. In Letter No. 287 of Tell el-Amarna one Abdu-Heba appears as governor of Jerusalem (*Urusalim*) and asks for help from the king of Egypt against his enemies (the Apiru) on the ground that "this land does belong to the king" (of Egypt). During this period all of Canaan was, in fact, an Egyptian possession. (GAQ, 72–75, 172–84; DSSE, 265–68; AGA, 47; ANET, 329; MTL, 48; ABB, 12)

Gen 14:19 —— *God Most High* In the excavations made in 1969–71 in the Jewish quarter of the old walled city of Jerusalem, a fragment was found of a jar for storing grain, with an ink inscription in Hebrew which reads in part, "Creator of the Earth." This phrase was probably preceded by the divine name *El*, which forms the first part of the compound name *El-elyon* ("God Most High") and which occurs in this verse of Genesis. The phrase also appears in a Phoenician inscription discovered in Karatepe, dating from the eighth century B.C., which reads, "El, the Creator of the Earth." According to the Israeli archaeologist Avigad, "we can assume that this vessel may have been intended for offerings to be brought to the temple, only a short distance away." (JR, 43)

Gen 15:1 —— *the word of the LORD came to Abram in a vision* An old Jewish tradition points out the very place in which the Lord established his covenant with Abraham. It is in the Hermon range at the foot of a hill called Meshed-a-Teir. The Muslims also consider it a holy site. A building with three domes, called Maqaam el-Halil, is built there. This identification, of course, can be neither proved nor disproved by archaeology. (BA, 43 [1980] 190)

Gen 15:2 —— *and the heir of my house is Eliezer of Damascus* The Hebrew text here is confusing and obscure due to the presence of *mesheq*, a term of unknown meaning. It is nevertheless probable that the word implies an ancient custom of northern Mesopotamia and eastern Syria, mentioned frequently in the Nuzi tablets, many of which are so-called adoption tablets. According to an ancient law, inherited lands could not be transferred outside the family; but a creditor sometimes employed the stratagem of having himself adopted as a son by the debtor, thereby collecting the debt by inheriting the property. Formerly adoption was employed in order to keep the family property from passing illegally to strangers. It would appear that if Abraham had had no son, he would have found himself obliged to adopt Eliezer and that the description *ben-mesheq* as applied to Eliezer, although traditionally translated "steward" (RSV, "heir") would rather mean "adopted son." Then the word *damesheq*, which follows and which means "Damascus" (but not "of Damascus" as it has usually been translated), would be a dittograph inserted by some copyist. (APB, 138)

Gen 16:2 —— *go in to my maid* According to our western standards, for a barren wife to give her maid to her husband so that he might have children by her is not only strange but reprehensible. Nevertheless, we have not only this case but also that of Leah and Rachel giving their maids to Jacob. This practice reflects not only existing customs but even laws that were in effect in Mesopotamia, where these patriarchs originated. Such a situation is mentioned in laws 144–46 and 170–71 of the Code of Hammurabi. In the archives dug from the ruins of the city of Nuzi, east of the Tigris River, there was found an interesting adoption contract which includes certain clauses pertaining to marriage. The case is that of a man named Shennima and his wife Kelim-ninu, and it is stipulated that "if Kelim-ninu does not bear [children], Kelim-ninu a woman of the land of Lullu (i.e., a 'foreign handmaid') as wife for Shennima shall take." The contract then adds that "as for the (concubine's) offspring, Kelim-ninu shall not send (them) away," which is just what Sarah did with Hagar and Ishmael, thus violating the established norms and giving rise to Abraham's displeasure (Gen 21:11). (ANET, 172–73; WB, I, 80)

Gen 16:11 —— *Ishmael* The name *ish-ma-il*, which corresponds to Ishmael, appears along with other biblical names as a personal name in the Ebla tablets. (BA, 43 [1980] 202)

Gen 17:23 —— *and he circumcised the flesh of their foreskins* Circumcision was a widespread practice in ancient times among most of the Semitic peoples (the Assyrians and Babylonians excepted) and also among the Egyptians. It is also practiced by the Arabs, a custom dating from times earlier than Mohammed. The same practice is observed by many tribes of Africa, Asia, and the American continent. A relief from the tomb of Ankhmahor, in Sakkara, Egypt, of the Sixth Dynasty (2350–2000 B.C.) portrays priests who are circumcising some young men, using flint knives (compare Ex 4:25, Josh 5:3). A stele in the Oriental Institute of the

University of Chicago, which is probably from Naga ed-Der, Egypt, and apparently dates from the twenty-third century B.C., contains the offering of an invocation in which the petitioner says that he was "circumcised, together with one hundred and twenty men." Among the Hebrews circumcision took on a solemn religious meaning as the visible mark of their covenant with Yahweh. (IDB, I, 269; WB, I, 57; ANET, 326)

Gen 19:28 —— *Sodom and Gomorrah* Prolonged explorations in the region south of the Dead Sea, carried out first by Albright and later by Glueck, appear to have settled beyond doubt the location of these and other "cities of the valley" (of the Jordan River and the Arabah; compare commentary on 13:12). Until relatively recent times, the consensus among biblical scholars had been that they were to the south of the Dead Sea and that the catastrophe described in chapter 19 and the subsequent rising of the water level due to increased silt deposits made by the Jordan River as it flows into the Dead Sea, left the site of these cities underwater. In recent years, however, hydraulic works in the Jordan have lowered the water level, thus leaving the southern end of the sea uncovered. Archaeologists who have examined the now dry area and studied the nature of the ground have come to the conclusion that this was unfit for the establishment of towns. Besides, no signs were found of the former existence of human settlements there, thus confirming the negative results obtained previously when divers searched under the waters then covering the site. On the other hand, the new explorations "have definitely established the correctness of the very early biblical tradition that the valley was very prosperous and densely peopled when Abraham came into the country" (Albright, APB, 48). The region, with its many accumulations of salt mounds left by evaporation, offers a fantastic spectacle. The present Israeli town of Sdom (or Sodom) preserves the name, but it makes no pretense of occupying the site of the biblical city. It is southwest of the Dead Sea and at some distance from its shores. As to the manner of destruction, there are both ancient and modern evidences of the presence of asphalt in the region. J. Penrose Harlan reconstructs the catastrophe as follows: "A great earthquake, perhaps accompanied by lightning, brought utter ruin and a terrible conflagration to Sodom and the other communities in the vicinity. The destructive fire may have been caused . . . through lightning or the scattering of fires from the hearths." (BAR-1, 59–70)

Gen 20:1 —— *and he sojourned in Gerar.* This town is at present identified with Tell Abu Hureira, on the north side of the Wadi esh-Sheira, halfway between Beersheba and Gaza. Excavations there have revealed an occupation dating from the Chalcolithic period. An abundance of potsherds has been found from the Middle Bronze II period (1800–1600 B.C.), within which falls the time of Abraham. The ruins indicate that Gerar occupied an area of about 180,000 square yards, an extraordinary extension for a town of those times. (IDB, II, 382; WB, I, 62)

Gen 21:3 —— *called the name of his son . . . Isaac.* "The name Isaac [*Yiṣḥaq*] is not found outside the Bible, but the Ugaritic epics contain the word, used in reference to a god, quite frequently, so we may safely translate it 'May (such-and-such a god) smile (favorably).' " (Albright, BA, 36 [1973], 19)

Gen 21:31 —— *that place was called Beer-sheba.* This name means "Well of Seven" or "Well of the Oath." In the excavations of the site, outside the Israelite gate, a deep well dating from early times appeared. This may be from the time of Abraham, but it cannot be proved that it is precisely the well mentioned in verse 25 or in 26:25 (q.v.). Recent excavations show that the region of Beersheba was occupied at least as early as 3500 B.C. No fewer than fifty populated sites have been located along the wadis or ravines of the area, two of which, Abu Matar and Safadi, have been completely excavated. They were small buried villages, some of them lying at a depth of more than 32 feet. They give evidence of a high degree of development in agriculture, animal husbandry, and implements, so much so that archaeologists are beginning to speak of a "Beersheba culture." (ABB, 27; ADHL, 3–8)

Gen 23:17 —— *and all the trees* A code of Hittite laws was discovered in Turkey at Boghazkoi, the ancient capital of the Hittite empire. Because the inhabitants of Kiriath-arba were Hittites, negotiation between Abraham and Ephron was in accord with those laws. Ephron preferred to sell the entire parcel of land and not the cave only because in such cases the purchaser would be under obligation to render certain services to the former owner. Hittite documents relating to the purchase and sale of land specify the exact number of trees within the property being sold. (BAW, 51)

Gen 23:19 —— *the cave of the field of Machpelah*   A very ancient tradition, dating at least from the time of the Second Temple, makes quite plausible the identification of this famous cave (where Abraham buried Sarah and which became the family burial place of the patriarchs) with the one located beneath the Haram el-Halil mosque in Hebron. This mosque was an earlier Byzantine church restored by the Crusaders in the twelfth century A.D., although its lower structure has been identified by Vincent as dating from the Herodian period. It may even have been built on the site of a still earlier structure. Within the mosque the supposedly exact sites of the tombs of Abraham, Sarah, Isaac, Rebecca, Jacob, and Leah are marked by cenotaphs. (EB, IV, 1205; WB, I, 70)

Gen 25:26 —— *his name was called Jacob.*   "The name Yaqub, 'May [such-and-such a god] protect,' is common in the Patriarchal Age, being found in both cuneiform and hieroglyphic texts as names of Northwestern Semites." (Albright, BA, 36 [1973], 19)

Gen 25:33 —— [Esau] *sold his birthright to Jacob.*   In one of the Nuzi tablets there appears a case in which a certain Tupkitilla transfers his inheritance rights to a grove to his brother Kurpazak in exchange for three sheep. (BAR-1, 23)

Gen 26:25 —— *Isaac's servants dug a well.*   This may have been the same well as the one mentioned in 21:25 (q.v.), simply cleaned out or enlarged. In excavations begun in 1969 in Tell Beersheba by the Israeli archaeologist Aharoni, a well was found at the top of the hill, about which Aharoni says, "We can add with certainty that we have to do here with the same well that was dug by the patriarchs." Nearby were found the ruins of a place of worship. (AR, No. 41 [1976], 8–10)

Gen 27:28 —— *dew of heaven, . . . fatness of the earth*   This expression appears to have been a very ancient literary formula common in the Middle East. It occurs, for example, in a fragment of the Ugaritic poem of Baal and Anath: "Sky-dew, fatness of earth," in the same sense of prosperity and abundance. (ANET, 136)

Gen 27:33 —— *yes, and he shall be blessed.*   Another possible translation is, "yes, and he stays blessed." According to the tablets of Nuzi (a town in the same general area from which the patriarchs came and whose customs and laws they appear to have followed), an oral blessing such as that given on one's deathbed was irrevocable and had full legal validity. This may explain the fact that Isaac's blessing of Jacob, even though fraudulently obtained by Jacob, had to remain in force. (BAW, 43–44)

Gen 28:18 —— *set it up for a pillar*   A great many ancient pillars (or steles) have been found in Palestine, as for example, the four discovered at Leijjun in Transjordan. It is clear that the erection of such pillars was a common practice in those times. These pillars were erected to commemorate important events, such as a divine manifestation or a military victory, as well as to solemnize a vow or an agreement, or to keep alive the memory of some ancestor or other notable person. (BAW, 51)

Gen 31:19 —— *Rachel stole her father's household gods.*   Like the Greeks, the Arameans and Canaanites also had penates, or household gods, represented in images that were placed on a small altar in the home. It was images of this kind (Hebrew *teraphim*) that Rachel stole from Laban to take with her. She did not do so out of mere religious zeal; she also had an economic interest, since the person who possessed the family *teraphim* was heir to the family possessions. Rachel wanted to make sure this right would belong to Jacob. This fact also explains why Laban was so anxious to recover his family gods. An Akkadian tablet from Nuzi, having to do with the adoption of one Wullu by a man named Nashwi, specifies that if Nashwi dies without a natural son, his adopted son, Wullu, "shall take the gods of Nashwi"—that is, Wullu would become the heir to all Nashwi's property. If, however, Nashwi should have a son of his own, the inheritance would be divided between him and the adopted son, but the former "shall take the gods of Nashwi"—that is, he would retain the rights of the principal heir. The excavations have produced a large number of household idols of this kind. They were of clay or bronze, and some of them were worn as amulets. (MLB, 28–30; BAW, 44; ANET, 219–20)

Gen 31:43 —— *all that you see is mine.*   In reproaching Jacob because he had fled and taken with him his daughters, his grandchildren, and the flocks, Laban was speaking not in a figurative but in a legal sense. The laws regarding property, inheritance, and similar matters which appear in the Nuzi tablets indicate the possibility that Jacob may not only have been the son-in-law (doubly so) of the Aramean patriarch but also his adopted son. Adoption as a way of confirming the possession of property was quite common in the region during those times. Jacob, his wives, his children, and his flocks would have been, in such a case, still under the patriarchal authority of Laban until the latter's death. (BAR-2, 26; BAW, 44)

Gen 31:46 —— *they took stones, and made a heap* The custom of erecting a heap of stones and a pillar, as in verse 45, was common in Bible times in the Middle East. Such a heap would serve to mark a boundary, to witness an agreement, to commemorate some note-worthy occurrence, or to mark a place that was regarded as sacred. Here and there in Palestine one may see such piles of stones made by Arabs for similar purposes. Since these stone piles lie on the surface and are exposed to the elements, it is difficult to assign to them any fixed degree of antiquity. In fact, they are not likely to be very old, since such monuments are easily set up and easily destroyed; but it is interesting that the custom still persists.

Gen 32:28 —— *Your name shall no more be called Jacob, but Israel* The earliest appearance of the name Israel outside of the Bible is on a tablet from Ebla which contains the form *ish-ra-il* (see comment on Ex 3:15), dating from the third millennium B.C. The name is also found in line 27 of the triumphal stele of Pharaoh Merneptah (about 1220 B.C.), which contains a list of the enemies conquered and subjugated by him in Canaan. This stele, now in Cairo, was discovered in the ruins of the burial temple of Pharaoh Merneptah in Thebes. The text says, "Israel is laid waste; his seed is not." It is problematic, however, just what is meant here by "Israel." If we are to understand it as meaning Israelites in general, it could be a reference to them at the time of the conquest (the dates more or less coincide); but if it refers to an already established people, we would have to place the date of the conquest more than a hundred years earlier, thus adopting a date close to that fixed by the so-called long or high chronology (about 1360 B.C.). What further complicates the problem is that nowhere else is there any evidence of such a crushing defeat of the Israelites at the hands of the

Egyptians. The hymn carved in the Merneptah stele celebrates such a defeat as would have left Israel practically annihilated—even discounting the customary hyperbole of eastern warrior kings. Could the text be anachronistic, assigning to Canaan and its inhabitants the name of the people that had left Egypt to go and settle there? Such an explanation seems unconvincing, so the problem remains. See comment on Ex 5:1. (ANET, 376–78; WB, I, 88)

Gen 34:20 —— *came to the gate of their city* The gate of the ancient city was the place where the authorities handled public matters and administered justice, and where ordinary citizens conducted business. Excavations in Shechem have uncovered one gate facing the northwest (found in 1913–14) and another (found in 1926) facing the east, both excavated by Sellin. They are beautiful examples of the way such gates were built. It is possible that Hamor and his son Shechem came to the authorities at one of these two, although the city may have had other gates besides these. (SW, 25, 26, 40, et seqq.; WB, I, 90)

Gen 35:18 —— *but his father called his name Benjamin.* The meaning of this name is usually given as "Son of [my] right hand," which may be equivalent to saying "Favorite son" or "Son (i.e., heir) of (my) strength." It is interesting to note that in the Mari tablets the name *Banu-Yamin* is used for a nomad tribe belonging to the larger group of the still rather mysterious *Apiru* (see comment on 49:27). Since people of that time took their orientation looking to the east (instead of to the north as we do today), "Son of the right hand" can also be understood to mean "Son of the south," a meaning which appears today in the Arabic name *Yemen*. The Mari tablets also mention *Banu-Simal*, "Sons of the left," referring to the north. (BA, 36 [1973] 18)

Gen 35:19 —— *Rachel died, and she was buried on the way to . . . Bethlehem* Visitors to the Holy Land today are shown (along the side of the road from Jerusalem to Bethlehem) a small structure that was built in 1841 and is known as Rachel's Tomb. It is supposed to be on the site where Rachel was buried, following a tradition handed down from the third century A.D. and mentioned first by Origen. Other structures preceded the present one, which the Arabs call Qubbat el-Rahil. Inside there is an ancient sarcophagus. Obviously it is not the authentic one belonging to Jacob's wife but one that represents it. A different and an even older tradition, which has biblical support (1 Sam 10:2), places the tomb of Rachel in the land of Benjamin to the north of Jerusalem. This site would be south of Bethel (35:16), and various locations have been proposed for it. The real and difficult problem is how to reconcile the two biblical traditions. The issue is complicated by the fact that the name Ephrath(ah) was given not only to Bethlehem but also to the territory of Ephraim, so much so that the Ephraimites are called Ephrathites in 1 Samuel 1:1 and 1 Kings 11:26. On the basis of Hebrew parallelism, some scholars have thought that Jeremiah 31:15 places Rachel's tomb near Ramah in Ephraim. In short, just as in the case of many other biblical locations, the identification of the place where Rachel was buried is highly uncertain. Barring some unexpected archaeological discovery, the problem may never really be solved. As to the name Bethlehem ("House of bread"), this is its first occurrence in the Bible, but outside the Bible it first appears in one of the Tell el-Amarna letters (fourteenth century B.C.), the one listed as EA No. 290, in which the town is mentioned as "of the land of Jerusalem, *Bit-Lahmi* by name." (EB, II, 1100; IDB, II, 122; WB, I, 93; ANET, 489)

Gen 37:3 —— *a long robe with sleeves.* This is probably a literal translation, but the Hebrew could also be translated *of many colors.* In the ruins of the palace of Zimri-lim at Mari, a fresco shows two persons dressed in long tunics with colored squares. Certain Egyptian frescoes, such as one found in a tomb at Thebes, portray Semitic Canaanite persons of high rank dressed in tunics with long sleeves and colored stripes while offering tribute. (WB, I, 94, 110–14)

Gen 38:3, 4 —— *Er, . . . Onan.* These names appear to be Hebrew equivalents of the names *Yaurru* and *Awnanu*, mentioned in Babylonian documents as tribes of the *Apiru* and ancestors of the First Babylonian Dynasty.

Gen 38:18 —— *She replied, "Your signet* The signet, or seal, was an important object in common use among persons of rank. It was a symbol of ownership and was used to seal contracts and other secret or confidential documents, and even, as in this case (verse 25), as a mark of personal identification. It was either round or (more frequently) oval and was pressed onto fresh clay before it was fired, or onto hot wax, which was left to cool showing its imprint. The seal itself was engraved with a reverse image, so that the impression would come out correctly. It sometimes carried some figure or symbol, in addition to the owner's name and usually the owner's occupation, office, or status. The seal was made from some precious stone and was normally inseparable from its owner, who wore it either mounted in a ring or attached to a cord around the neck. Archaeologists have discovered many specimens of such seals (over two hundred) and of impressions made from them (over six hundred). In Egypt seals were used whose reverse bore the form of a scarab, symbol of the sun god. Some of the impressions made from them appear in fragments of handles from clay jars and would seem to have been used as public or official seals to certify the contents or the capacity of the vessel. The word *lamelech* ("of the king," "for the king," or "royal") often appears, perhaps certifying in some cases the authorized or legitimate measure. When biblical names occur on such seals, this fact is mentioned in the corresponding passages of this volume. In Mesopotamia cylindrical seals were used which could be rolled onto a surface, producing a repeated ribbonlike design. (DOTT, 218–26, plate 13; EB, VI, 554–56)

Gen 39:7, 12 —— *Lie with me*   The literature of ancient Egypt accuses its women of being frivolous, cruel, liars, and unfaithful. The Egyptologist Gaston Maspero accepts this characterization. Whether generally true or not, it is indeed interesting that in Egyptian literature a case is cited so similar to that of Joseph and Potiphar's wife that it makes one wonder—especially since the story comes from the period of Ramses II—whether it may be a version of the story of Joseph that was preserved by tradition, although in distorted form. It is the story of two brothers, Anubis and Bata, in which the wife of the former tries to seduce her brother-in-law, saying to him, "Come, let us pass an hour (together); let us lie down." The young man refuses with the reply, "You are for me as a mother, and your husband is for me as a father." Like Potiphar's wife, Anubis' wife accuses the one who has scorned her of having tried to seduce her. (ETB 78–80)

Gen 40:8 —— *We have had dreams, and there is no one to interpret them.*   The Egyptians developed quite an art of interpreting

dreams—a remote and empirical foreshadowing of the famous
theories of Sigmund Freud on the subject! They went so far as to
produce manuals or "Dream Books," with keys to interpret dreams,
a matter in which they were more or less on a par with the
Babylonians. The Chester Beatty Papyrus III (about 1300 B.C.), now
in the British Museum, contains materials from the Twelfth Dynasty
(2000–1800 B.C.) in hieratic script (it is probably from Thebes) and
gives over two hundred examples of dreams with their respective
keys for interpretation. Each column has the heading "If anyone
himself sees in a dream," followed by a list of dreams and before
each one the rating of "good" or "bad" (the latter in red ink). For
example, it is a good omen if one is given white bread, if he sees a
large cat, or if he sees the moon shining; but it is a bad omen if he
sees himself in a mirror or catching birds or looking into a well. One
cannot help but note analogies between some of these concepts and
the interpretations given by Joseph to the dreams of the wine steward
and the chief baker. (ANET, 495; ETB, 76–77; WB, I, 101)

Gen 41:29, 30 —— *seven years of great plenty . . . seven years of
famine* In Egypt there was a still more ancient tradition of "seven
years" of scarcity and famine, known as early as the twenty-eighth
century B.C. The narrative that appears in an inscription on a rock
on the island of Siheil, near the Upper Falls of the Nile, is placed
in that period. Pharaoh Netjer-er-khet writes to the governor of the
island of Elephantine concerning the great distress which he has
undergone because in his time the Nile had not overflowed "for a
space of seven years." The situation was causing anguish: "Grain
was scant, fruits were dried up, and everything which they eat was
short. Every man *robbed* his companion. They moved without going
(*ahead*). The infant was wailing; the youth was *waiting*; the heart
of the old men was in sorrow, their legs were bent, crouching on
the ground, their arms were *folded*. The courtiers were in need. The
temples were shut up; the sanctuaries held [nothing *but*] air.
Every[*thing*] was found empty."

Then the god Khnum appeared to the king in a dream, announcing
that after the seven years of famine there would come a time of
plenty: "I am Khnum, thy fashioner. . . . I know the Nile. When he
is introduced into the fields, his introduction gives life to every
nostril, like the introduction (of life) to the fields. . . . The Nile will

pour forth for thee, without a year of cessation or laxness for any land. Plants will grow, bowing down under the *fruit*. . . . The starvation year will have gone. . . . Egypt will come into the fields, the banks will sparkle, . . . and contentment will be in their hearts more than that which was formerly." Note that in this narrative the order is reversed: the seven years of famine come first, and then the time of plenty. (ANET, 31, 32)

Gen 41:41 —— *I have set you over all the land of Egypt.* There has been much research and discussion as to the identity of the pharaoh who was the protector of Joseph, as well as the pharaohs of the oppression and of the exodus, but the fact remains that there is no complete certainty about them. The chronology of the events of the period is not clear, and the opinions of scholars not only differ but are often irreconcilable. Nevertheless, even in the absence of a complete consensus, it is possible to arrive at a conjecture which is highly probable. Accordingly, the pharaoh who raised Joseph to the rank of second in authority in Egypt and who then welcomed the Israelites and favored them with a place to settle was probably one of the dynasty established by the Hyksos, a group of peoples from northern Mesopotamia who invaded and conquered Egypt. Some of the Hyksos were themselves Semites. Their capital was Avaris in the Nile Delta and near Goshen, the land where the Israelites settled. The Hyksos dominated Egypt from around the eighteenth century B.C. until the first half of the sixteenth century B.C. (1580), when they were driven out by the Egyptians, and the Eighteenth Dynasty was established. (ETB, 16–23; EB, III, 1226–28)

Gen 41:42 —— *his signet ring . . . a gold chain* From literary evidence and from paintings in ancient Egypt we know that the second in authority after the pharaoh (his prime minister or vizier) bore the title "Bearer of the Seal of the King of Lower Egypt." Not only was the gold chain a costly gift, it also indicated that the vizier was charged with the control of food supplies. (ABB, 31)

Gen 41:43 —— *in his second chariot* Ancient Egyptian chariots, such as the one of Tut-ankh-amen, have been found by archaeologists and can be seen in the Cairo Museum. The chariot used by Joseph on this occasion was certainly like one of them.

Gen 42:6 —— *with their faces to the ground.* A number of reliefs and frescoes discovered by archaeologists illustrate this typical oriental manner of showing humble subjection and submissive homage toward persons of high rank. For example, in a fresco from a tomb in Thebes, Egypt, dating from the fifteenth century B.C., there appears a group of Canaanites in an attitude of homage. They can be identified by their pointed beards and long tunics. Some of them are prostrated in the manner described in this passage; others are kneeling with the palms of their hands turned forward; still others are standing behind them and offer gifts to the monarch. (WB, I, 110)

Gen 47:1 —— *My father and my brothers . . . have come from the land of Canaan* A painting from the tomb of Khnum-hotep III in Beni Hasan, Egypt, pictures the arrival of a caravan of Asiatic people of Semitic type, headed by a prince named Abishar and consisting of men, women, and children, together with their animals and other possessions. Although the scene is from around 1900 B.C., some two centuries before the immigration of Jacob and his sons, this painting helps one imagine what the patriarchal family must have looked like when it reached Egypt. Also it illustrates the fact that migrations from Canaan to Egypt, "the ancient world's granary," were frequent, especially in times of scarcity and famine. (UTB, 34)

Gen 47:31 —— *Then Israel bowed himself upon the head of his bed.* The beds used from ancient times in Egypt, especially by persons of some means, were similar to beds as we know them today. Specimens of them have been found in a number of Egyptian tombs. The Semites from Canaan did not usually sleep in beds, but rather on skins spread on the floor. The Egyptians also used pillows, at times so numerous that stools or steps were required in order to climb onto the bed. However, they also made use of headrests in place of pillows; these were made of wood, concave in form, with a base or pedestal 8 inches or more in height. Specimens of these have been found in the tombs of Egypt. It is probable that it was this kind of rest upon which Jacob bowed himself. (WB, I, 119)

Gen 49:27 —— *Benjamin is a ravenous wolf* In the tablets unearthed in the ancient Mesopotamian city of Mari, reference is made to the campaigns of King Zimri-lim against a warlike tribe known as the

Banu-yamina, who came from the desert south of the Euphrates. In affiliation with the Amorite peoples they carried out invasions toward the north, both attacking and plundering. Their name means "Sons of the right hand," just as the meaning of the Hebrew *Ben Yamin* (Benjamin) in the singular form (see comment on 35:18). The characterization of the progenitor of the Israelite tribe of Benjamin, in the blessing of Jacob upon his sons, accords with what is known of the *Banu-yamina* from the Mesopotamian documents. This gives rise to an interesting question: Is there actually some relationship between these people and the Benjaminites? Yet how could there be, if at least three centuries separated the battles of Zimri-lim and the formation of the tribe of Benjamin? But since, as noted in the comment on 35:18, the Mesopotamian archives also mention an Amorite tribe called the *Banu-simal* ("Sons of the left hand," or "People of the north"), in all probability this and the other designation are not actually patronymics, but are simply descriptions of these peoples as coming either from the south or from the north. *Banu*, like the Hebrew *benei* (literally "sons of"), does not always mean "sons" in the literal genealogical sense. (BAR-1, 16, 17)

Gen 50:2, 3 —— *commanded . . . the physicians to embalm his father, . . . forty days were required* Like other Semites, the Hebrews did not normally embalm the bodies of their dead, nor did they practice cremation; their custom was simply to bury a body, and they considered it a terrible fate for a dead person to remain unburied. Jacob and Joseph are the only exception to this rule, as far as our information goes. The reason for embalming them was no doubt to preserve their remains so that they might later be taken back to Canaan and given an appropriate burial there.

The Egyptian process of embalming was long and complicated, as may be seen from the time it required—according to the Greek historian Herodotus, seventy days, and according to this passage, forty. But for the biblical writers forty was often a round number expressing an extremely long time, rather than an exact mathematical figure. The specific procedure used in Egypt is not known; it remains a secret to this day. In the tomb of Tut-ankh-amen were found bags containing some of the materials used, that is, natron and chaff, and in the tomb of Amen-em-opet (Nineteenth Dynasty) a fresco portrays part of the embalming procedure—but only a part of it, and without revealing the true secret, namely, the formula and the method of preparing the substance used for the embalming. (WB, I, 123)

Gen 50:26 —— *So Joseph died, being a hundred and ten years old* This was considered in Egypt to be the limit of a ripe old age. In *The Instruction of the Vizier Ptah-hotep* (Papyrus Prisse), written during the Middle Kingdom (2050–1785? B.C.), this royal official says, in closing, "What I have done on earth is not inconsiderable. I attained one hundred and ten years of life. . . ."

and they embalmed him, and he was put in a coffin Since Joseph was considered almost as though he were of royal lineage, his body was treated practically like that of one of the pharaohs. Many coffins, or sarcophagi, have been found in Egyptian tombs. They were usually made of fine wood and were richly ornamented. Some were made of stone, either granite or basalt, and were sculptured with relief work. Many embalmed bodies, some of which are extremely well preserved, have been found in these sarcophagi. The Egyptian art of embalming has never yet been surpassed. If, as we may suppose to have been the case, the embalming of Joseph was done as carefully as was done for the pharaohs or for a person of as high a rank as he held, we may be sure that his body could have been preserved intact to this very day. (ANET, 414)

EXODUS

Ex 1:8 —— *a new king . . . who did not know Joseph.* As in the case of the pharaoh who befriended Joseph (see Gen 41:41), it is very difficult to establish the identity of the pharaoh of the oppression. The main problem consists in fixing the chronology by synchronizing the data from secular history with the information in the biblical narrative. Scholarly opinion has been divided into two camps: those who favor the so-called long or high chronology, with earlier dates, and those who adopt the so-called short or low chronology, with later dates. There is a difference of some 150 years between them. According to the former, the pharaoh of the oppression would have been Thutmose III (1490–36 B.C.). But according to the latter, to which the majority of scholars are at present inclined, he would have been no other than the famous Ramses II (1290–24 B.C.), who ruled for some sixty-seven years, and whose very well preserved mummy may be seen in the Cairo Museum. Among numerous statues of him, the largest and most famous are the four in the façade of the temple of Abu Simbel. There remains also a very beautiful one, of granite but of smaller size, which may have come from Karnak. Ramses was a grand builder. The biblical statement that the Israelite slaves built two store cities, Pithom and Raamses (or Rameses), evidently named after him, makes the identification of Ramses as the pharaoh of the oppression all the more probable. However, this identification has not ceased to raise problems. (ETB, 24–30; EB, VI, 106–7; IDB, IV, 11; WB, I, 127)

Ex 1:11 —— *Pithom and Raamses.* The remains of Pithom—in Egyptian *Pr-itm,* "house of (the god) Atum" (or Tem)—have not been

31

identified with complete certainty. According to some authorities they are located at Tell el-Maskhutah in the Wadi Tumilat zone of the Delta. Some of its monuments are now in the so-called Garden of the Steles at Ismailia. It was at first believed that the brick buildings found there were among those the Israelites built, but this opinion has been abandoned by archaeologists. These ruins were excavated in 1883 by E. Naville, who identified them as Pithom. Other authorities, however, locate this city at Tell er-Retabeh, excavated in 1905–6 by Petrie, who thought he had found Raamses, an opinion afterward considered by others to be mistaken. Remains of a temple built by Ramses II were found at that site. Wright, who favors the er-Retabeh identification, believes that the ruins of el-Maskhutah are those of Succoth (compare 12:37). There seems to be more certainty concerning the identification of Raamses. Its ruins are located at Tell el-San, where granite pillars, pedestals of statues, and bas-reliefs have been found. This was Ramses' capital, built on the site of Avaris, the former capital of the Hyksos rulers. When rebuilt in later times, it was named Tanis; and a block of stone decorated with heads of prisoners was taken from the palace of Ramses and used in the monumental gate of the city. Remains of castles, among them a slab almost 20 feet long, were also found. Both cities were in the Delta, in the zone called Goshen and also Rameses (Gen 47:1, 11), where the Israelites were settled. (ETB, 53–57; BA, 58, 61; EB, V, 1127, VI, 100–3; IDB, III, 821, IV, 9)

Ex 1:14 —— *with hard service, in mortar and brick* Reliefs and paintings have been found which illustrate the Egyptian practice of imposing forced labor on prisoners and slaves, especially in tasks of construction, beginning with the making of bricks. In the Bologna Museum there is a bas-relief that shows a forced-labor chain gang of black people being watched by foremen or officers armed with sticks, while a scribe registers data on a tablet. A painting from Rekh-mi-Re's tomb carries the following title: "Prisoners led by His Majesty for the construction of the temple of Amon who are making bricks to build once again the temple at Karnak." (ETB, 81–84)

Ex 1:16 —— *upon the birthstool* The Hebrew word here translated *birthstool* literally means "pair of stones" or "double stone." Lexicographers and commentators differ as to its meaning in this particular passage. In Jeremiah 18:3 the same word refers to the potter's wheel (or rather *wheels*, that is, the two disks that rotate one above the other). Neither the Septuagint nor the Vulgate translates the word. The dictionaries note the dubious sense of the term and offer two probabilities: (1) it may be a euphemism to refer to the genitals, either masculine or feminine, or (2) it may designate a birthstool because of a certain resemblance to the potter's bench. A. B. Ehrlich, in his marginal notes to the Hebrew Bible (1908–14), favors the former interpretation, while other Jewish commentators prefer the latter. As a matter of fact, the context allows either interpretation. In support of the second alternative, the Lexicon by Brown, Driver, and Briggs mentions a terra-cotta figure, dating from the fourth or fifth century B.C., which represents a woman about to give birth. She is sitting on a stool according to the ancient custom. In the inscription on an Egyptian stele of a penitential hymn to a goddess, the author says, "I sat upon the brick(s) like the pregnant woman." The editor adds the following note to this sentence: "The Egyptian women in childbirth sat upon a support of bricks, the 'birth-stones' of Exod. 1.16." In a nonliteral version the essential meaning of this verse is clear. For instance, the Good News Bible avoids a direct rendering of the debatable Hebrew word and simply translates the whole clause as "When you help the Hebrew women give birth." (ANET, 381)

Ex 2:3 ——— *a basket made of bulrushes, and daubed it with bitumen and pitch* In the Assyrian legend of Sargon of Agade (c. 2300 B.C.) occurs a curious parallel to the story of the child Moses. Sargon says, "My mother was a changeling, my father I knew not. . . . My changeling mother conceived me, in secret she bore me. She set me in a basket of rushes, with bitumen she sealed my lid. She cast me into the river which rose not (over) me. The river bore me up and carried me to Akki, the drawer of water. Akki, the drawer of water, lifted me out as he dipped his e[w]er. Akki, the drawer of water, [took me] as his son (and) reared me." A very ancient custom is hereby illustrated, that is, baskets waterproofed with bitumen in order to use them as a sort of tiny boat. The contrast between the two cases is apparent. The child Moses is placed in the waterproofed basket in order to preserve his life. Sargon, the unwanted baby, was sent down the river and abandoned to his fate. (ANET, 119)

Ex 2:5 —— *the daughter of Pharaoh* It has not been possible to identify this princess. If the pharaoh of the oppression was Ramses II (see comment on 1:8), she must have been his daughter. There seems to exist, however, no notice whatever about her in Egyptian documents. It has been suggested that she was Hatshepsut, the daughter of Thutmose I, who became Queen of Egypt upon the premature death of her brother and husband Thutmose II. This identification would require the adoption of the so-called long chronology (see comment on 1:8), which is not now generally accepted among scholars.

Ex 3:1 —— *Horeb, the mountain of God.* Horeb is an alternative name for Sinai, a name applied also to the whole range of mountains in the peninsula and even to the peninsula itself. There is no complete certainty as to which of the imposing and craggy mountains of the area should be identified with this "mountain of God," where Moses received the law and which later played an important role in the prophet Elijah's life. The choice appears to lie between two massive mountains: *Yebel Serbal* and *Yebel Musa*, as the Arabs call them. In about the fourth century A.D. Christian monks decided in favor of the first, but by the end of the same century opinion shifted in favor of the second, which the Arabs also call *Tur-Sina*. Topographical considerations more in accord with the data provided by the biblical narrative favor this alternative. There are still some who propose a "Sinai" farther north, or to the east of the Gulf of Aqaba, and even in the region of Petra, but without adequate support. Also the Ras el-Safsafa lying to the northwest of the Yebel Musa has been suggested, while still others have proposed a location in the area of Midian. The Yebel Musa is 7,600 feet high, the Serbal 6,725 feet, and the Safsafa about 6,500 feet. (EB, VI, 726–30; WB, I, 134; IDB, IV, 376–77; DEB, II, 679)

Ex 3:15 —— *The LORD, the God of your fathers* As explained in a footnote in the Revised Standard Version, the word LORD stands for the divine name YHWH. It has been deduced from this passage that the name Yahweh was first revealed at this time and was not known before. Accordingly, its earlier mention in the Bible (for example, in Gen 2:4) had to be considered an anachronism. This interpretation seems to be supported by 6:3, where the Lord tells Moses that he did not make himself known to the patriarchs by that name. This does not necessarily mean, however, that the name did not exist before, but only that God revealed himself to the patriarchs under some other name, for instance, El-Shaddai (traditionally translated as "God Almighty"). In this same verse Yahweh introduces himself as the God of the patriarchs. This passage may simply mean that from then on Yahweh would be the personal name by which God would maintain his particular relationship to his chosen people.

The excavations at Ebla, some 30 miles south of Aleppo (started in 1964 by Paolo Matthiae of the University of Rome), uncovered between 1974 and 1976 over 15,000 clay tablets. Their inscriptions in cuneiform script began to be deciphered by Pettinato of the same institution. They have been dated from the time of Sargon of Agade (or Akkad). The Eblaite language is Semitic. According to Pettinato, in certain names, which he considers to contain a reference to God, the ending *ia* (*ya*) occurs as the equivalent of *il* ("God"). The matter has been hotly debated, but it seems probable that these endings do correspond to the Hebrew forms *yah* or *yahu* (well known abbreviations of *Yahweh*) and *el*, the shortening of *Elohim* ("God"). Curiously enough, in the Ebla tablets the name *ishrail* (Hebrew, *Israel*) also occurs as *ishraia* (or *ishraya*). If this equivalence proves certain, it would then mean that the name Yahweh has a northern Canaanite predecessor rather than a Midianite or Kenite one, as so far suggested. (The form *Jehovah* had its origin in a misreading of the Hebrew, dating from about the fourteenth century A.D. In ancient times Hebrew was written without vowels, so that the divine name appeared only with consonants, as YHWH. The original pronunciation is unknown, since from about the fifth century B.C. it ceased to be pronounced for fear of profaning the sacred name. Instead, it was simply read as *Adonai* ["Lord"]. Between the fifth and the ninth centuries A.D. a system of vowel pointing was developed, and the vowels in the Hebrew word *Adonai* were given to the consonants YHWH as a signal or reminder to the readers. Since in Hebrew these vowels are more exactly *e-o-a*, Christian readers, unaware of what they stood for, took them as belonging to the sacred name, and began to read it as "Jehovah.")

The pronunciation Yahweh is not completely certain. It is only an approximate reconstruction according to a more or less general consensus among scholars. There are also considerable differences of opinion regarding the etymology or original meaning of YHWH.

(JPW, November 30, 1976; AEB, 248–49; UTB, 62; author's notes from a lecture by Mitchell Dahood, of the Pontifical Biblical Institute, Rome.)

Ex 5:1 —— *Moses and Aaron went to Pharaoh*   The death of the king of Egypt is mentioned in 2:23. If the pharaoh of the oppression (1:8) was Ramses II, this would have been the king who had died. The pharaoh of the exodus, then, would have been his son and successor, *Merenptah* or *Merneptah*, who would have kept the Israelites under the harsh slavery established by his father. There exist not only statues of Merneptah but also his mummy, as impressively preserved as that of Ramses. The identification of Merneptah as the pharaoh of the exodus meets, however, with a problem resulting from the mention of Israel in his famous stele of Thebes (see Gen 32:28–29). It reads, "Israel is laid waste, his seed is not." What does this mean? Three explanations have been proposed: (1) It could be a reference to other Hebrew groups defeated during a campaign about which the stele says "Canaan has been captured." (2) It might be an allusion to Hebrew groups settled on the other side of the Isthmus of Suez. (3) The Israelite slaves in Egypt could have revolted and then been brutally punished by the pharaoh. (4) There seems to be room for still another explanation: "laid waste" might be understood as completely subdued and hence helpless slaves. And the phrase "his seed is not" could be an exaggerated reference to the effort to deprive the Israelites of descendants by killing their male children (1:16). (ETB, 30–34)

Ex 7:12 —— *every man cast down his rod, and they became serpents.*   According to the biblical narrative the magicians of Egypt imitated Aaron by making their rods become serpents. A scarab from Tanis, the very region which the Israelites occupied in Egypt, represents a snake charmer performing one of his tricks before three gods. A scarab is a small ceramic or a precious stone in the shape of a black beetle, usually having its flat side engraved as a seal. (ETB, 91–93)

Ex 13:17 —— *by way of the land of the Philistines*   This was the road that paralleled the Mediterranean coast, the most direct route between Egypt and Canaan. It was a part of the great route between Egypt and Mesopotamia by which armies marched in one or the other direction. The Egyptians also called it "the road of Hor" (the god Horus). It was garrisoned by a chain of forts. These are represented in a relief, dating from about 1300 B.C., in the temple of Karnak. They are also described in a document of Ramses II, from the middle of that century. In a site between el-Arish and Gaza, Dothan uncovered in 1980 the foundations of a fifteen-room structure, dating from the fourteenth century B.C. This was probably an official residence belonging to a very important Egyptian settlement, the most northeastern garrison town along the coastal route at the time of the exodus. ("The land of the Philistines" is a retrospective reference aimed at proper identification for readers at the time the book of Exodus was written. The Philistines actually settled in that region about a hundred years later.) Had the Israelites followed that road, they would have been forced to engage in battle with the Egyptian garrisons stationed along it. (WB, I, 140; *Time*, March 23, 1981, p. 35)

Ex 14:22 —— *into the midst of the sea on dry ground*   The topography of the zone extending from the Delta southward to the beginning of the Sinai desert has been greatly altered, due not only to the passing of so many centuries but in modern times by the construction of the Suez Canal. It is now impossible to locate even approximately the place of the crossing of the sea which the Hebrews called the Sea of Reeds, but which is called the Red Sea in almost all versions of the Bible. Strictly speaking, biblical references to the Sea of Reeds do not refer to what is at present called the Red Sea, which lies between Africa and the Sinai and Arabian peninsulas. Ordinarily the biblical reference is to the eastern tongue of the Red Sea, known today as the Gulf of Aqaba. This is made clear by the reference to the port of "Ezion-geber, which is near Eloth [Eilat] on the shore of the Red Sea" (I Kings 9:26). Only in the accounts of the departure from Egypt and the march along the western side of the Sinai peninsula does the phrase "Sea of Reeds" refer to the present Gulf of Suez. One should not conclude that the crossing of the sea was at the northern extremity of the Gulf of Suez, for in 15:22 it is clearly stated that after crossing the sea the Israelites "went into the wilderness of Shur," a region situated north of the Sinai peninsula and bordering the Mediterranean. This seems to indicate that the crossing of the "Sea of Reeds" took place east of Raamses, not very far from that city. This would have been in the so-called lake region, much to the north of the Gulf of Suez. One may conclude that the swamps and lakes in this zone were regarded as belonging to the "Sea of Reeds." Reeds would not grow in the Red Sea proper, but they are abundant in the lake region. In the light of the biblical data, one must conclude that the crossing of "the sea" occurred somewhere in the area between the Gulf of Suez and the Mediterranean, east of the Nile River. Unfortunately in this case archaeology cannot be of help, for in an event of this kind it is clear that no archaeological evidence could remain. Excavations made in the area prove only that it was well populated and that, especially to the north, the Egyptians had watchposts looking toward the wilderness.

Opinions are divided as to the route of the exodus as well as the place of the crossing, which occurred right at the start of the march toward the Sinai. According to the traditional view, the Israelites left Raamses, reached Succoth, camped at Etham "on the edge of the wilderness," and then moved in a southeasterly direction toward the Sinai peninsula. In accordance with this opinion, the crossing of the sea would have been closer to the Gulf of Suez than to the Mediterranean. It would have occurred in the swampy region which in some periods of the year would be joined to the waters of the gulf itself and therefore considered a part of the gulf. Since the biblical narrative states that after the crossing of the sea the Israelites "went into the wilderness of Shur," it would be necessary to assign to this area a much greater extension toward the south.

According to an alternative opinion, the Israelites would have gone to the northeast after leaving Succoth. They would have gone diagonally toward the Mediterranean and would have passed between the Egyptian fortified posts of Migdol and Pi-ha-hiroth before camping in Baal-zephon. The "sea" mentioned in 14:2 would then be the Mediterranean, with Migdol and Pi-ha-hiroth somewhere along its coast. Supporters of this view locate Baal-zephon on the shoal or key which separates Lake Sirbonis from the Mediterranean proper. When "a strong east wind" blows, the waves of the Mediterranean cover the key. According to this hypothesis, the Israelites entered the key with the Egyptian cavalry at their heels. When they had finished their crossing and were already safe on the mainland, the Egyptians went in to some depth. Then a sudden change in the direction of the wind caused a violent flooding of the key, and the Egyptians were drowned. After their persecutors' disaster, the Israelites went on turning from the Mediterranean coast to the south, and entered the wilderness of Shur. According to this view, Lake Sirbonis would be the "Sea of Reeds." That lake now consists of salt water, but at that time—so the supporters of this hypothesis claim—it contained fresh water from the Delta in which reeds could grow. This hypothesis seems to find support in the biblical narrative, for it says that the Lord commanded Moses to tell the people "to turn back and encamp in front of Pi-ha-hiroth." To "turn back" means clearly a change of direction, an "about-face." This would mean proceeding toward the northeast, instead of continuing forward. However, there are serious difficulties with this view: (1) According to the biblical account, Baal-zephon would have to be situated east of Pi-ha-hiroth, though the expression "in front of" might mean simply "in the sight of." In that case Baal-zephon could well have been west of Pi-ha-hiroth. (2) Whenever in the Bible reference is made to the Mediterranean it is called not merely "the sea" but "the great sea" (*yam haggadol*). It seems improbable that the text could identify the *yam suf* ("Sea of Reeds") with Lake Sirbonis (today Lake Bardawil). (3) The biblical narrative says that the east wind "made the sea dry land," and not, on the contrary, "flooded the land," as this hypothesis would require. (4) Since in 13:17 it is clearly stated that the Israelites did not go "by the way of the land of the Philistines" (see comment on that verse), it would have been inconsistent with the Lord's command if they had taken precisely that route, the most direct one but at the same time the one best guarded by the Egyptians. The crucial problem is that it has not been possible so far to identify with enough certainty all the sites mentioned in this episode.

Two other theories about the crossing and the Egyptian disaster have recently been advanced. One is proposed by Hans Goedicke, chairman of the Department of Near Eastern Studies at Johns Hopkins University. According to Goedicke, the Israelites were mercenaries escaping from their service to Egypt and were pursued by the Egyptian army in order to force them to return. The drowning of the pursuers was due to a formidable tidal wave coming from the Mediterranean as a result of the eruption of a volcano on the island of Thera (Santorini), north of Crete. This wave reached the Egyptians south of Lake Menzaleh and drowned them when the Israelites had just climbed to a safe height at the wilderness border. To support his theory, Goedicke has had to push back the date of the exodus almost two centuries, to the reign of Queen Hatshepsut, for the eruption took place in 1477 B.C. He believes that a hieroglyphic inscription of Hatshepsut contains the Egyptian version of the story.

Goedicke's theory has been much debated. One of the strong dissenters is Charles Richard Krahmalkov of the University of Michigan, who suggests still another possibility. First of all, he interprets the Hatshepsut inscription as a reference to Asiatics other than the Israelites, and he points out that in this story the drowned ones are the fleeing people, not the pursuers. He believes the Song of the Sea (15:1–21) is the earliest narrative of the event, where the description seems to refer to a storm at sea. For these and other reasons he suggests that the crossing took place much farther south, in the region of Thebes, where the Israelites embarked on ships from the port of Qoseir and succeeded in reaching Arabia or the Sinai peninsula. The Egyptians, following them, were also on ships, but were overtaken and drowned by a storm. Both theories raise many problems, and it is difficult to decide which one is more preposterous. (BAW, 60–62; EB, IV, 1,277–79; IDB, II, 197–98; WB, I, 141–44; OLB, 47–50; ABB, 38–41; TBAR, 3, No. 2 [1977], 22–31; 7, No. 5 [1981], 42–54)

Ex 20:1 —— *And God spoke all these words* In this way the text of the Ten Commandments is introduced. Its parallel is found in Deuteronomy 5:1–21. One of the oldest manuscript fragments known to be extant is the Nash Papyrus, named for its original purchaser. It contains a portion of the Ten Commandments and is dated from the second or first century B.C., according to certain authorities. Others assign it to the Maccabean period, while still others date it from the first half of the first century A.D. The text is that of the book of Exodus, but in 20:16 it reads with Deuteronomy *shaw'* ("unfounded") instead of *shequer* ("deceptive" or "false"). It also lists the sixth and seventh commandments in inverted order. The Nash Papyrus is kept in the Library of Cambridge University. (TOT, 24, plate 6; WB, I, 152)

Ex 21:12 —— *Whoever strikes a man* The section on manslaughter, assaults, and injuries covers up to verse 27. The corresponding section of the Code of Hammurabi consists of twenty laws. In the specifications and the punishments there are certain similarities, but there is a very important difference: the Code of Hammurabi discriminates in favor of the "nobles" or the "members of the aristocracy," and against the slave or commoner in deciding the degree of fault and in specifying the reparations and punishments. When it makes any distinction at all, the Mosaic code tends to favor the slave. (ANET, 175)

Ex 21:16 —— *Whoever steals* (that is, kidnaps) *a man . . . shall be put to death.* (See also Deut 24:7.) The corresponding law in the Code of Hammurabi reads: "If a seignoir has stolen the young son of a(nother) seignoir, he shall be put to death." According to T. J. Meek, the word *awelum*, here rendered seignoir ("lord"), means in this context a person of noble rank or a free person. It will be noted at once that the Hebrew law makes no such distinction; anyone who kidnaps a man, whatever his rank, shall be put to death. (ANET, 166)

Ex 21:22 —— *When men . . . hurt a woman with child* This law deals with a fight among men in which a pregnant woman is accidentally struck and caused to miscarry. If the harm is not serious, the penalty is a fine whose amount is fixed by the husband. If the harm is serious, the punishment is equal to the harm caused (the law of talion). An Assyrian law which corresponds to this same case does not specify a fight. A person guilty of provoking an abortion had to pay an indemnity of two talents and thirty minas of lead, receive fifty blows with sticks, and "do the work of the king for a full month." (ANET, 181)

Ex 21:28 —— *When an ox gores* Similarity of life and customs among various primitive societies makes their laws also similar. A famous Code of Eshnunna, dating from the first part of the second millennium B.C. (even older than the Code of Hammurabi), was found in Tell Abu Harmal, near Baghdad. It includes the following laws: "If an ox gores (an)other and causes (its) death, both owners shall divide (among themselves) the price of the live ox and also the equivalent of the dead ox. If an ox is known to gore habitually and the authorities have brought the fact to the knowledge of the owner, but he does not have his ox dehorned, and it gores a man and causes (his) death, then the owner of the ox shall pay two-thirds of a mina of silver. If it gores a slave and causes (his) death, he shall pay 15 shekels of silver." (ANET, 163; WB, I, 156)

Ex 22:18(17) —— *You shall not permit a sorceress to live.* An Assyrian law punished with death any prosecuted and convicted man or woman who "made up magical preparations and they were found in their possession." Not only eyewitnesses but also earwitnesses were admitted in the trial, but their declarations had to be made under oath before the king. (ANET, 184)

Ex 22:26 —— *your neighbor's garment* (See also Deut 24:12, 13.) The law commanded that a person's garment or mantle received in pledge had to be returned to the owner before sunset because he would need it as a covering during the night. A potsherd from the seventh century B.C., excavated at Mesad, contains a reaper's complaint before an official: "Let my lord the official (or governor) hear the complaint of his servant. As for your servant—your servant was reaping in Hasar Asam (?). Your servant had reaped. . . . Then came Hasavyahu son of Shovai, and took away your servant's garment. . . . All my fellow workers, who were reaping with me in the heat, will testify for me. . . ." (UTB, 180)

Ex 23:19 —— *You shall not boil a kid in its mother's milk.* Much more than what might be considered as sentiment was included in this peremptory prohibition. A ritual text from Ugarit mentions this pagan practice as part of an established ritual. Maimonides also said that this prohibition was due to a pagan rite. (BAR-2, 41, note 8)

Ex 23:24 —— *and break their pillars in pieces.* The excavations have uncovered many steles (pillars) dedicated to pagan gods with their images and corresponding inscriptions. When unearthed, they are usually found broken in pieces, and sometimes it is clear that the breaking was intentional. Some of them may have been broken by the Israelites during the conquest of Canaan. In Beth-shan, for instance, a stele dedicated to the god Mekal was found. It bears the god's image and an inscription in his honor. It was evidently broken deliberately. (WB, I, 157)

Ex 23:33 —— *if you serve their gods* The cuneiform tablets from Ras Shamra (Ugarit), excavated in 1919 in Syria, have thrown considerable light on Canaanite religion, about which we previously had only the references found in the Old Testament and in Phoenician writings. The main god was *El* ("god"). His consort was Asherah, and from them seventy gods and goddesses were born. The principal one was *Baal* ("lord"), the god of rain and vegetation, whose surname was Zabul or Zebul. Baal was really a title, the god's personal name being Hadad. He is often represented brandishing lightning. He had various local or regional representations, and so the plural form *Baalim* sometimes occurs. His consort was Anath, goddess of love and war, identified with Astarte. Other Canaanite gods were Dagon, Resheph, Shulman (or Shalim, Shalem), and Kathar (or Koshar). (ANET, 129–55; BAW, 101–20)

Ex 24:4 —— *And Moses wrote*   Writing was, of course, already known in the time of Moses. Since Moses was adopted into the royal family, he received the best education of that epoch in Egypt. He no doubt knew the Egyptian cursive script that had been in use since the end of the third millennium B.C. In Serabit el-Hadem, in the region of the Sinai, primitive Semitic inscriptions (thirteenth century B.C.) have been discovered in a script called Proto-Sinaitic because of where they were found. The Paleo-Hebraic script originated at approximately the same time. According to the so-called short chronology, this was precisely at the time of Moses and the exodus. The Hebrew script called "square," from which the present Hebrew printed letters derive, developed toward the year 1000 B.C. along with the Phoenician script, which had a strong influence on it. Some authorities think Moses could have used a cuneiform alphabetic script, because the similar Ugaritic script already existed in the sixteenth to fourteenth centuries B.C., the epoch assigned by scholars to the Ras Shamra (Ugarit) documents. This assumption, however, seems improbable, if not altogether impossible. (THS, I, 33, 34; CHB, I, 12, 13; WB, I, 159)

Ex 25:18 —— *And you shall make two cherubim of gold*   The cherub in all of its various forms was a common figure in the ancient Middle East. It was a fanciful or mythical creature, with a human face, wings, the body and feet of an animal, either an ox or a lion, sometimes with a tail of either one or the other. The cherub probably represented the supernatural combination of the characteristic qualities of man, fowl (especially the eagle), and either ox or lion. The winged bulls of Mesopotamia and the Egyptian sphinxes are varieties of the cherubim. Those discovered by the archaeologists are of various dimensions and made of various materials: stone, brick, mosaic, ivory, gold, etc. The cherub is associated with gods or kings as a symbol of power and majesty. The image of the "cherub" as a little angel, sometimes represented only as a small winged head, is an artistic creation of an epoch much more recent than that of the Bible. It is therefore an anachronism to represent the cherubim of the ark and the temple in the form of angels. A fragment of a stone cherub has been found in Jerusalem, and in a royal quarry there is an outline of a cherub carved in stone. (TOJ, 34–35; MTL, 101)

Ex 25:31 —— *And you shall make a lampstand of pure gold.* By means of the description in this passage, of the lampstand for the portable sanctuary of the wilderness, it is possible to have a rather precise idea of the form of the temple lampstand. The same type of lampstand, though in a simplified form, is still employed in Jewish worship. It was not an ordinary lamp holder nor a common lampstand. Lamps found by archaeologists from the Bronze and Iron ages for use with seven wicks have a very different shape. Representations of the *menorah* (Hebrew name of the sacred lampstand) from ancient times are uncommon. Among the earliest is the one which appears on a coin of the Hasmonean king Mattathias Antigonus (40–37 B.C.). Undoubtedly the most famous is the one that appears in the Arch of Titus in Rome. It is shown being carried in the triumphal procession which celebrated the capture of Jerusalem by Titus (A.D. 70) and the sacking of Herod's temple. The lampstand was a part of the plunder. The coat of arms of the present state of Israel is the menorah, as it appears in the Arch of Titus, with the name Israel in Hebrew characters inscribed at its foot, and surrounded by olive branches. (WB, I, 163)

Ex 28:30 —— *the Urim and the Thummim* It has not been possible to ascertain the nature of the Urim and the Thummim, which formed part of the high priest's equipment. The contexts in which they are mentioned indicate that they were used somehow in the casting of lots. In an Akkadian myth the bird god Zu usurps the heavenly sovereignty by means of his possession of the "divine tablets of destinies," which he has stolen. This suggests that the capacity to decide the lot or destiny of humans is an attribute of divine sovereignty. (ANET, 111–13)

Ex 29:12 —— *upon the horns of the altar* The first altar for animal sacrifice ever found in Palestine is the one excavated in Beersheba by Aharoni. It was not found in its original condition, for its stones had been used in the building of a wall. Not all of them were found, but the archaeologists used those that were found to reconstruct the altar as far as possible. The "horns" are the upper corners, diagonally projecting upward. Its height is about 63 inches to the tips of the horns (the three cubits prescribed in 27:1). According to Aharoni it dates from the eighth century B.C. and possibly earlier. The fact that it had been dismantled and its stones used to build a wall could be explained in the light of 2 Kings 18:22 (see the discussion at this passage). (TBAR, 1, No. 1 [1975], 8–9, 15)

Ex 30:1 —— *an altar to burn incense upon* We know the shape of this kind of altar not only from the description given in this passage but also because in several archaeological sites many similar small altars have been excavated. They undoubtedly were designed to burn incense and were made of stone or clay; some of them were perhaps for domestic use. Eight of them dating from the Iron Age were found in Megiddo. Another, also found there, dates from the time of the Israelite monarchy. (WB, I, 169)

LEVITICUS

Lev 7:32 —— *the right thigh . . . to the priest* This means literally "the shoulder" of a sacrificial victim, which belonged to the priest. Among the ruins of the Canaanite sanctuary at Lachish a number of animal bones were uncovered, and all of them were the upper part of the right foreleg, namely, the portion reserved for the priests. The rest of the victim would have been carried away by the worshiper for the family meal. The similarity with the Mosaic prescriptions for the sacrifice of the peace (or reconciliation) offering seems to indicate that certain ritual practices were widespread in the Middle East. They were incorporated into Israelite worship from their common cultural source, after being stripped of their pagan application. (BAW, 116)

Lev 19:23–25 —— *three years . . . fourth year . . . fifth year* The law in the Code of Hammurabi most like this one prescribes a total period of five years, but the distribution is different and has another significance. In this passage the fruit must not be gathered and eaten, the product of the fourth year is consecrated totally to the Lord, and only the product of the fifth year may be eaten. According to the Babylonian code, the first four years of a field rented to a farmer for cultivation are devoted to its "development." In the fifth year the owner and the tenant divide the fruit half and half, but the owner has the choice of his half. The originality of the Hebrew law is evident. (ANET, 169)

Lev 19:36 —— *just weights* Weights of different periods and also measures of capacity have been uncovered in various archaeological

46

sites. The weights generally are made of stone, are spherical in shape, and are identified by having their names engraved on them. The measures of capacity are usually containers, mainly jars, with the name of the measure inscribed on it. Because of their rustic manufacture, they are not "accurate" or "just" in a precise modern sense. However, they served as normative standards in a given period and region, although they differed according to time and place. For this reason the equivalences in terms of modern weights and measures are only approximate.

Lev 20:13 —— *they shall be put to death*   The Assyrian law against homosexual intercourse made the punishment fall on the active sodomite. Punishment consisted in delivering him first to be violated by other men and then to suffer castration. Hebrew law made no difference between the active and the passive homosexual: both were guilty of an abomination and were put to death. (ANET, 181)

Lev 26:30 —— *and I will destroy your high places, and cut down your incense altars*   Pagan worship took place in "high places" or shrines generally built on the tops of hills, mountains, or other heights. Before the building of the Jerusalem temple, the Israelites made use of the high places they found already in Canaan, after purifying them from their idolatrous elements and consecrating them to the cult of Yahweh. They also built sanctuaries expressly for Yahweh (1 Sam 9:12; 1 Kings 3:4). There were some periods, especially under the monarchy, when pagan cults infiltrated Israel. In some of these sanctuaries heathen rites were no doubt mixed with the worship of Yahweh. Not until 1964, however, were the ruins of one of these places of worship actually found. Aharoni discovered in his excavations at Arad in the Negev "the first Israelite temple that archaeology has ever found." It consisted of a courtyard divided in two sections, of which the smaller could have served as a vestibule. At the entrance to the main room the bases of two stone columns were found. In a corner of the courtyard were found the remains of a great altar built of unhewn stones, which was used for holocausts (compare Ex 20:25). The sanctuary proper consisted of two sections: the first corresponding to the Holy Place (Hebrew *heikhal*), and the second, somewhat smaller, corresponding to the Holy of Holies (Hebrew *debir*). Ascent to the latter was by three steps, on the second of which were two small altars. A stele lay fallen to the ground in the interior, "the first absolutely certain example of an Israelite *maṣṣebah*" (Aharoni). Two potsherds also were discovered, inscribed respectively with the names *Meremoth* and *Pashhur*. These raise the question as to whether the names designated the priestly lots for service (compare Ezra 8:33; 2:38). Since a royal citadel existed in Arad, which defended the south of Judah, Aharoni felt inclined to think that this was the citadel's sanctuary, but he quotes Mazar's opinion that it belonged to the Kenites, who descended from Moses' father-in-law and to whom reference is made in Judges 1:16. According to some authorities the Arad temple was schismatic, and the worship of Yahweh was mixed with pagan rites. As for the incense altars (Hebrew *hammanim*, singular *hamman*), the lexicons formerly gave "statues," "images," and "sun pillars" as the possible translational equivalents, and these are consequently the renderings found in traditional versions. However, in the ruins of Palmyra (present-day Tadmor) a small altar was discovered, dating from the first century B.C. and bearing the inscription *hamman*. This differs from the altar proper for burnt offerings, which is called in Hebrew *mizbeah*. This find is a clear indication that the *hamman* was a portable incense altar, which perhaps was placed on top of the other altar. (NDBA, 28–44; APB, 108; BAH, 26)

NUMBERS

Num 2:2 —— *shall encamp each by his own standard, with the ensigns of their fathers' houses* The Israelites followed the very ancient custom of using military banners or standards. We do not know just what theirs were like, but there are a number of frescoes and bas-reliefs in Egypt and Mesopotamia which give some idea of what they could have been like. Among the nonbiblical scrolls of Qumran, there is one called the *War,* which describes the formations of the "Sons of the Light," their banners, and the mottoes of the banners they carried before them during and following a battle. (DSSE, 127–29; LRQ, 209–11)

Num 13:19 —— *camps or strongholds* The "camps" were aggregates of tents or huts which were often formed outside the walls and under the protection of walled cities. Sometimes the camps were surrounded by rudimentary defenses of adobe. At times they developed into more or less extensive suburbs, even to the point of becoming a so-called lower city, because the fortified town was generally built upon a height. Some such camps became so important that the wall system was expanded so as to include them. This was, for example, the case in Jerusalem. Ruins of these adjuncts to walled cities have been excavated in Hazor and other sites.

Num 13:22 —— *seven years before Zoan in Egypt.* This reference makes it possible to calculate the epoch when Hebron was founded, since the date of the foundation of Zoan may be determined from an ancient Egyptian stele. Zoan (in Greek, Tanis), lying east of the Nile Delta, was the capital of the Hyksos pharaohs. The so-called

Stele of the Year 400 was found at San el-Hagar, the site of ancient Zoan. When Ramses II made that city his capital, he erected this stele to commemorate the fourth centenary of the foundation of the city. This occurred toward the end of the eighteenth century B.C. Hebron was founded at about the same time, so that it did not yet exist in the time of Abraham. This accounts for the expression "Kiriath-arba (that is, Hebron)" in Genesis 23:2; 35:27. The sacred writer thought an explanation was necessary for the better understanding of his contemporaries. It seems that the city was founded with the name of Kiriath-arba at the old site, which in Genesis 35:27 is explicitly identified with Mamre. It was like saying, "Mamre, afterward called Kiriath-arba, present-day Hebron." (WB, I, 213; BAW, 47)

Num 13:33 —— *the sons of Anak* Some Egyptian potsherds from about 1800 B.C. contain lists of enemies of the royal house. Among them is mentioned a tribe of Palestine called *Iyaneq*, practically the equivalent of *Anak*. Their relation to the "sons of Anak" is uncertain, but "it is the only evidence ever discovered for the aboriginal names preserved by the Israelites" (Wright). No archaeological evidence has so far been found for the existence of such "giants" (as some versions translate this passage). The height of these people, although somewhat notorious, could not have been greatly abnormal. (ANET, 328; BAW, 29)

Num 14:45 —— *and pursued them, even to Hormah.* In his excavations of 1971 and 1974 Aharoni identified the site of Hormah with the Tell Masos in the Negev, a little to the southeast of Beersheba. Arad (see comment on 21:1) and Hormah were the two main fortified cities of the Hyksos in the region from about 1800 B.C. Aharoni uncovered the remains of the fortified embankments at Hormah. The city declined in importance after the Egyptians had liberated themselves from Hyksos domination toward the middle of the sixteenth century B.C. The excavators also found the remains of the very rudimentary first Israelite settlement of the last part of the thirteenth century B.C. (AR, 41 [35], 1976)

Num 19:15 —— *which has no cover fastened upon it* A vessel in such a condition was ritually unclean. In order to cover it tightly, a vessel had to be molded in such a way that the cords fastening the cover could be tied firmly. A clay vessel found in Hazor clearly shows how this was done. It has four handles, and to match them, the cover has four protuberances with a hole in each. The cords were passed through each handle and the corresponding hole in the cover, thus permitting the cover to be tightly fastened to the vessel. By this hermetical sealing, contamination of the contents could be avoided. (WB, I, 218)

Num 20:21 —— *refused to give Israel passage through its territory* This refusal by the king of Edom was repeated by the king of Moab (21:22). Accordingly, Israel had to take a roundabout route. Glueck's explorations in the 1940s revealed the existence of a chain of fortresses along the borders of both Edom and Moab, north and south, east and west. It was impossible, therefore, to force a passage through those territories. (BAR-1, 53)

Num 21:1 —— *Arad* The excavations at Tell Arad, east of Beersheba and some 15½ miles south of Hebron, first uncovered ruins dating from the first century B.C. and later others from the eleventh century B.C. In the 1972 excavations ruins were found going back to the third millennium B.C. According to the excavator, Aharoni, the most exciting findings were almost two hundred potsherds with inscriptions and a sanctuary of the tenth century B.C. (see comment on Lev 26:30). The plan of this sanctuary shows a "Holy of Holies," a "Holy Place," and two pillars in front. These, however, were situated in the interior of a vestibule (Hebrew *ulam*) and not in front of it, as in the temple of Jerusalem. (ADHL, 89–99)

Num 21:18 —— *with the scepter and with their staves.* It does seem strange that a well could be dug with only a "scepter" and "staves," especially in the wilderness, where it is usually necessary to dig to a great depth in order to reach water. But it seems that in this case it is a matter of a rather shallow well that could in fact have been dug with sticks. Such places can be seen even today; they are called *temileh* by the Arabs. They are found in some valleys of the Negev where there is wet soil surrounded by dry sand. Occasionally even some green vegetation is found in these places. By scraping the mud with sticks, water can be made to seep out, sometimes in quantities sufficient to form small pools. Archaeological excavations are not, of course, necessary to reveal such sites, but such superficial finds help to explain this passage. (ABB, 57)

Num 22:5 —— *sent messengers to Balaam the son of Beor*   In the light of Babylonian texts Balaam would appear to have acted like one of the Mesopotamian soothsayers called *barus*. For their soothsaying and predictions they used sophisticated methods following a special ritual. Balaam's "omens" over Israel are preceded by sacrifices. These are repeated when Balaam does not find the omens favorable for the Moabites. The third time, Balaam gives up the auguries, and instead of cursing Israel as the king of Moab wanted, he blesses them. "The story is quite understandable when Balaam is studied as a Babylonian *baru*" (Wright). In 1975 about a dozen panels were discovered which had tumbled down from the walls of a temple at Deir Alla in Transjordan. The inscriptions are written in cursive Aramaic script. They date from the eighth or seventh century B.C. and contain a nonbiblical account about Balaam and his visions, prophecies, and acts. He is called "seer of the gods" and evidently came to have a prominent role in the religious traditions of the region east of the Jordan. (ABB, 57, 58; BAH, 14; BAW, 73)

Num 24:17 —— *the sons of Sheth.*   Being in synonymous parallelism with Moab, this phrase seems to refer to the nomadic tribe called *Shutu* by the Egyptians. A painting in an Egyptian tomb represents a caravan coming from Shutu, whose chief, called Ibsha, is designated as a "ruler of a foreign country." This painting is from the nineteenth century B.C. Egyptian documents of the thirteenth century B.C. describe the campaigns of Ramses II in the lands of the *Shoshu*, who seem to be the same people. (ABB, 59)

DEUTERONOMY

Deut 6:4 —— *Hear, O Israel* As a summary of the Jewish faith, this passage has become famous. It is commonly called the *Shema* (Hebrew word for "Hear"). It appears together with the Ten Commandments in the Nash Papyrus, dating from the second century B.C. This is not a portion of a scroll, but a separate sheet. Perhaps it was used for teaching or for formal worship (see comment on Ex 20:1). (BAW, 216)

Deut 7:5 —— *break down their altars, and dash in pieces their pillars* The ruins of Canaanite sanctuaries found in the excavations give evidence of their almost complete destruction by the Israelite conquerors of the territory. In the museum related to Hazor, established in the kibbutz Ayelet Hazahar ("Hind of the Dawn," title of Psalm 22), close to the ruins, the steles and a small statue of a god from the Holy of Holies of one of these sanctuaries are exhibited in the same arrangement in which they were found. The idol's head has been put back on the statue because the statue was found decapitated, with the head lying separately.

Deut 8:7, 8 —— *a good land, . . . a land of wheat and barley, . . . of olive trees and honey* In *The Story of Si-nuhe*, an Egyptian narrative from the beginning of the second millennium B.C., the official Si-nuhe, who was voluntarily exiled in Asia, describes Syria-Palestine in similar terms: "It was a good land, named Yaa. Figs were in it, and grapes. It had more wine than water. Plentiful was its honey, abundant its olives. Every (kind of) fruit was on its trees. Barley was there, and emmer. There was no limit to any (kind of) cattle."

Many manuscripts (some in papyrus) of this story have been found, indicating that it was very popular. (ANET, 19; WB, I, 260)

Deut 8:9 —— *a land whose stones are iron, and out of whose hills you can dig copper.* Glueck's explorations in the Negev, and especially in the Arabah, made it possible to locate many sites where copper was extracted and refined in ancient times, much before the exploitation of the famous Timnah mines. Glueck said that "the amazing correctness of historical memory in the Bible" has been proved. (BAR-1, 6)

Deut 9:1 —— *cities great and fortified up to heaven*   The excavations in Jericho, Lachish, Gezer, Megiddo, Beth-shan, Hazor, and other ancient cities in Palestine have revealed a system of fortifications which is very remarkable for that epoch. The system included walls, ramparts, moats, and towers, which by their height, thickness, and strategic location were almost impregnable. At least they were able to resist long sieges. The ruins also reveal the effects of conflagrations and devastation by superior forces.

Deut 11:12 —— *from the beginning of the year to the end of the year.*   In 1908 Macalister discovered at Gezer a tablet of soft limestone, dating from the tenth century B.C., which is considered to have been a kind of school "slate." It contains an inscription, probably a mnemonic ditty, about the twelve months of the year as related to agriculture. It has been called "The Gezer Calendar." It reads as follows:

> His two months are (olive) harvest;
> His two months are planting (grain);
> His two months are late planting;
> His month is hoeing up of flax;
> His month is harvest of barley;
> His month is harvest and *feasting*;
> His two months are vine-tending;
> His month is summer fruit.

For some time this had been considered the earliest known Hebrew writing, until in recent years a clay tablet was uncovered at Izbeth Sarte, possibly the ancient Eben-ezer, in the outskirts of Tel Aviv. It bears eighty Hebrew characters, and it seems to come from the eleventh century B.C. The inscription is quite blurred, and at the time of the present writing it has not yet been deciphered. (ANET, 320; BAW, 183; ANEP, 84; DOTT, 201-3, plate 11; TBAR, 2, No. 4 [1976], 6)

Deut 13:16(17) —— *a heap for ever* The heaps of ruins are called in Hebrew *tel* and in Arabic *tell*. They are sometimes actual hills or huge mounds built up by successive layers of debris from ancient towns. They are very numerous in Palestine. Many of them have been excavated and identified as ancient biblical cities.

Deut 16:21 —— *You shall not plant any tree as an Asherah* The Hebrew word *asherah*, here used for a tree, is also the name of an important Canaanite goddess, the consort of the god El, father of the gods. In turn she is called "the creator of the gods." Her symbol, to which also her name was given, was a stump, stem, or post, probably of phallic form, erected in her sanctuaries. Several representations of this symbol have been found. For example, a piece of ceramic from Cyprus shows three women dancing around an *asherah*. There is also a bronze model found in Susa and exhibited now in the Louvre Museum. It dates from the twelfth century B.C. and is known as the *Sit Shamshi*. It is believed to represent a ritual ceremony taking place at dawn. Two completely naked persons are seen at the moment of an ablution. Around them are pictured temples, big jars, sacrifice altars, several stumps, and other cultic objects. It undoubtedly is a ceremony at a *bamah* ("high place"). (ANEP, 203, 324; TB, 20; MLB, 79; WB, I, 270)

Deut 18:12 —— *whoever does these things is an abomination to the* LORD The context refers to sorcery, divination, spiritism, and other similar practices. Excavations at different sites have uncovered a great number of figurines, charms, amulets, and other objects connected with sorcery, fertility cults, demon exorcism, and pagan superstitions that at times propagated themselves in Israel to such an extent that legislators, prophets, and some rulers had frequently to warn the people against them.

Deut 21:17 —— *a double portion* Israel shared with other eastern peoples the right of a firstborn to a double portion when an inheritance was being distributed among him and his brothers. An ancient Assyrian law grants the firstborn son the privilege of choosing his two portions before his brothers by turn select theirs. In the case of a cultivated field, the firstborn son took one portion first, then cast lots with his brothers for his second portion. (ANET, 185)

Deut 22:23 —— *and lies with her* Verses 23–29 deal exclusively with cases of the violation of a virgin. Corresponding Assyrian laws also cover cases of the violation of married women and of adulterous intercourse consented to or solicited by a married woman. The main difference is that in the case of a violated virgin, her father has the right to take the wife of the violator, to cause her to be ravished, and to keep her without returning her to the husband. (ANET, 181, 185)

Deut 24:5 —— *When a man is newly married, he shall not go out with the army* This seems to have been a common exemption among Semitic peoples, as may be seen in a verse of the Ugaritic poem called "The Legend of King Keret." In describing the general mobilization of an army, it emphasizes that "E'en the new-wed groom goes forth." (ANET, 143)

Deut 25:5 —— *her husband's brother shall go in to her, and take her as his wife* Levirate (from the Latin *levir*, "husband's brother") was a custom of marrying a widow with no children to a near relative of the deceased husband. It was widely practiced in the Middle East, and it continues among present-day Arabs. The main reason for this custom was to keep an inheritance within the family. The Hebrew levirate included this motive, but the main reason was the perpetuation of the deceased husband's name or descent. The text of the Assyrian laws is damaged at this point, but it seems to allow the option between the brother-in-law and the father-in-law. Among the Hebrews, however, the latter alternative was considered improper (Gen 38:26). (ANET, 182)

Deut 25:11 —— *and the wife of the one draws near* For a case similar to the one described in this passage, the Assyrian law only punished the woman who in a fight had seized her husband's adversary by his genitals and caused injury to them. The punishment was to cut off her hand and even to gouge out both her eyes, depending upon the seriousness of the injury. The Hebrew law does not mention the precise injury. Punishing the woman by cutting off her hand seems to be because what she did was indecent, whether or not she inflicted injury on the man she assaulted. (ANET, 181)

Deut 28:68 —— *the LORD will bring you back in ships to Egypt, . . . for sale to your enemies as male and female slaves* The acquisition of Asiatic slaves by either purchase or capture is frequently represented in Egyptian frescoes and bas-reliefs. In one of the latter, two ships may be seen loaded with slaves—men, women, and even children. They are perhaps from Canaan, judging from their clothing, their hairstyles, and, in the case of the men, the pointed beard with which Egyptian artists usually depicted Semites. This bas-relief dates from the second half of the third millennium B.C. (WB, I, 291)

Deut 33, 34 —— Among the biblical manuscripts discovered in Masada, the Jewish fortress near the Dead Sea, are fragments of these two chapters, as well as of the book of Leviticus. As in the case of other biblical manuscripts in that find, the text agrees with the traditional Masoretic text.

JOSHUA

Josh 1:11 —— *to go in to take possession of the land which the* LORD *your God gives you to possess.* The conquest of Canaan by the Israelites has been dated as occurring in the thirteenth century B.C. This dating is based in part on Albright's study of the political geography of Palestine at the time the Amarna letters were written (fourteenth century B.C.). The main cities of Palestine at that time were Gezer, Jerusalem, Lachish, and probably Hebron. In chapters 10 to 14 these four are mentioned, but also five others, a fact which points to an epoch later than the fourteenth century B.C., when the number of city-states had increased owing to the fact that the power of the first four had declined. The traditional view of the Israelite conquest of Canaan has been that of a single and extensive campaign led by Joshua, but this view now finds less and less support among scholars. The increasingly accepted theory is that the Israelite invasion followed two main routes: one from the south, for which archaeological evidence is somewhat uncertain, and the other (best described by the biblical account) through the east, across the Jordan and then toward the north. This was the drive led by Joshua, for which the best archaeological evidence is that offered by the discoveries at Hazor (see comment on 11:10, 11). It is more and more widely believed that the Israelite conquest was not the result of a single campaign but that it took place by stages covering some two hundred years. The biblical narrative itself really seems to give support to this theory, for it states that the tribes did not at once take possession of all the territory assigned to them. Some Canaanite settlements remained in the midst of or along Israelite territory. A

58

notable example is Jebus, in the territory of Benjamin, which David had to capture around the year 1000 B.C. in order to make it his capital, Jerusalem. (BAW, 76; BRA, 33, 41)

Josh 2:15 —— *she dwelt in the wall.* Rahab's house "was built into" the wall of Jericho, so that one of its windows looked out from the outward side of the wall. No remains from Joshua's time are left among the ruins of ancient Jericho (see comment on 6:20), but from excavations in the ruins of other ancient cities, the fact that sometimes the inhabitants built their houses "into" the walls has been fully substantiated.

Josh 3:16 —— *the waters coming down from above stood* It seems that a sudden damming occurred in the Jordan, allowing the Israelites to cross the almost dry bed of the river. According to the biblical account this happened "at Adam, the city that is beside Zarethan." Adam has been identified with Tell el-Damiya, near the confluence of the Jabbok River with the Jordan. At this point a deep·ditch is formed in the river, and its eastern bank consists of earthen walls whose base is easily eroded by the stream. A sudden collapse of the banks must have produced such an obstruction to the normal flow of the water. A similar phenomenon has occurred in more recent times, namely, in 1267, 1906, and 1927. To the north of Tell el-Damiya is Tell Umm Hamad, which supposedly is the site of the ancient Zarethan. (WB, II, 24)

Josh 6:4 —— *the priests blowing the trumpets.* These trumpets were made of rams' horns. It is understood that the harsh sound of the horns, along with the war cry raised by the people, was designed to cause panic among the enemy ranks, as in the case of Gideon and his three hundred chosen soldiers at a later time. It must have been a common military practice in biblical times. The Qumran scroll known as the *War of the Sons of Light Against the Sons of Darkness* offers an interesting parallel: "The priests shall give with the six assault trumpets a shrill and intermittent blast to direct the battle. The Levites and all the corps of blowers of rams' horns shall sound, on their part, a mighty war blast to intimidate [literally, "to melt the heart of"] the enemy." (1QM 8:8–10; DSSE, 134; MMY, 8, 8–10, p. 101)

Josh 6:20 —— *the wall fell down flat* As one enters modern Jericho

from the north, there is Tell es-Sultan, the mound of ruins of ancient
Jericho. Excavations indicate that it was a walled city at various
times during the site's occupation. According to Kenyon, Jericho
was the earliest city of this type (8000 B.C.). During excavations
made in 1930–36, J. Garstang found signs of walls violently destroyed—as if they had fallen forward—and debris which indicated
a great conflagration. Since at that time these remains were dated
to the beginning of the fourteenth century B.C., it was believed that
they were the ruins of the Jericho of Joshua's time and of the walls
that collapsed when he besieged the city. However, the excavations
conducted by Kenyon from 1952 to 1958 give us a different picture.
They show, says Kenyon, "that almost all traces of the Late Bronze
Age town of the time of Joshua . . ." and even almost all remains
later than the third millennium B.C. (Early Bronze Age) ". . . had
been destroyed by erosion, and that the identification of one of the
lines of town walls as belonging to this period [Joshua's] was
mistaken" (AHL, 314). The traces of conflagration found by Garstang
would have belonged to the Middle Bronze Age, when all the
buildings "were violently destroyed by fire" (ibid., p. 197). The same
may be said of the fallen walls. "The excavations have revealed
clear evidence of collapses from an earthquake with the face of the
wall fallen straight forward onto the contemporary ground level"
(ibid., p. 105). Since time immemorial the basin of the Jordan has
been a typical seismic zone. (POTA, 73–80; AHL, 195–220; ADHL,
19–28; BAW, 78–80; BRA, 33, 38)

Josh 6:26 —— *at the cost of his youngest son shall he set up its
gates.* This probably refers to a ritual human sacrifice which seemed
to have been customary among pagans when they laid the foundations
of important buildings. In the excavations of ancient Jericho the
skeleton of a child was discovered in the foundations of the ruins
of a building, probably a sanctuary. First Kings 16:34 is an allusion
to the fulfillment of the curse in this passage. Similar interments
have been found in Tanis, Megiddo, Taanach, and Gezer. (AHL,
154; ETB, 100–2)

Josh 7:21 —— *a beautiful mantle from Shinar* Costly mantles and
other garments from Babylon and other places in Mesopotamia
(Shinar) were famous because of their fine weaving. In statues and
figurines excavated in that area males are generally represented as

wearing skirts woven in imitation of sheep fleeces. A statue of a woman, found in Khafaja in the Tigris region, dating from about 2500 B.C., shows her dressed in a full tunic or wide mantle of this type. The temptation to seize a mantle of this type is easily understandable. (WB, II, 32)

Josh 8:28 —— *So Joshua burned Ai*   This city is spoken of as being "beside Bethel" (12:9), and it is always mentioned elsewhere as lying close to Bethel or together with it. For this reason it has been identified with the ruins of Et Tell, some 10 miles north of Jerusalem. These ruins were excavated by J. Marquet-Krause. J. Simons questions this identification of the site, for in his opinion the Hebrew preposition translated "beside" (Bethel, 12:9) denotes a greater proximity than that of Et Tell (1¼ miles away). However, if the identification is correct, the archaeological finds raise a problem concerning the biblical account, according to which Joshua attacked, captured, and destroyed the city. Kenyon says, "The excavations showed, however, that the site was abandoned at the end of the Early Bronze Age, and was not reoccupied until well on in the Iron Age." This means that the site was in ruins and desolated from more or less the year 2000 until 1200 B.C. The conquest under Joshua took place toward 1220 B.C., when Ai would not have had the importance the biblical narrative assigns to it, even if at the time it had been repopulated. Besides questioning the identification, other explanations have been proposed in order to maintain the historicity of the biblical account: (1) The reference would be to the conquest of Bethel, of which Ai would be considered another name, because of their close proximity; (2) Bethel's defenders might have used the ruins of Ai as a fortified post and consequently as a part of the city's system of defense, and even as a part of the city itself for defensive purposes; (3) in the course of the centuries between the historical event and the final drafting of the book of Joshua (which seems to have occurred during the exile, and into which the traditions of the tribe of Benjamin were incorporated), a popular explanation of the ruins of Ai had developed. The name means "heap of stones," and gradually the history of Ai and the history of Bethel, being so close to each other, merged. It is interesting that in spite of Bethel's importance, its conquest is not recorded as a separate event. Indeed it is said that the people of Bethel joined the inhabitants of Ai in the battle against the Israelite attackers. It is possible therefore that the citadel of Bethel, where the king resided, was located in Ai. Accordingly, he is called "the king of Ai." On the other hand, in the list of the kings defeated by Joshua both "the king of Ai" (12:9) and "the king of Bethel" (12:16) appear, which seems to make the third explanation difficult to accept. As already noted, the book of Joshua omits all direct reference to the conquest of Bethel, but Judges 1:22–24 does report it. The excavations in Bethel (1934, 1955, 1960) have indeed shown that in the thirteenth century B.C. the city experienced a tremendous destruction, including a fire which left an accumulation of debris to a height of almost five feet. Albright and Wright attribute this destruction to the capture of the city by the Israelites. As to Ai, it seems that the most plausible of the proposed solutions is the third one, which was offered by Albright. (AHL, 115; APB, 234; BAW, 80–81; GTS, 270; EB, I, 945–48; DDB, 183–84)

Josh 10:1 —— Adonizedek king of Jerusalem This is the first time Jerusalem is mentioned by that name in the Bible. It was then a city-state inhabited by Amorites. Among the tablets discovered in 1887 at Tell el-Amarna, Egypt, there are 150 letters written from Canaan, when that region was under Egyptian rule. Five of them (Nos. 286–90) were written by a certain Abdu-Heba (or Abdi-Hiba), a governor of Jerusalem (*Urusalim*) and a vassal of the pharaoh. Judges 1:8 mentions the complete destruction of the Amorite Jerusalem. Later on it was settled by the Jebusites, under whom it continued as an independent city until the time of David (see comment on 2 Sam 5:9). (ANET, 487–89; MTL, 48–49)

Josh 10:32 —— the LORD gave Lachish into the hand of Israel This city has been identified with Tell ed-Duweir on the route toward Beersheba. It was excavated between 1932 and 1938 by J. L. Starkey, who was later brutally assassinated by Arabs. Stratum (or level) VI shows impressive traces of the city's violent destruction by its Israelite conquerors, including a third layer of ashes belonging to the epoch of around 1220 B.C. By this and other evidence it has been possible to fix the date with some precision. For example, a bowl was found belonging to the last Canaanite stratum and carrying the inscription "fourth year." This seems to be a reference to the reign of Pharaoh Merneptah, about 1225–14 B.C. After that the city remained practically without inhabitants, perhaps even until the time of David. A platform dating from the Davidic period has been discovered, upon which stood a palace which probably belonged to the provincial governor. There are also remains of fortifications built by Rehoboam. Stratum II shows the destruction suffered by the city during the second invasion by Nebuchadrezzar (589–87 B.C.). (BAR-2, 302–6; EB, IV, 888–93; WB, II, 39; BAW, 82–83)

Josh 10:34, 35 —— *Eglon . . . he* [Joshua] *utterly destroyed* As in the cases of Bethel / Ai and Lachish, the excavations at Eglon (modern Tell el-Hesi), carried out between 1890 and 1893 first by Petrie and then by Bliss, showed traces of the destruction caused by the Israelites. These traces were considered as dating from the end of the thirteenth century B.C. (BAW, 83)

Josh 10:38 —— *Joshua, . . . turned back to Debir and assaulted it* This city was also called Kiriath-sepher. Its ruins, identified with Tell Beit Mirsim and thoroughly excavated by Albright between 1926 and 1932, provided traces of the tremendous destruction that followed the Israelite assault. "It was found to have been completely destroyed, the fortifications demolished and the town burned in a conflagration so intense that the layer of ashes was in some places three feet thick" (Wright). However, Martin Noth and especially Moshe Kochavi do not agree with the identification maintained by Albright and other archaeologists, such as Aharoni. They believe that ancient Debir is Khirbet Rabud (excavated by Kochavi), located some 12 miles southwest of Hebron. (APB, 63–126; BAW, 83; TBAR, 1, No. 1 [1975] 5–7)

Josh 11:1 —— *Hazor* Excavations in and around the site of this great city of northern Canaan have shown that the earliest human settlements took place in the period of the Bronze Age which archaeologists call Early II (2600–2300 B.C.), stratum XXI, the deepest of these excavations. This verse is the first biblical reference to Hazor, but references to it in Egyptian and Mesopotamian documents and inscriptions are very numerous. It is first mentioned in the so-called Execration Texts, Egyptian lists of actual or potential enemies used in magical rites designed to make curses fall upon them. They are dated to the nineteenth or eighteenth century B.C. Hazor is also mentioned several times in the famous royal archives of Mari. This leads to the belief that Hazor was considered to be a very important city. It is the only Canaanite town mentioned in those texts, except for its neighbor Dan. These references show that the renowned King Hammurabi had ambassadors in Hazor. We also learn that there was a king of Hazor called Ibni-Adad (Akkadian for Yabni-Adad), a suggested equivalent of Jabin. This would mean that it was a dynastic name, and for this reason it was given to the king of Hazor defeated by Joshua. According to Yadin, who excavated Hazor, almost all the pharaohs mention Hazor among the conquered Canaanite cities. In the Tell el-Amarna letters a certain Abdi-Tirshi, king of Hazor, is mentioned. For some time there was uncertainty as to the site occupied by Hazor, but in 1926 Garstang identified it with certainty as the Tell el-Qedah (see comment on 11:10, 11). The more formal excavations at the site, carried out by Yadin, have thrown very important light on both prebiblical and postbiblical Hazor. Strata XIV–XXI date back to the Late Bronze II period (fourteenth century B.C.). Strata I and II date to the Persian (fourth century B.C.) and the Hellenistic (second and third centuries B.C.) periods. After that the site was never again inhabited permanently. (HYY)

Josh 11:4 —— *all their troops, a great host, . . . with very many horses and chariots.* Ivory bas-reliefs excavated at Megiddo show the kind of Canaanite infantry and chariots that Joshua had to confront in the decisive battle of "the waters of Merom." The chariots are light and are manned by archers, while each foot soldier carries a shield and the typical curved sword, similar to a sickle. These bas-reliefs date from the thirteenth and the beginning of the twelfth centuries B.C., precisely the period of the Israelite conquest of Canaan. (WB, II, 41)

Josh 11:10, 11 —— *Joshua . . . took Hazor, . . . and he burned Hazor with fire.* Because Jabin, king of Hazor, was at the head of the coalition of rulers defeated by Joshua in the battle of Merom, the Israelite leader attacked, captured, burned, and destroyed his city, at a time when it was the most important one of northern Canaan, "the head of all those kingdoms." It has two sections. One is a mound over 130 feet high (Tell el-Qadah), almost 2,000 feet long, and on the average 650 feet wide. Here the acropolis, or "upper city," was situated. To the north of it there is a rectangular plateau, measuring some 3,300 by 2,300 feet, with traces of a fortified surrounding wall. This was the "lower city."

Up to twenty-one strata, the deepest corresponding to the third millennium B.C., were uncovered in the mound by the excavations carried out by Yadin between 1955 and 1958 in nine areas of the enormous compound. The bare-rock foundations were reached. Other important levels belong to a period starting with Solomon, who gave back to the city much of its former importance, and extending to 732 B.C., when Tiglath-Pileser III captured and destroyed it. The "lower city," founded around 1750 B.C., flourished between 1550 and 1220 B.C., when all of Hazor fell into Joshua's hands. In the fourteenth century B.C. Hazor became the largest city in Canaan, but after its destruction by the Israelites, it was never fully repopulated. The excavation at the "lower city" did not uncover more than five levels of occupation. The lowest level gave evidence that its founders were Hyksos and that they built its earliest fortifications. The acropolis never recovered from its destruction by the Assyrians, and it experienced afterward only a temporary, limited, and occasional occupation. Traces were found, however, of successive citadels built on its westernmost flank. They correspond respectively to the Assyrian period, then to the Persian period (fourth century B.C.), and finally to the Hellenistic (second century B.C.) period.

In its best epoch Hazor had as many as 40,000 inhabitants. According to ancient standards, it was therefore a city of extraordinary size. In stratum XIII, which corresponds to the thirteenth century B.C., the excavators found impressive signs of a terrible destruction, not only by demolition but also by a formidable conflagration. There were thick layers of ashes and of brick debris, especially at the city's gates, decapitated idols of stone, and other revealing indications. Yadin says, "The striking similarity between the size of Hazor as revealed by the excavations and its description in the Bible as 'the head of all those kingdoms,' plus the insistence of the biblical narrator that Hazor—and only Hazor—had been destroyed by Joshua and burned, leave little doubt, it seems, that we actually found the Canaanite city of Jabin that was destroyed by Joshua. In that case, the excavations at Hazor provided, for the first time, decisive archaeological data for fixing both Joshua's dates and, indirectly, the date of the Exodus from Egypt." In other words, the excavation at Hazor, on the basis of the ceramics found in

stratum XIII, dates the capture of Hazor by Joshua, and consequently
the Israelite invasion of Canaan, as occurring in the thirteenth
century B.C. This provides practically unimpeachable support for
the so-called lower or short chronology. Accordingly, the exodus
would have occurred toward the beginning of that century and the
entry of the Israelites into Canaan during the last third of it. (HAZ;
BAR-2, 191–224; ADHL, 57–66; HYY, 145)

Josh 11:13 —— *mounds*   The Hebrew word for "mound" is *tel*, which
some versions translate as "hills." But a *tel* is an artificial hill,
generally formed by successive layers of debris. Ancient people
simply built a new town upon a previous one, which had usually
been destroyed by war. Accordingly, through the centuries, mounds
of ruins were formed, many of which have now been explored and
excavated. With the exception of Hazor, Joshua did not burn the
cities built upon such mounds, perhaps because they generally were
of some importance, since the sites had been rebuilt again and again.
A *tel* (in Arabic *tell*, a word used in many names of places) is a very
common feature in Palestine.

Josh 11:23 —— *And the land had rest from war.*   Albrecht Alt and
his school claim that there was actually no military conquest of
Canaan by the Israelites, but rather a gradual and pacific penetration.
Opposing this theory, Yadin writes: "The biblical narrative, in broad
lines, tells us that at a certain period, the nomad Israelites attacked
the city-states organization of the Holy Land and destroyed many
of its cities, setting them on fire, and slowly but surely replacing
them with new unfortified cities, settlements to start with; at the
same time, they were unable to dislodge certain cities which
continued to live side by side with the new invaders. . . . This
description . . . is exactly the picture which the archaeological finds
present to us: a complete system of fortified cities collapsed, to be
replaced by a new culture of which the material aspect can well be
defined as the first efforts of semi-nomads or nomads to settle down."
(JPW, August 3, 1976)

Josh 12:22 —— *Carmel*   This is a town identified with the present
Khirbet el-Karmil, some 9½ miles south of Hebron. It must not be
confused with the two other places with the same name. The Carmel
mentioned in 1 Samuel 15:12 is situated some 3 miles north of the

town mentioned in Joshua 12:22. And there is the famous Mount Carmel on the shore of the Mediterranean, which towers over the present city of Haifa and which is so much associated with the prophet Elijah. (GTS, ¶¶ 42–44, 319[c/2], 322[19], 685, 738)

Josh 15:7 —— *En-rogel* This is a spring situated southeast of the point where the valleys of Hinnom and of Kidron meet. The name means "Fuller's Fountain," and it certainly is the one called in Nehemiah 2:13 "the Jackal's Well" (others translate, "the Snake's Well"). It is identified with the present well which the Arabs call Bir Ayub ("Job's Well"). It is really a cistern some 33 feet deep, built with huge blocks of coarsely dressed stone, which can be dated, according to some authorities, to at least the last years of the monarchy of Judah. The ancient spring or brook probably disappeared during the earthquake of Uzziah's time which altered the configuration of the whole area to a considerable degree (Amos 1:1; Zech 14:5). This is the theory of Josephus, and it is subscribed to by some scientists. Others believe that the change in the nature of the spring occurred when the kings of Judah built the pool of Siloam in order to irrigate the "King's Garden," and especially after the construction of Hezekiah's tunnel (see comment on 2 Kings 20:20). The water which leaks into the cistern flows only in winter. Above the cistern there arises to a height of some 40 feet a sort of second level covered by a vaulted chamber. Many successive modifications of the structure have taken place during the centuries. This fact helps to explain the present dilapidated condition of the ruins. (MTL, 156–58; AR, No. 39 [1975], 4–6)

Josh 15:9 —— *the spring of the Waters of Nephtoah* Also mentioned in 18:15, this spring was one of the points marking the boundary between the tribes of Judah and Benjamin. It is identified with Ain Lifta, near the village of Lifta, to the west of Jerusalem. The redundancy in the phrase "spring of the Waters" has given room for the suspicion that the Masoretic text here may have suffered an alteration both in the vocalization and in the division of words. The Hebrew consonantal text *my nftwh* could be read *mynftwh*, which could be the Egyptian name Mer-ne-Ptah adapted to Hebrew. The translation would then be "the spring of Mernephtah" (an Egyptian pharaoh). A papyrus containing notes of a frontier official in the region of the Delta, with information about the journey between

Egypt and Asia in the time of this pharaoh (thirteenth century B.C.), mentions the arrival of an Egyptian official whose title was "Chief of the Bowmen of the Wells of Mer-ne-Ptah . . . on the mountain range." If the reference is to a place in Palestine where Jerusalem is located, then this mention could give support to the emendation of the original Hebrew as indicated above. (ANET, 258)

Josh 15:22 —— *Adadah* So the Masoretic text reads here, but 1 Samuel 30:28 reads "Aroer." It has been suggested that here the original text suffered an alteration and that "Adadah" probably should read "Ararah." In Hebrew the letters *r* and *d* in handwriting look very much alike and can easily be confused. Robinson identified the site in 1838 in Khirbet Ararah (or Arareh), some 12 miles southwest of Beersheba. This identification is generally accepted by modern archaeologists, including Glueck. The ruins of Adadah were excavated in 1975 by Biran, with the cooperation of Rudolph Cohen, directing a team of students from the Nelson Glueck School of Biblical Archaeology. Five levels of occupation, dating from the eighth and seventh centuries B.C., were discovered. According to Biran there was a possibility of finding levels of previous occupations at a greater depth. (JPW, May 27, 1975, 13)

Josh 15:47 —— *Ashdod, its towns and its villages* This important coastal city was one of the Philistine city-states. It has been fully identified with Tell Ashdod, near the abandoned village of Isdud, and has been excavated under the direction of Moshe Dothan. It presents twenty levels of occupation, from the beginning of the third millennium B.C. to the seventh century A.D. From these several levels have been recovered ceramics, remains of walls and houses, scarabs and cylinder seals, the corner of a Philistine fortress, figurines, cultic objects, common graves, and other finds. (ADHL, 129–37)

Josh 15:62 —— *the City of Salt* The Hebrew name is *Ir ha-Melah*. It was one of the six cities in the wilderness of Judah. It is almost certain that it was located at a place now occupied by the ruins of the Qumran monastery, northwest of the Dead Sea. P. Bar Adon, however, assigns it to a site excavated by him in 1967 on the shore of the Dead Sea, some 10 miles south of Qumran. He identifies Qumran rather with ancient Secacah (verse 61). At any rate, he considers that the place belonged to Qumran. Until all these discoveries were made, Ir ha-Melah was considered as entirely unknown. (BA, 36 [1973] 118)

Josh 18:1 —— *the whole congregation . . . assembled at Shiloh* The identification of Shiloh with the ruins of Khirbet Seilun, about halfway between Shechem and Bethel, has been made since the time of Eusebius and St. Jerome. Robinson verified it in 1838. The site was first excavated in 1926 by Danish archaeologists. They continued their work in 1929 and 1932 but left it unfinished. In the time of Joshua the tabernacle with the ark of the covenant was moved from Gilgal to Shiloh. In Samuel's time there existed in Shiloh a sanctuary proper (1 Sam 3:3), but its ruins have not been found. However, traces of the Israelite occupation lasting until 1050 B.C. have been uncovered. Approximately in that year the Philistines destroyed the town. By the time of Jeremiah the site was already completely in ruins and laid waste (Jer 7:12). In 1980 the Israeli government sent a team of archaeologists to the place in order to initiate new and thorough excavations, but since it is located in Arab territory, serious political disturbances among the people of the area began to occur and apparently the project was suspended. (IDB, IV, 329–30; BAW, 89)

Josh 19:6 —— *Sharuhen* According to Albright and other archaeologists this town or frontier post, which was part of Simeon's share in the allotment of Canaanite territories, has been clearly identified with Tell el-Farah, southeast of Gaza, in the southwestern limits of the territory where the Israelites settled. It was an important Hyksos center, at one time occupied by Pharaoh Shishak. It is mentioned in Egyptian inscriptions, according to some of which it was besieged by Pharaoh Ahmose three years after the expulsion of the Hyksos from Egypt. Pharaoh Thutmose III had a garrison in it. The excavations have uncovered remains of Hyksos fortifications and of an Egyptian citadel. (APB, 53; WB, II, 58)

Josh 19:35 —— *Hammath* The name means "hot spring," and it is identified with the hot springs about 1½ miles south of Tiberias. Some ruins of the thermal baths of the Israelite epoch have been found there. (TANT, 45)

Josh 19:46 —— *over against Joppa.* This very ancient port on the

Mediterranean (called *Yafo* in Hebrew), which has been in existence and active until the present day, is here mentioned in the Bible for the first time. It has been known also as Yafa, Jafa, and Joppe. Witness to its antiquity is contained in a manuscript of the Nineteenth Dynasty (Papyrus Harris 500, in the British Museum), dated to about 1300 B.C. It tells of the capture of Joppa by Thoth, a general of Thutmose III (or Men-kheper-Re), sometime between 1490 and 1436 B.C. Excavations started in 1950 have revealed remains of a rampart of beaten earth from the time of the Hyksos (eighteenth century B.C.), of buildings and ceramics from the seventeenth to the fourteenth centuries B.C., of the gate of Ramses II with portions of the adjacent walls, traces of a destruction with conflagration occurring in the thirteenth century and another in the twelfth century B.C., remains of the Persian and Hellenistic periods (among them an inscription with the names of Ptolemy Philopator and his wife Bernice), a fragment of a Hasmonean wall, parts of a building of New Testament times, and also remains of the later Roman and Byzantine periods. (ADHL, 113–18; ANET, 22–23)

Josh 24:1 —— *Then Joshua gathered all the tribes of Israel to Shechem* Shechem is mentioned at least three times in ancient Egyptian documents. The first two occurrences correspond to the Eleventh Dynasty, toward the beginning of the second millennium B.C. One of them is found in one of the so-called Texts of Execration in a list of Asiatic towns, many of which are in Palestine. It is there called *Skmimi*. The other mention occurs in the Khu-Sebek inscription, concerning an Asiatic campaign of Pharaoh Sen-usert (Sesostris) III (1880–40 B.C.), in which it is said: "His majesty proceeded northward to overthrow the Asiatics. His majesty reached a foreign country of which the name was Sekmem." The third mention appears in a satirical letter (Papyrus Anastasi I) of the Nineteenth Dynasty (thirteenth century B.C.). It says, "Where does the mountain of Shechem come?" Thus the city was known by its biblical name since very early times. It also is mentioned by name in Letter No. 289 of Tel el-Amarna, where it is said that Labayu "gave the land of Shechem to the 'Apiru'." Other letters were written by Labayu himself, who appears as the chief, lord, or king of the region of Shechem. These letters belong to the end of the fifteenth and the beginning of the fourteenth centuries B.C. The city was evidently very important and constituted a main center of opposition to the authority of the pharaohs. This may help to explain the curious fact that Joshua did not have to conquer Shechem and that he apparently considered it as already belonging to him, or at least closely allied to him. If the people of Shechem were in a sense also Hebrews, even though they had not gone down to Egypt with Jacob and his sons, their descendants at the time of the Israelite conquest would have recognized their kinship with the invaders and would have welcomed them as brothers liberating them from Egypt, whose suzerainty neither they nor their ancestors had ever accepted. Archaeological evidence confirms that the city was not attacked and taken by storm at the time of the Israelite conquest. The narrative in Genesis 34 could well preserve the tradition of this kinship relation between Shechemites and Israelites. (BAR-2, 258–65; ANET, 230, 477, 489; BAW, 76–78)

Josh 24:30 —— *And they buried him . . . at Timnath-serah* The name of this place is given in Judges 2:9 as Timnath-heres (Hebrew *heres* means "sun"). Perhaps the worship of the sun was practiced in that place, and this may be the reason why the Israelites changed the name. *Serah* means "corruption," in this case an allusion to the pagan cult. An ancient tradition, which dates from at least the fourth century A.D., locates Joshua's burial place in one of the funeral caves of Khirbet Tibnah (or Timna), an archaeological area where remains of the time of the Israelite conquest have been found. This could be the site of Timnath-heres. But, as in the case of many other identifications, this one relating to Joshua's tomb is very doubtful. (WB, II, 67)

JUDGES

Judg 1:6 —— *and cut off his thumbs and his great toes.* The brutal mutilation of enemy prisoners was a very common practice in ancient times. One of the bronze panels of the palace door of Shalmaneser III (middle of the ninth century B.C.), found near the ruins of ancient Calah at Tell Balawat, represents Assyrian soldiers in the act of mutilating enemy prisoners from Kulisi in the region of the sources of the Tigris. One of them has already cut off his prisoner's feet and is shown chopping off his right hand. (WB, II, 72)

Judg 1:28 —— *they put the Canaanites to forced labor* Forced-labor levies are a very old practice. The Israelites themselves had been subject to them in Egypt. They also found and continued them in Canaan. In one of the Tell el-Amarna letters (fourteenth century B.C.), Biridiya, governor of Megiddo, in a report to the pharaoh mentions one of these levies which he assigned to agricultural labor. Forced-labor levies were generally imposed on vanquished enemies. Solomon used them for his construction projects (WB, II, 74)

Judg 2:13 —— *the Baals and the Ashtaroth.* The god Baal and the goddess Ashtart were the main Canaanite deities. They were related to natural phenomena and to fertility. Because they had local and regional representations, their names frequently appear in the plural. *Ashtaroth* is the Hebrew plural for Ashtart (Moabite *Istar* and Greek *Astarte*). The Hebrews called her *Ashtoreth*, giving the name an ending that would sound like the word *bosheth*, which means "infamy" or "shame." At several sites the excavations have brought to light a great number of seals, small statues, figurines, as well as many bas-reliefs in which these divinities are represented.

Judg 4:2 —— *Jabin king of Canaan, who reigned in Hazor* In this case the excavations in Hazor by Yadin raise a problem, namely the chronological divergence between what is stated in this passage and what has been clearly revealed by archaeology. According to archaeological findings (see comment on Josh 11:10, 11), it was Jabin's Hazor that Joshua destroyed in the thirteenth century B.C. In the next century (the time of the judges) Hazor was already an Israelite city. The reference to Jabin in the book of Judges must therefore be an apparent anachronism. The problem results from locating this Jabin in Hazor; he may have been a later person by the same name. Neither Jabin nor Hazor is mentioned in Deborah's song, which seems to be the earliest report of the event. Several solutions have been proposed to explain the discrepancy. Yadin gives the following: "The narrative in the book of Joshua is therefore the true historical nucleus, while the mention of Jabin in Judges 4 must have been a later editorial interpolation." It would seem, however, that the interpolation may have been the phrase "of Hazor," for the Jabin of the time of the Judges could have been, as suggested above, a different person. (HYY, 12, 13, 249–55)

Judg 5:2 —— *The Israelites were determined to fight* (GNB; RSV: ". . . the leaders took the lead in Israel.") The Hebrew literally reads, "When the [warriors'] hair of the head is let loose." In the so-called Stele of the Vultures, discovered in Lagash (Tello), Sumer (now in the Louvre Museum), King Eannatum is represented in battle. He rides in his war chariot, and his hair is shown coming out of his helmet and falling down his back. Also the soldiers of his heavily armed phalanx (but seemingly not those of his light infantry) have their hair loose. It seems that the loosening of the hair was a ritual sign of preparation for war which the Israelites adopted. This custom persists among nomadic Arabs today. Deuteronomy 32:42 seems to refer to the same warlike practice. (MLB, 15, 16)

Judg 6:5 —— *coming like locusts for number* Coming in vast number like clouds, locusts are a common plague in the Middle East. The analogy was, therefore, natural and appropriate to designate a countless multitude. It is thus a frequent figure of speech occurring in the Bible, and it was a common form of expression among Semitic peoples in general. So in the Ugaritic legend of King Keret reference

is made to a huge army "like locusts that dwell in the steppe."
(ANET, 144)

Judg 8:6 —— *Are Zebah and Zalmunna already in your hand* The
Hebrew is literally, "Is the palm [of the hands] of Zebah and
Zalmunna already in your hand . . . ?" This expression may be
understood not only in a figurative sense as victory over an enemy
but also in a literal sense. The custom of cutting off and exhibiting
the hands or other members of the bodies of enemies, in order to
prove their utter defeat, was very common in the wars of the Middle
East. This practice appears in bas-reliefs such as those of Ramses
II in Abydos (thirteenth century B.C.). It shows the pharaoh's scribes
counting the cut-off hands of enemies piled up in heaps. (WB, II,
89)

Judg 9:6 —— *the pillar at Shechem.* This may be the great stele or
monolith (Hebrew *maṣṣebah*) that Sellin found in his excavations at
Shechem in 1926. The Drew-McCormick expedition in 1962 rebuilt
the temple's courtyard and restored the pillar to its approximate
original place in it. It is made of white stone, finely polished, with
rounded corners. It is 58¼ inches wide and 16½ inches thick. Its
original height is not known, but the height of the remaining fragment
is 57 inches on one side and 24¼ inches on the other. It seems that
it was located 35 feet from the entrance to the temple. (SW, 85, 86)

Judg 9:46 —— *the stronghold of the house of El-berith.* The description of the material stage of this dramatic passage is somewhat
uncertain. The "stronghold" (Hebrew *tseriah*, literally "chamber,"
"cellar," "vault") could have been the building whose ruins were
discovered in 1926 in Shechem and which seems to have the
characteristics of a type of fortress. The Hebrew word has been
sometimes translated as "crypt" (burial vault), but excavations have
not revealed any sign of the existence of a crypt proper in the ruins
of the temple, only underground cisterns or silos of very limited
capacity. There is some possibility that the *tseriah* was a sort of
storeroom of the temple. On the whole, Wright says "In Judges 9
. . . we have a most important correlation between the archaeological
discoveries and biblical tradition." (SW, 87–91, 124)

Judg 14:1 —— *Samson went down to Timnah* Tell Batash, about 4½
miles west of Beth-shemesh, was recognized as the site of the ancient

city associated with Samson's feats. But it was only in the summer of 1977 that a formal excavation of the place was undertaken. It revealed the existence of a Canaanite city destroyed by a great fire about 1200 B.C. The Philistines built their city upon its ruins. Pavements, ovens, silos, ceramics, and other remains of this Philistine city have been uncovered. At the time of the Israelite monarchy the city of Timnah had a wall 13 feet thick, and the great gate occupied an area of over 19 square yards. (JPW, August 23, 1977)

Judg 16:29 —— *Samson grasped the two middle pillars* In the summer of 1972, in excavations at Tell Qasileh, on the north bank of the Yarkon River, a mile or so from where it empties into the Mediterranean, the remains of a Philistine temple was discovered—the only such temple that had been found up to 1974. In the center of the floor of what was the main hall can be clearly seen the stone bases of two huge wooden pillars which had served to support the roof. (BA, 36 [1973], 43, 47, 48)

Judg 18:12 —— *that place is called Mahaneh-dan* This name means literally "Dan's encampment." Archaeological excavations at this site have shown that the earliest Israelite settlement was, in fact, a mere encampment. Only pits (or ditches) and silos have been found dating from that period. "The silos probably were used for storage while the people lived in tents or huts" (Biran). Afterward, when the Danites abandoned this semisedentary stage, they built houses. (BA, 43 [1980], 173)

Judg 19:15 —— *They went into town and sat down in the city square* (GNB; RSV: "he went . . .") Compare the verses that follow. The reference seems to be not to an open space in the center of the city but to a small square located at its entrance, between the outer and the inner gates and protected by the walls, like the one discovered when the ancient city of Dan was being excavated (1966–68). Compare 2 Chronicles 32:6, where it is explicitly said, "in the square at the gate of the city." These small squares situated at the gate of the city were common in walled towns, such as those of the old city of Jerusalem, especially at the Damascus and Jaffa gates, which still exist. (BA, 37 [1974], 48)

Judg 20:40 —— *the whole of the city went up in smoke to heaven.* When in 1922–23 Albright excavated Tell el-Ful, site of the Gibeah of Benjamin, he found the ruins of a fortress. In its deepest level, corresponding to about 1200 B.C., there were clear signs of a great fire. "This confirmation of the biblical narrative," Albright writes, "is particularly interesting, since the historicity of the story in question had often been doubted." Ruins from the time of Saul (end of the eleventh century B.C.) were also found at that place. Saul was a native of that city. (APB, 47)

RUTH

Ruth 4:1 —— *And Boaz went up to the gate and sat down there* In 1979 the gateway of the Canaanite city of Dan, dating from about 1900–1700 B.C., was found. It consists of two towers and a remarkable arch, formed by three courses of huge mud-brick blocks. After a relatively short period of use, it was buried for some reason under a massive rampart built at a later date for the city's defense. Its marvelous preservation is due to this fact. This gateway is, of course, much older than the gate referred to in this verse. But the ruins of the Israelite gate of the time of Boaz have also been uncovered. This happened during the excavations of 1966–68. Near its entrance great blocks of stone were found. They formed a bench 15 feet long, apparently like those that would be at the gates of other towns. The elders, judges, and other city notables would sit on such a bench to conduct their business. (Also see verse 2, and compare Gen 19:1, Ps 69:12 et seqq.) (TBAR, 7, No. 5 [1981], 20–28; BA, 37 [1974], 45)

Ruth 4:10 —— *from the gate of his native place* (See 4:1.) In the course of time the term "gate" also came to mean the "meeting" or "assembly," not only of the authorities in particular but even of the people in general (compare 3:11). In the Code of Hammurabi there is a law in which the Babylonian word *babtum* (literally "gate") is used in the same sense. For that reason Meek translates it as "city council." (ANET, 171)

77

THE FIRST BOOK
OF SAMUEL

1 Sam 1:24 ―― *a three-year-old bull*   As pointed out in the footnote to this verse, the Masoretic text reads "three bulls." With its vocalization and division of words, it literally means "with bulls three." But with a different vocalization and division it can be translated as "a three-year-old bull." This rendering is supported by a Qumran scroll and by the old Greek and Syriac versions. It is supported also by the tablets found in Nuzi, according to which in the Middle East a bull was not considered mature enough to be acceptable for sacrifice until it was at least two years old. (WMTS, 41)

1 Sam 4:4 ―― *who is enthroned on the cherubim*   Archaeological excavations have uncovered figurines of Mesopotamian and Canaanite gods represented as kings seated upon thrones flanked by cherubim. Sometimes they appear standing upon animals, most commonly lions. For example, a bas-relief found in Maltaya, north of Mosul, represents a procession of five gods and two goddesses. All of them are shown standing upon diverse animals, except one of the goddesses, who appears seated on a throne which in turn is placed upon an animal. This throne has cherubim carved on its base. (ANEP, 181, 314)

1 Sam 6:4 ―― *and five golden mice*   The Philistine priests and diviners advised sending to the Israelites as reparation golden figures of the tumors and the mice that had made them suffer so severely. This was no doubt regarded as a means of ridding themselves of these plagues. In the Middle East excavations have uncovered figures of rats and mice evidently used in some magic ritual. In the ruins of the temple at Gebal (Byblos) one image of a mouse is made of alabaster; it may have had this ritual use. (WB, II, 119)

1 Sam 6:7 —— *a new cart* In a bas-relief of Ramses III, portraying this pharaoh's campaign against the "Sea Peoples" (Philistines and kindred peoples) there are some exact representations of the Philistine carts. Like carts used by many peoples in Africa and America, their wheels were made of single, solid, circular blocks of wood. The upper section of a cart was formed by crossed wooden bars in the shape of a cage. In such a cart the Philistines returned the ark of the covenant to the Israelites. (WB, II, 120)

1 Sam 8:11 —— *the ways of the king* Samuel's description of the privileges belonging to a king is based on the practices followed by Canaanite kings for centuries and made known by the tablets in cuneiform script discovered at Ras Shamra (Ugarit). These tablets reflect the same practices followed by Israelite monarchs beginning with Solomon.

1 Sam 9:24 —— *So the cook took up the leg and the upper portion and set them before Saul* The leg of an animal was considered the choicest piece of meat. It was therefore served to the owners of the house and to guests of honor as a token of preference. In Egyptian reliefs representing sacrificial feasts and banquets, whole legs are commonly shown being set before honored persons. The Hebrew word translated as "the upper portion," although obscure (see footnote in RSV), seems to refer (with a slight emendation of the Hebrew text) to "the tail." This would have been the rich fat tail of a special breed of sheep common in Palestine (*Ovis laticaudata*). It was the portion of sacrificial victims reserved for the priest (see Ex 29:22). The suggested emendation is supported by the Aramaic version (Targum) and by the Babylonian Talmud ('*Aboda Zara* 25a). (WB, II, 125)

1 Sam 13:21 —— *and the charge was a pim* For centuries and even until very recent times, this obscure verse has been translated by rendering the word *pim* in its literal sense of "mouths," even though this meaning makes no sense in the context. The Septuagint seemingly had a different Hebrew text for the first part of the verse. Since Jerome noticed that *pim* could also mean "cutting edges" he rendered it with that meaning in the Vulgate. The KJV understood "file," perhaps because in a sense mouths (*pim*) can bite. Recent archaeological finds have at long last clarified at least the first part of this verse. In excavations at Lachish and other sites, stone weights with the word *pim* carved in them were discovered. These weights were about ¼ ounce, more or less two thirds of a shekel. As can be seen, the RSV took notice of this discovery.

The Hittites were already acquainted with iron. In fact, they had known it since before the twelfth century B.C., and they jealously guarded the secret of its production. The Philistines, however, had in some way come upon the secret and maintained the monopoly of its application to the manufacture of tools and agricultural implements, whose use they introduced into Palestine. That situation lasted until Saul and David broke their power. (BAW, 91–94)

1 Sam 15:34 —— *and Saul went up to his house in Gibeah of Saul.* Saul's native city, which later took on his name, has been clearly identified as Tell el-Ful, some 3 miles north of Jerusalem. Among its ruins a tower and a double casemate wall have been found. The latter formed one of the four corners of a citadel built during the first period of the Israelite monarchy. In the time of Saul the place was occupied by a Philistine garrison. Some have conjectured that the first Israelite king may have later used it as his residence. This is the reason why in some archaeological texts it is called "Saul's fortress." The name Saul is a very old one. In the Ebla tablets (third millennium B.C.) it appears as *sa-u-lum*. (WB, II, 134; POTA, 81–85; BAW, 122–23; BA, 43 [1980], 202)

1 Sam 17:4 —— *a champion* The Hebrew word is *ish-habbenayim*, commonly translated as "champion," "paladin," "challenger." The term *benayim*, being the dual form of *bayin* and apparently meaning "intermediate space," can be translated literally as "man of the intermediate spaces." In this particular case it would mean "man between two (armies)." The context shows that such a person was a duelist representing an army. In single combat with an enemy duelist, it was his task to decide the battle's fate. This expression occurs only twice in the Bible, here and in verse 23. But in one of the nonbiblical scrolls of Qumran (the so-called War Scroll), it appears some fourteen times, either in a dual form or as the simple plural *bayinim*. In this scroll it designates a heavily armed infantry corps, which constituted the center ("between the two wings") of a combat formation. We would now call such soldiers "shock troops." It would therefore seem that Goliath belonged to such a select corps of especially armed warriors.

1 Sam 17:35 —— *I caught him by his beard, and smote him and killed him.* In Tell Halaf, the biblical city of Gozan, an orthostat has been uncovered which represents a man fighting a lion. (An orthostat is a block of dressed stone used as the base of a wall constructed of adobe or fired brick.) Overpowering a lion seems to have been one of the typical feats of a traditional hero. (UTB, 114)

1 Sam 17:40 —— *five smooth stones* In this case it has not been necessary to appeal to archaeology. Smooth stones like the ones chosen by David for his sling in the combat with Goliath can still be easily gathered in the valley of Elah (or "of the Terebinth"), where the battle took place. Archaeology has uncovered in various excavations a great number of slingstones. This rustic weapon, so simple and yet so terrible when skillfully handled, was very common, not only in David's time but for centuries before and after him. In many countries slings are still used for chasing away wild animals which threaten the flocks. (BAW, 124–25)

1 Sam 23:29 —— *Engedi.* The oasis of Engedi, famous since ancient times, is now the site of a small Israeli village on the western shore of the Dead Sea. In David's time it was surrounded by a craggy, desolate, and inhospitable area. In Joshua 15:62 it is mentioned, perhaps by an anachronism, as one of the "cities" of Judah. Remains of buildings constructed long before the sixth century B.C. have been uncovered there. The archaeological excavations at the site in 1949, 1961, and 1962 have revealed that it flourished primarily toward the end of the kingdom of Judah, perhaps under Josiah, when it may have been a royal possession. The discoveries confirm that its main industries were the making of perfumes and wine (Song 1:14). (ADHL, 67–76)

1 Sam 25:14 —— *Abigail, Nabal's wife* In a seal made of red carnelian, found apparently at Ashkelon, the name "Abigail" appears. This seal did not belong to Nabal's wife, for it reads, "Of Abigail, the wife of Ashayahu." It belongs to the Ustinov Collection in Jaffa. (SPA, 105)

1 Sam 31:10 —— *They put his armor in the temple of Ashtaroth* This temple was in Beth-shan, the ruins of which have been excavated at Tell el-Husn, north of the Israeli city of Beth-shean. Several temples have been uncovered there. The one in the north of the mound was dedicated to Ashtaroth and is located in the stratum that corresponds to the twelfth century B.C. With some changes it was in use until David's time (toward the end of the eleventh century B.C.). This is almost certainly the temple where the Philistines put Saul's armor after his defeat and death at Mount Gilboa. What were the Philistines doing so far to the north and so near to the Jordan, when their own territory was in the southwest of Palestine on the shore of the Mediterranean? Excavations have revealed that when this region was part of the Egyptian empire, Beth-shan was a stronghold used by the pharaohs to protect the fertile grain-producing Plain of Esdraelon. Many traces of this Egyptian occupation have been found. The pharaohs used Philistine mercenaries to man the garrison, and descendants of these evidently remained in control of Beth-shan and the surrounding region even until the time of the early Israelite monarchy. In their excavations there archaeologists have uncovered numerous artifacts from the Philistine period. (WB, II, 159; BAW, 95–97)

The city of "Ur of the Chaldeans," considered by some to be Abraham's native town, was the prosperous center of a brilliant civilization. Among its ruins is this stepped tower or pyramid called a ziggurat. The tower of Babel may have been similar to a ziggurat (Gen 11:4, 28).

Excavations in Tell es-Sultan, the mound of ruins of ancient Jericho, indicate that it was a walled city since ancient times. However, almost all traces of the town of Joshua's time have been lost, since almost all remains later than the third millennium B.C. were destroyed by erosion in the course of many centuries (Josh 6:20).

Presumably, the Holy of Holies of Solomon's temple stood on the huge rock preserved under the Islamic sanctuary known for that reason as the Dome of the Rock (1 Kings 6:16).

The Siloam inscription found near the southern end of Hezekiah's tunnel (2 Kings 20:20).

Mosaic of the church at et-Tabgha (Mt 14:19).

Remains of a storehouse stand among the ruins at Beersheba. The town flourished under Israelite rule (2 Kings 23:8).

Ruins of Herod's funeral monument, called the Herodium (Mt 2:1).

"Moses' seat" of the Chorazin synagogue, a seat reserved for the president or main teacher or for an important guest speaker (Mt 23:2).

A broken slab found in Caesarea with the only inscription bearing Pilate's name so far discovered (Mt 27:2).

A section of the retaining wall of the esplanade where Herod's temple stood. It was formerly called the Wailing Wall but now simply the Western Wall. It is considered the holiest of the places sacred to Judaism (Mk 13:1).

THE SECOND BOOK
OF SAMUEL

2 Sam 1:21 —— *nor upsurging of the deep!* The Hebrew literally reads "neither fields of offerings," which does not seem to make sense. RSV, in the footnote, marks the rendering "nor upsurging of the deep" as a correction or emendation of the Hebrew text. It finds support in an interesting textual parallel found in the Ugaritic poem about Aqhat. There Daniel (or Danel) pronounces a curse or prediction, using the same words as in the RSV translation. (ANET, 153; UT, 245)

2 Sam 2:13 —— *and met them at the pool of Gibeon* (This name is also given as Gibon and Gabaon.) Excavations in 1956–57 and 1959–60 have uncovered an admirable hydraulic system in connection with this pool. The pool or reservoir proper lies at a depth of about 80 feet. There are two sections which are reached by a spiral stairway with 79 steps attached to the walls of a pit which averages 37 feet in diameter. The pool or reservoir measures 22 feet by 11 feet. A tunnel 170 feet long leads from it and descends by 43 steps to an additional depth of almost 80 feet. This tunnel originally led to the lower part of the city. (EB, III, 643–47; POTA, 110–14; ADHL, 139–46)

2 Sam 2:16 —— *and thrust his sword in his opponent's side* In the ruins of Gozan (Tell Halaf) an orthostat was found which depicts two warriors killing each other in the same way as described in this passage: that is, grabbing each other by the forelock and stabbing at each other with their swords. This may have been the usual way of fighting a personal duel. (UTB, 114)

83

2 Sam 2:23 —— *smote him in the belly with the butt of his spear*   In this way Abner, who was being pursued by Asahel, was able to kill him without having to turn around in order to smite him with the spear's point. The butt of the spear was also made of metal and was used to stick the spear in the ground or as a goad when driving oxen or horses. It appears in one painting dating from the Iron Age. In addition to spearpoints, a great number of spear butts have been found in excavations. As this passage shows, a spear butt could be lethal. (WB, II, 166)

2 Sam 4:3 —— *Gittaim*   See also 2 Kings 12:17(18), where this name appears as Gath. It should not be confused with the Gath which was one of the main Philistine cities. It is identified with the present Tell Ras abu Hamid, near modern Ramleh. It is the same town called Gath in 1 Chronicles 7:21.

2 Sam 5:8 —— *the water shaft*   This is how the Hebrew *tsinor* is translated here. Its meaning is uncertain. But it evidently refers to a part of the old subterranean system that conveyed water to the city from the Gihon spring. It could be the shaft discovered in 1867 by Warren, a kind of secret passage between the spring and the city and used in the case of a siege. It seems that this shaft was discontinued when Hezekiah built his underground aqueduct (see 2 Kings 20:20, 2 Chron 32:30). In 1910 an assistant of Parker succeeded in getting into the city by climbing through this shaft, apparently as Joab did (compare 1 Chron 11:6). The shaft still exists and has recently been explored and cleared of debris. According to Kenyon, "The story of Joab's entry into the city by an underground tunnel, to create a diversion within the wall which enabled David to break in, is one of the most dramatic of the Old Testament. Archaeology has almost certainly identified the route. . . . There is . . . a strong probability that it [the tunnel] belongs to the Jebusite city, and that it was thus the channel up which Joab crawled." Vincent shares this opinion and tells of having himself been a witness to the feat of Parker's assistant, who was aided by a Welsh miner. J. Simons discusses the matter at length and suggests that the correct translation is "to reach the shaft" of the spring, and not "get up," as RSV and other versions read. He believes that it would therefore be understood that Joab climbed the hill by sheer force until he reached the upper mouth of the *tsinor*, which he then blocked, thus preventing access to the spring from above. Mazar summarily reviews the debate on this matter and proposes abandoning Vincent's theory, which others have followed. He believes, with J. Braslavi, that the *tsinor* was the horizontal conduit that carried the water from the spring to a pool under the shaft, and not the shaft itself. Since the word translated "to reach" also could very well be literally translated "to hurt" or "to strike," what Joab did would have been to reach the water conduit on the side of the spring, namely, at the foot of the hill, and to block it so as to leave the city without water. In verse 8 the Hebrew text consists of what is called an anacoluthon, an unfinished sentence, and it further obscures the meaning by the curious reference to "the lame and the blind." However it all happened, Joab performed a courageous and decisive feat that precipitated the fall of the Jebusite city. (AHL, 242–43; JAT, III, 632; JOT, 168–73: MTL, 168–69)

2 Sam 5:9 —— *the city of David. . . . the Millo* The site of the city of Jebus (the Jebusite Jerusalem, captured by David and then designated as his capital) has since ancient times been located on the southeastern hill of the city, to the south of and outside the present Turkish wall. Since 1867 a great number of excavations have been made in and around Jerusalem. The most important are those carried out under the direction of Kenyon from 1961 to 1967. The oldest ruins so far recovered are those belonging to the Jebusite wall (1800 B.C.), including those of a gatè. The duct which conveyed the waters from the Gihon spring and which David used to capture the city was also uncovered. Ruins corresponding to later times will be mentioned in connection with the respective passages. The Millo (literally "filling") was apparently the name given to the earth fill which leveled a ravine originally separating the southern extremity of Mount Moriah (known today as the Temple Mount) and the southern hill. This area was called the Ophel, a name also given by extension to the hill itself. On the terrace that resulted from the fill, an important fortification, which retained the name Millo, was evidently constructed later. So far, however, no identifiable remains of this fortification have been found during the extensive excavations in that area. Some archaeologists believe it was located at the site where Macalister discovered traces of a breach, possibly the one mentioned in 1 Kings 11:27. If so, the Millo originally would have served to fill it. Solomon would have then converted it into an actual fortification (JOT, 116, 131). Mazar, however, believes that the Millo "may well have been the terrace on the eastern slope of the southeastern spur, forming supporting walls for the structure above. It seems to have been here that the more splendid buildings of the City of David were built" (JR, 6). "Around the terraces was a supporting wall which stabilized the fill and formed a straight platform for the large building from the 8th–7th centuries B.C. This building was apparently the 'Beth Millo' (the house of the filling) mentioned in 2 Kings 12.22 as the place where King Joash was murdered. The Beth Millo was apparently a huge fortified building included in the fortification system of the Ophel; it was constructed on the terraces which were built on the hill slope. The Beth Millo was razed at the time of the destruction of the First Temple (586 B.C.)." (TBAR, 6, No. 4 [1980], 53)

In Lachish archaeologists discovered a great terreplein or platform which had a covering of stone. It is some 23 feet high, and it seems that a fortress or palace was built upon it. Remains of a similar structure were found in Beth-shemesh also. It appears that the Ophel was substituted for the Millo in the time of the kings of Judah, who built a new fortress with that name between the City of David and the Temple Mount (compare 2 Chron 27:3; 33:14). Mazar has undertaken important excavations at the site. It is believed that a segment made of undressed stones, which was discovered by Warren to the southeast of the southeastern corner of the Temple Mount's retaining wall, belongs to the old Ophel wall (compare Neh 3:26). (TCD; BAW, 126–30; JAT; JOT; MTL, 50, 171–73, 198–99)

2 Sam 18:24 —— *between the two gates* (See 19:8[9].) The stronger walled cities had an outer and an inner gate, with a covered passage or narrow entrance hall between them. Along the sides of the passage were usually rooms occupied by guards. Excavations have uncovered remains of such city gates at Megiddo, Samaria, and other places. In modern Jerusalem, the Damascus Gate, the Lions' Gate, and Sion's Gate, although not in all details like the ancient ones, give some idea of the system of protection offered by a double gate.

2 Sam 19:8(9) —— *Then the king arose, and took his seat in the gate.* In the excavations at the gate of the ancient city of Dan (1966–68), a type of stone platform was found, having traces of four small pillars at its corners. The bases of two of these pillars were found in place and another nearby. Apparently the pillars served to support a canopy or awning. It is possible that the place where David used to sit before the people was similar to this structure (compare 1 Kings 22:10). Others suppose, however, that it could have been a kind of altar or podium for an idol (see 2 Kings 23:8; Ex 8:3, 4). (BA, 37 [1974], 47; TBAR, 7, No. 5 [1981], 24)

2 Sam 24:16 —— *Araunah* In Hebrew this name has a definite article. This fact, and also certain passages in the texts of Ras Shamra (Ugarit), suggest the possibility that it is a title rather than a proper name and that the *araunah* might have been a type of feudal baron (or "king"). If it was a Jebusite title, the alternative translation in verse 23 could very well be, "King Araunah gives all this to the king" (that is, to David). The word could be of Hurrian origin, namely, *iwirne* or *ewrine*, meaning "lord" and referring to a ruler. (IDB, I, 195; JR, 4)

THE FIRST BOOK OF THE KINGS

1 Kings 2:10 —— *and was buried in the city of David.* It has not been possible to identify with complete certainty the exact location of the royal burial grounds, in spite of the extensive excavations carried out in the area where the City of David stood to the south of the Temple Mount. Some tombs have been discovered there, and some of them are of such size and structure that they seem to have belonged to important persons, possibly kings or other members of Judah's royal family. There is one of unusual size, the largest so far found in those places, in the interior of which is seen the place of a sarcophagus 4 feet wide. It consisted of a double vaulted chamber, 50 feet long and 8 feet wide. (TCD, 69–71; WB, II, 204)

1 Kings 3:1 —— *Solomon . . . took Pharaoh's daughter* From one of the Tell el-Amarna letters, we know that Pharaoh Amen-hotep III refused to give his daughter in matrimony to Kadashmanenlil, king of Babylon, who had asked for her hand. He gave this reason for his refusal: "From of old, a daughter of the king of Egypt has not been given to anyone" (supposedly meaning to any foreign king or prince). The Greek historian Herodotus records another case of such a refusal, that of the pharaoh Amasis to Cambyses, king of Persia. Solomon's case was truly an exception, an evidence of the extraordinary political importance of this king. The royal father-in-law of Solomon has not been identified. It all depends on what chronology is adopted. He could have been Psusennes II, but more likely it was his predecessor Siamon, also a king of the Twenty-first Dynasty. (BAR-2, 91–93)

88

1 Kings 6:2 —— *The house which King Solomon built for the* LORD The plans for the construction of the famous temple of Solomon seem to have had two antecedents: the tabernacle of the wilderness and the temples of the Canaanites. Some authorities suspect that certain elements in the description of the tabernacle given in Exodus 26 and 36 were retroactively influenced by the structure of Solomon's temple. However, it appears that the structure actually existed as it is described. It was divided into two rooms: one a rectangle, called the Holy Place, which was the sanctuary proper (Hebrew *qodesh*), and the other a square room, called the Holy of Holies (Hebrew *qodesh haqodashim*). The two rooms were separated by a curtain. The ark of the covenant was in the latter. In some Canaanite temples discovered at different places, a similar floor plan has been found: a main hall, and at the rear a smaller enclosure in which, in certain cases, some cultic objects have been found. To this class belong the sanctuaries excavated at Hazor, at Tell Tainat (in Syria), and near Nahariya, to the north of Haifa. A space for a vestibule appears in front of each of them, so that there were actually three areas, as in Solomon's temple. Since the architects and foremen that worked for Solomon came from Tyre, it is understandable that they would think in terms of the Canaanite temples so familiar to them. Apart from the general plan, Solomon's temple was unique in its disposition, structure, and above all in its ornamentation. The tabernacle's *qodesh* came to be called *hekhal*, a word of Sumerian extraction, also meaning palace (*ekallum*). The inner room, called *debir*, a term of uncertain meaning, continued to be called *qodesh haqodeshim* (Holy of Holies). The tabernacle did not have a vestibule or the two columns in the front which Solomon's temple had. The Israelite sanctuary excavated at Arad has a floor plan similar to that of the temple (see comment on Num 21:1). Several model reconstructions of Solomon's temple have been attempted. An excellent model of the central building, including its interior, is one built by E. G. Howland and P. L. Garber and exhibited at Agnes Scott College, Decatur, Georgia. Another really extraordinary model is the one forming part of the huge model of Herodian Jerusalem, which is shown at the Holyland Hotel in modern Jerusalem. It was probably Ernest Renan who first suggested that Solomon's temple was a royal chapel, an annex to his palace, a theory today subscribed to by many exegetes and archaeologists (compare Amos 7:13). Temples of this type have been excavated at several sites, as in Mari and Tell Tainat. This theory is not altogether incompatible with the fact that the temple was first of all the "House of Yahweh," placed under the immediate and personal protection of the king for its preservation and maintenance. At the same time it was the sanctuary where he, his family, and his court worshiped God. (IDB, IV, 498–506, 534–38; EB, VI, 838–41, 908–13; WB, II, 213; ADHL, 101–11; TOJ, 23–25)

1 Kings 6:16 —— *an inner sanctuary, as the most holy place.* The esplanade of the holy mount underwent a very great change with the destruction of Solomon's temple by the Babylonians when they captured Jerusalem for the second and last time. With the building of Zerubbabel's temple later, and afterward with the construction of Herod's magnificent temple, all traces of the Solomonic sanctuary were no doubt lost. According to the prevailing opinion among archaeologists, it is almost certain that Solomon's temple stood where the Dome of the Rock now stands. It is also probable that the underlying rock is the one that served as the foundation for the Holy of Holies. It shows signs of having been used as a quarry, perhaps by the builders of the Roman Aelia Capitolina. (MTL, 81, 98; TOJ, 17)

1 Kings 6:20 —— *and twenty cubits high* Verse 2 gives the height of the temple as 30 cubits (about 45 feet). Here the height of the inner sanctuary is only 20 cubits (30 feet). If the building had a single roof at the same level, the difference of 10 cubits (15 feet) is indeed difficult to explain. It has been suggested that perhaps there was another story above the *debir* or Holy of Holies. Another possibility, however, seems more satisfactory, namely, that this room was built on a higher level than the main sanctuary or Holy Place. As Carl Watzinger pointed out, in ancient temples the inner recess generally stood at a higher level than the outer sanctuary. (See the comment at Lev 26:30 concerning this detail of the temple excavated at Arad.) (WMTS, 260–61)

1 Kings 6:36 —— *three courses of hewn stone and one course of cedar beams.* As may be seen in the remains discovered in Ugarit, Beth-shan, Megiddo, and more recently in Herod's palace at Masada, this form of construction was known and practiced in Palestine at least since the second millennium B.C. It consists of inserting a course of planks or beams of wood in a wall of stone in order to strengthen it. It was the method employed in the reconstruction of the temple in Jerusalem upon the return from the exile (Ezra 6:4), according to Cyrus' instructions. (WB, IV, 226)

1 Kings 7:8 —— *Pharaoh's daughter*   In the ravine or valley of Kidron there is a monument in the shape of a cube, with a funeral chamber in its interior. Over the entrance there was evidently a Hebrew inscription that was intentionally erased. According to a popular tradition this is the "Tomb of Pharaoh's Daughter," referring to the princess mentioned in this passage. This identification, however, is very doubtful. It may stem from the fact that its architectural style shows Egyptian influence. (EB, II, 251)

1 Kings 7:19 —— *the capitals . . . were of lily-work*   This reference is to the capitals of the two pillars that stood in front of the temple's vestibule. It is not possible to know what their exact shape was. In the excavations at such sites as Megiddo, Samaria, and Hazor, fragments of capitals and even whole capitals made of stone have been unearthed. They belong to the style called Proto-Ionic or Proto-Aeolian, being earlier than the famous classic forms of Greece: Ionic, Doric, and Corinthian. The capitals consist of a central angle and two volutes on the sides. Egyptian capitals in the shape of lotus flowers are well known. It seems that the capitals of the temple pillars had a special, perhaps even exclusive form, now impossible to reconstruct. A further complication is due to the fact that the Hebrew word *shushan* (or *shoshan*) usually translated "lily," probably served to designate various kinds of flowers.

1 Kings 7:21 —— *pillars at the vestibule . . . Jachin; . . . Boaz.* Archaeology has not been fortunate enough to find the precise remains of these pillars which stood in front of the temple nor of the similar pillars of the Herodian temple. The Babylonians must have completely destroyed the former, and the Romans likewise the latter. There are literary references, however, to pillars like these in other temples, and pillars of this kind have been uncovered in excavations in Israel. Phoenician temples, like that of Melkart in Tyre, are known to have had pillars at the front. The meanings of the names *Jachin* and *Boaz* are uncertain. Several hypotheses have been proposed concerning them. As far as the literal meaning of the Hebrew words is concerned, Jachin means "He [Yahweh] establishes" (or "affirms"), and Boaz (if vocalized as "Beoz" rather than Boaz) means "by the power" (of Yahweh). Perhaps the meaning of these names can never be known with certainty, nor what they symbolized in such a singular situation, for they were not a part of the vestibule's structure. According to the general consensus, they stood detached from it, not serving as a support for anything. (TOJ, 26–27; MTL, 101, 103)

1 Kings 7:27 —— *stands of bronze*   The description of these pieces of the temple's furniture makes it possible to suppose that they were probably of the same shape as some miniatures discovered in Cyprus, dating from the eleventh and tenth centuries B.C. These miniatures are possible replicas of larger stands used in the temples. One of them, found in a tomb and very well preserved, has the shape of a four-wheeled rectangular box, with a ring or circular brim in its upper part. At each side of the "box" two sphinxes appear, facing each other. The upper ring obviously served to hold a bowl. (WB, II, 217)

1 Kings 9:1 —— *the house of the* LORD   This literal expression (or "the house of God") is used to designate the temple. This use was verified in a rather interesting way when, in the ruins of the Israelite temple of Arad in the Negev, a potsherd was found bearing an inscription dated to the time of the kingdom of Judah and mentioning the temple precisely with these words, "the house of Yahweh" (the Lord). (MTL, 53)

1 Kings 9:15 —— *the wall of Jerusalem and Hazor and Megiddo and Gezer*   Solomon is recorded in the Bible as one of the greatest builders in Israel's history. First he built the temple and palaces and fortifications at Jerusalem, and after that the cities mentioned in this verse, as well as others. "Yet, with all that," writes the eminent Israeli archaeologist Yadin, "Solomon remains one of the most elusive builders in the country, archaeologically speaking." Nothing is left of his great constructions in Jerusalem, except perhaps a small stretch of a casemate wall which Kenyon found in her excavations at the City of David (southeastern hill) in 1961–67. (At least that wall was in the style of construction believed to be Solomonic.) Some idea of Solomon's palace may be had by comparison with what the excavations at Zenjirli, Ugarit, Mari, and Ebla reveal about the royal palaces in those cities. Although they were of much earlier times, it is probable that their structures persisted for centuries as a model.

In his remarkable book *Hazor: The Rediscovery of a Great City*, in which he renders a detailed description of his excavations at this site, Yadin gives to chapter 12 the title "The Search for Solomon." The quotation given above is from that book. In the following pages he says: "Some of what I am about to relate may sound like a detective story, but the truth is that our great guide was the Bible; and as an archaeologist I cannot imagine a greater thrill than working with the Bible in one hand and the spade in the other. This was the true secret of our discoveries of the Solomonic period" (p. 187). Yadin's finds were truly extraordinary. The most notable was without any doubt that of the main gate of the citadel or acropolis, with a considerable stretch of the adjacent casemate wall, and not far from it a garrison barracks. The gate consisted of three guardrooms at each side of the entrance passage, according exactly with the plan of the Solomonic gates of Megiddo and Gezer, with two towers flanking the entrance. A pavement and a drain were found between the barracks and the wall. In one of the barrack rooms a small and stylized animal head was found. It has a sun disk and a cross of equal arms on its forehead. It may represent the head of a bull or of a horse. In Middle Eastern paganism the bull is associated with the gods and the horse with the sun cult ("the sun chariot"). In one of the casemates, a Red Sea conch shell used as a trumpet (*shofar*) was picked up, and one of Yadin's laborers, a professional shofar blower in a synagogue, managed to get some sound out of it. Yadin says: "It may be assumed that this one was used by the soldiers near the wall for alarm signals."

For Megiddo, see the comment on 1 Kings 10:26. "Perhaps the most spectacular Solomonic fortification at Megiddo is the city gate on the northern end of the mound" (Wright). The study of its ruins shows that it was a double gate, to which access was gained; if one was on foot, by climbing a steep stairway, or if riding a cart or chariot, by a ramp. After passing through the first gateway, one had to make almost a 90-degree turn to the left in order to get to the main gate, which was flanked by impressive towers. This was really a quadruple gate. Each of its entryways, situated one after the other, was protected by its own guardrooms. Wright points out that the plan of the temple gate which Ezekiel (40:5–16) describes with so much detail shows the same disposition as the Megiddo gate. More recent excavations carried out at the site under the direction of Yadin (1960, 1967, 1971–72) uncovered remains of the Solomonic wall. Previously, a later wall was considered to be such. Also ruins of a fortress-palace were located; these were in the same style of construction as the Solomonic gate, imported by Solomon from Phoenicia. Fitted blocks of well-dressed stone (ashlars) are the main characteristic of this style. Yadin's excavations cleared up an archaeological error of previous excavators, namely, attributing to Solomon the famous stables. As a matter of fact, the Solomonic stratum in the Megiddo ruins really lies beneath the one formerly thought to be Solomonic. In all probability the fortress-palace was the governor's residence where Baana ben Ahilud (4:12) lived. The Irish archaeologist Macalister, Gezer's first excavator (1902, 1905, 1907, 1909), announced the discovery there of a "Maccabean castle." In 1958, Yadin launched the theory that these ruins were actually those of the Solomonic gate and wall, for in the drawings of the Macalister report he found a remarkable likeness to Solomon's fortifications at Hazor and Megiddo. However, the excavations carried out from 1965 to 1973 under William G. Dever left no room for doubt. As Dever puts it, "Solomon did indeed rebuild Gezer" (compare verse 17). After the time of Solomon the city experienced other reconstructions up to the Maccabean period, and there are remains of these. (JR, 6; BAW, 132–33; MTL, 53; HYY, 187–231)

1 Kings 9:26 —— *a fleet of ships at Ezion-geber*   Glueck's excavations at the head of the Gulf of Aqaba in 1935 did not uncover the remains of the Solomonic port itself, but they did uncover the relatively well-preserved ruins of a building Glueck first identified as a copper and iron smeltery and refinery. Veins of these minerals are found in that region. Glueck dated this building as of the tenth century B.C., that is, the time of Solomon. The site, called Tell el-Kheleifeh, was identified by him as the location of Ezion-geber-Elath. To the north of these ruins, at Timnah, very old mines were discovered, which at least for some years the modern state of Israel again worked. All over this wilderness area small, primitive furnaces have been found in which minerals received a preliminary smelting. Slag heaps, too, abound in the area, as well as walled enclosures and ruins of huts, all of which seem to give strong support to Glueck's theory. These may have been forced-labor camps, which agrees with the biblical references concerning the labor levies which Solomon imposed on foreigners. According to Glueck, all this would demonstrate that the great king had in that area a large industrial center, based on the exploitation of minerals and employing thousands of workers. This thesis naturally provoked great interest. If Glueck's theory was right, an unknown aspect of Solomon's activities would have suddenly been revealed. But not everybody accepted his theory. The Israeli scholar G. Cornfeld, for example, believes that the region's primitive furnaces are older than the twelfth century B.C. (ABB, 109) and that therefore they have nothing to do with Solomon. The proposal was made that the building believed by Glueck to be the Solomonic refinery could have rather been a warehouse. In an article published in 1965 (BA, 28 [1965], 70), Glueck himself accepted this possibility, although he insisted in attributing to Solomon the copper mines and metallurgical activities in the area. Beno Rothenberg, who had been Glueck's photographer and who later excavated Timnah, published in 1972, after Glueck had passed away, conclusions contrary to those of Glueck. Rothenberg did not find evidence of mining activities in the area later than the twelfth century B.C. (See comment on Gen 4:22.) (BAW, 135–37; TBAR, I, 1, 10–12, 14, 16; OSJ, 106–37)

1 Kings 9:28 —— and they went to Ophir, and brought from there gold Where was this almost legendary place or country, which produced gold not only in great quantity, as inferred from the biblical texts, but also of an excellent quality? Numerous places have been proposed, and for each of them some persons have insisted on finding some support. The matter has been profusely debated. Places as far away as South Africa, Malaysia, Spain, and even Peru have been suggested, as well as closer regions such as India, Ceylon (now Sri Lanka), Somalia, and Armenia. (The identification with Peru was proposed as early as toward the end of the sixteenth century A.D. by Thomas of Malhenda. It was supported by writers of the time, such as the Inca Garcilaso, Juan of Pineda, Gregorio Garcia, and Bernardo of Alderete.) In 10:11 it is also said that "almug wood and precious stones" were brought from Ophir. It has not been possible to identify the wood. Those who translate *almug* as "sandal" find in this a proof in favor of India, for this aromatic wood is typical

of that country. In Genesis 10:29 the word is the name of an eponymous person, and this seems to point to Arabia. Explorations carried out since 1932 by the engineer Karl Twitchell in the Arabian peninsula led to the localization of a site of several square miles with evident traces of an extensive exploitation of gold ore. Arabs call this place Mahd adh Dhahab, "Cradle of Gold." From 1934 to 1954, a British company extracted important quantities of gold from that place and discovered in the region fifty-five other ancient mines, although of much less importance. In 1972 a joint team for geological exploration (Saudi Arabia and United States) marked more than forty places with beds of gold, and also traces of their having been exploited in antiquity. This has reinforced the theory of an Arabian Ophir. The gold from this region would have been brought in Solomon's time to some seaport on the Red Sea. Ships would have then carried the gold northward to the head of the Gulf of Aqaba, where Ezion-geber stood and where the Israeli port of Elath stands today. It could also have been carried by land to Jerusalem, in a more or less direct route. Mahd adh Dhahab is between Medina and Mecca. Will the explorations in that area finally clear up the centuries-old mystery of the location of Ophir? (TBAR, 3, No. 3 [1977], 1, 28–ɔ3)

1 Kings 10:18, 19 —— *a great ivory throne, . . . and two lions standing beside the arm rests* In sculptures and reliefs from the ruins of ancient buildings, it is common to represent royal thrones flanked by lions, a symbol of strength and courage. The lions of Ahab's throne most probably were also made of ivory. In the excavations at Samaria, his capital, two ivory lions were found, but they are represented as crouching, not standing. They have perforations that "indicate that they may have decorated the arms or steps of a throne" (ANEP, 264, figure 129). In the Palestine Archaeological Museum in Jerusalem, there is an ivory inlay representing the Egyptian god Horus. It may have been the central piece on the back of a throne (ANEP, figure 566).

1 Kings 10:26 —— *the chariot cities* In the excavations at Megiddo, one of the more extensive ever made in Palestine, archaeologist P. L. O. Guy found in 1928–29 at stratum IV the ruins of large stables (or so they were considered then) constructed of dressed stone, with two rows of stone pillars and some drinking troughs, also made of stone. The pillars served not only to support the roof but also, since they had holes pierced in the stone, to tether the horses. It is believed that the place had room for some three hundred horses. The pavement was of a mortar as hard as cement. The mention of Megiddo in 9:15 made it seem that this was one of "the chariot cities" referred to in this verse. Ever since that excavation, these ruins have been called "Solomon's stables." Later studies, however, have led to a rejection of this identification. It is now believed that these stables belonged rather to Ahab. It is nevertheless possible that Solomon did have stables at Megiddo, and that Ahab's stables were built with materials left from Solomon's earlier construction. The masonry is perhaps of Phoenician type. In more recent times some scholars even doubt that these are ruins of real stables at all. They have proposed that the building was more likely used as a warehouse. (BAR-1, 247; LTR, 35)

1 Kings 10:28 —— *Solomon's import of horses was from Egypt and Kue* In Assyrian inscriptions *Musri*, a region in northern Syria, is often mentioned as famous for its horses. This fact suggests that perhaps that name should be read here in the Hebrew text, instead of *Misrayim* (Egypt). In fact, with the exception of the final *m*, the consonants are the same in both names. (It is so translated in the GNB.) Kue (Hebrew *qeveh*) is Cilicia in Asia Minor. The fact that the two names appear together seems to be a strong support for the reading *Musri*, for the two places then would represent the same general area.

1 Kings 12:25 —— *Jeroboam built Shechem* This means he rebuilt this city, which was already known from ancient times. This reconstruction included the repairing of the ancient Canaanite wall. "At least one fragment of this repair, comparable in type to the Solomonic wall at Megiddo, has been unearthed" (Wright). Also two gates of the city, one to the east and one to the northwest, have been uncovered. It is supposed that there was also a southern gate. Its ruins may lie under the houses of the modern village of Balatah. The repair and fortification works undertaken by Jeroboam would have included these gates. (BAW, 148; SW)

1 Kings 12:28, 29 —— *two calves of gold. . . . he set one in Bethel, and the other he put in Dan.* Repeatedly the Bible denounces idolatry as the "sin which he [Jeroboam] made Israel to sin" (15:26). Main centers of idolatry were Bethel in the south and Dan in the north of his kingdom. In 1974 the excavations of the ninth archae-

ological expedition took place at Tel Dan. They were directed by
the Israeli archaeologist Biran. A structure was discovered which
he considers to be the vestibule (or propylaeum of the shrine or
sanctuary, *bamah*) which would have stood at the center of the
great religious enclosure associated with the worship of Jeroboam's
golden calf. There are signs of a first stage in the construction at
the time of Jeroboam I (tenth century B.C.), of a second stage
belonging to Ahab's reign (ninth century B.C.), and of a third stage
in the epoch of Jeroboam II (eighth century B.C.). (See 12:30; 16:30–
33; 2 Kings 14:24.) In later excavations, archaeologists found that
rather than a single cultic location there was a whole *temenos* or
sacred area, with several structures devoted to worship. It is for
this reason that in the reference in verse 31 the Hebrew text uses
the plural. In previous excavations remains had been uncovered of
some small shrines that would have been part of the great compound,
and of a monumental stairway belonging to the main structure. It
has been suggested that the worship was not rendered to the golden
calf itself, but to Yahweh though already mixed with pagan elements.
Heathen gods were often represented as standing on a bull, the
symbol of strength. If that were the case, then the calf would have
simply been the pedestal of the invisible God. (JPW, August 26,
1975; BA, 37 [1974], 26–51; BA, 43 [1980], 168–82; TBAR, 7, No.
5 [1981], 20–37)

1 Kings 14:2 —— *and go to Shiloh* Excavations by a Danish expedition under the direction of Hans Kjaer (1926, 1929, 1932) showed
that this city was destroyed by the Philistines (a fact not mentioned
in the Bible) at the time when they defeated the Israelites and
captured the ark of the covenant (toward 1050 B.C.), but that the
site was settled again, as indicated in this passage (see also Jer 41:5).
(TBAR. 1. No. 2 [1975], 3–5)

1 Kings 14:25 —— *Shishak* This pharaoh's Egyptian name is *Sheshonq*. An inscription at Karnak contains an allusion to his conquests
in Palestine (see comment on 2 Chron 12:2, 7).

1 Kings 15:18 —— *Ben-hadad the son of Tabrimmon, the son of
Hezi-on* A votive stele discovered near Aleppo in Syria is inscribed
by one "Bar [Aramaic for the Hebrew *Ben*] Hadad, the son of Tabr
. . . [the rest is illegible] of Hazia," a person identified with Ben-
hadad I of Damascus. (WB, II, 233)

1 Kings 15:21 —— *and he* [Baasha] *dwelt in Tirzah.* The ruins of Tirzah have been identified with Tell el-Farah, to the northeast of Shechem and south of Beth-shan. The excavations at this site have uncovered remains of buildings of the period of the Israelite monarchy. They show that, although the city was founded in the fourth millennium B.C. and had had very fine fortifications in the second millennium B.C., its high point was reached at the beginning of the ninth century B.C., under Baasha's dynasty. (WB, II, 234)

1 Kings 15:22 —— *and with them King Asa built . . . Mizpah.* For a majority of archaeologists the Tell en-Nasbeh, some 7 miles north of Jerusalem, is the site of ancient Mizpah, fortified with stones carried by a labor levy from Ramah, about 2 miles south. As may be seen from the ruins found there, the fortifications were formidable. At certain points the walls were up to 26 feet thick, and their present remains reach a height of 25 feet. These ruins have been dated as belonging to the fortifications built by King Asa. (BAW, 151–52)

1 Kings 16:24 —— *and called the name of the city which he built, Samaria* According to this passage, Omri transferred his capital from Tirzah (identified with Tell el-Farah) to the newly founded Samaria. Kenyon writes, "This accords remarkably well with the evidence at Tell el-Farah. Omri's first four years were occupied with the struggles with his rival, Tibni. Only then was he free to concentrate on his capital. He began to build, but abandoned his work. On pottery evidence, where Tell el-Farah stops, Samaria begins. . . . When Omri decided to move to Samaria, he took with him his court, and probably most of the inhabitants of Tirzah." The hill of Samaria is one of Palestine's most thoroughly explored archaeological sites; it has produced more finds than any other since 1908, when an expedition from Harvard University started the excavations. The ruins represent sixteen periods, seven of which belong to the Israelite epoch. Remains have been found of the walls of Omri, Ahab, and Jeroboam II, as well as of the royal palace in the time of these monarchs. In the precinct of the palace numerous potsherds have been found, the majority of them inscribed with ink. There was also an important aggregate of ivory artifacts. The ceramic remains were abundant and of great value for archaeology.

The city's western gate was of imposing dimensions and of singular importance for the reconstruction of the gates of walled cities of that period. Also ruins of the Assyrian, Babylonian, and Hellenistic periods were discovered. A splendid round tower of the Hellenistic period was found, which according to Parrot is "the best preserved of all the monuments of the Hellenistic epoch known today in Palestine." Ruins of the Roman and especially of the Herodian period are imposing. Herod the Great named the city *Sebaste*, in honor of Augustus, a name that is preserved in modern *Sebastiye*. That was the period of the city's greatest splendor. Remains of its walls were found, as well as of the street called "of the porticoes," the temple of Augustus, the temple of Kore, the theater, the basilica, the forum, the stadium, and tombs. In the time of Jesus, Samaria was more pagan than Jewish. This was an additional motive for the rejection of the Samaritans by the Jews. (AHL, 261; SCKI; BAW, 153–56)

1 Kings 16:29 —— *Ahab the son of Omri* Aja-al-bu of Siril ("Ahab of Israel") is mentioned in an obelisk of Shalmaneser III as one of the kings who, headed by Hadadezer (the Bible's Ben-hadad), fought against the Assyrian monarch in the battle of Qarqar (854 B.C.). According to this inscription, Ahab took with him to the battle 10,000 footmen and 2,000 chariots, the latter more than half of the total of allied chariots which participated in the fight. The ruins of a citadel-residence, of a warehouse (or granary) excavated at Hazor, and of the stables discovered at Megiddo are remnants of Ahab's constructions. (BAW, 156; ANET, 279)

1 Kings 16:31, 32 —— *and served Baal, . . . in the house of Baal* Jezebel was the daughter of the king of Tyre, and so it is almost certain that the Baal whose cult Ahab introduced in Samaria as a compliment to his queen was Melkart, the god of Tyre. Among other images of this god provided by archaeology is the one that appears in a stele in which the image is identified as Amrit and which probably represents him. (It is now in the Louvre.) The god is shown standing on a lion which advances upon the mountains. He is attired in Egyptian clothing and is depicted as a hunter, for hanging from his left hand he carries a lion's cub. At other times he was represented as a warrior. (MLB, 58)

1 Kings 20:1 —— *Ben-hadad the king of Syria* Shalmaneser III's inscriptions mention several campaigns against Hadadezer of Damascus (sometimes called "Adad-idri of Damascus"), the biblical Ben-hadad (Ben-hadad II), the chief of a coalition of kings who were enemies of Assyria. Among these campaigns is described the battle of Qarqar, in which the coalition was utterly defeated by the Assyrians. In the Aleppo Museum there is a stele of one Bar Hadad, probably the son of Ben-hadad II (see comment on 16:29). (ANET, 276–81)

1 Kings 20:14 —— *the servants of the governors* These were not ordinary servants. The word so translated is *nearim*, literally "boys" or "young men." Sometimes this word was applied to soldiers in general or to selected troops. (One is reminded of Catalonia's militiamen called *mozos de escuadra*, literally "squad boys.") An Egyptian letter from the end of the thirteenth century B.C. speaks of an army which goes out "to crush those rebels called Nearin," probably in Phoenicia. And in one of the chronicles of Ramses II's Asiatic campaign, "the Nearin-troops of Pharaoh" are mentioned. In this case they were Egyptian troops, or perhaps Canaanite mercenaries. (ANET, 476, 256)

1 Kings 21:15–16 —— *the vineyard of Naboth . . . to take possession of it.* From a legal document inscribed in a tablet of the fifteenth century B.C., found in Alalakh, Syria, one may deduce that the property of a legally executed culprit passed into the king's possession. It is possible that in this passage reference to a similar law or custom is implied. (WB, II, 247)

1 Kings 22:34 —— *between the scale armor and the breastplate* Metal scale armor or coats of mail of that epoch consisted of many pieces in order to allow for the warrior's movements. As in this case, the vulnerable points were the junctures. A curious leather relief from the chariot of Pharaoh Thutmose IV (fifteenth century B.C.) depicts a soldier of a Canaanite chariot with an arrow stuck in the joint of his breastplate and the sleeve of his lorica. (WB, II, 249)

1 Kings 22:39 —— *the ivory house* No doubt Ahab's palace was so called because of the abundance of ornaments and other objects made of ivory. In the ruins of what is thought to have been this king's palace in Samaria, hundreds of these precious objects have been unearthed. "And there can be no doubt that these fragments came from its furniture [the palace's], though they were mostly recovered from the debris of the destruction caused by the Assyrians in 720 B.C." (Kenyon, AHL, 266). The ivory artifacts recovered from Ahab's palace are kept in the Rockefeller Museum in Jerusalem.

THE SECOND BOOK OF
THE KINGS

2 Kings 3:11 —— *who poured water on the hands of Elijah.* This may be a literal reference to a ritual act, such as the one represented in the model of *bamah* (or sanctuary) called *Sit Shamshi*, kept in the Louvre (see comment on Deut 16:21). Two naked worshipers in a squatting position are shown getting ready for the ceremony. One of them is about to pour water in the other's hands. But in a context like the present one the clause denotes merely a personal assistant or servant. (MLB, 79–80, and note 4)

2 Kings 3:26 —— *the king of Moab saw that the battle was going against him* The famous monolith known as the stele of King Mesha, found in 1868 in Transjordan (at present in the Louvre Museum, Paris), gives an account of this battle. Mesha tells how Moab freed itself from the oppression of Omri and his dynasty. According to his version, King Mesha was the one who took the initiative in this encounter, by order of his god Chemosh, and who inflicted on Israel a serious defeat. The Moabite king announces that this defeat was such that "Israel has perished for ever." Some scholars believe, however, that this sentence is a reference to the extermination of Omri's dynasty by Jehu's coup d'etat. (MLB, plate VIII, 84–90; DOTT, 195–98, plate 10; ANET, 320)

2 Kings 7:1 —— *at the gate of Samaria.* Usually markets were installed at the gates of ancient Israelite cities. In the Samaria excavations there was found behind the fortified gate of the city an open space which may have been the marketplace.

2 Kings 7:2 —— *the captain on whose hand the king leaned* This expression refers to the king's field adjutant. In reliefs representing Assyrian chariots, the king is accompanied not only by the charioteer or driver but also by a third person, on whose arm the king literally leans in order to stand firm when the chariot is running at full speed (NAOT, 37)

2 Kings 8:15 —— *And Hazael became king in his stead.* This king of Syria (Damascus) is mentioned in Aramean and Assyrian inscriptions. He was a warrior king who succeeded in keeping the Assyrians at bay and in snatching from Israel the regions east of the Jordan At Arslan Tash (Hadathah) on the Euphrates, two interesting pieces of carved ivory were found. One, which decorated the side of a bed has this Aramaic inscription: "Bar Ama to our lord Hazael, in the year. . . ." The other was a tablet found nearby, possibly also an ornament of the same bed. It represents a bearded person, dressed in Aramean and Phoenician style. It could be a god, but some scholars believe it is a portrait of Hazael himself. An inscription of Shalmaneser IV says that "Hazael, son of a nobody, seized the throne." (WB, II, 264; WMTS, 281; UTB, 166)

2 Kings 9:30 —— *put on eye shadow* (GNB; RSV: "painted her eyes.") Hebrew literally "put her eyes in black powder," that is antimony. Archaeology has found abundant testimony, especially in frescoes and toilet articles, of this very old feminine custom of painting the eyelids and eyelashes black with antimony, a very costly cosmetic preparation and therefore a sign of fine economic circumstances. It was prepared on a base of antimony sulfide powder mixed for its application with oil or fine grease. Jars for antimony some of them made of horn, have been found in excavations. Keren happuch, the name of Job's third daughter, means "Horn of antimony." (EB, 536–37; BAW, 194)

2 Kings 10:32 —— *Israel. Hazael defeated them* In the inscription of Shalmaneser III are mentioned two campaigns against the king of Damascus. In the first the Assyrian monarch defeated him on Mount Senir, opposite the Lebanon. But Hazael succeeded in escaping, so Shalmaneser chased him all the way to Damascus, his capital, where he besieged him. He failed to capture the city, but he did cause great destruction in Hazael's kingdom. In the second campaign he took from Hazael "four of his larger urban settlements," but Hazael retained Damascus. It seems that the Assyrian monarch finally gave up the attempt to conquer Syria, which relieved the pressure on Hazael so that he was able to attack Israel. (ANET, 280; EB, III, 1096–97)

2 Kings 10:34 —— *the rest of the acts of Jehu*   In London's British Museum may be seen the famous monument called the Black Obelisk of Shalmaneser III, king of Assyria. It shows Jehu, prostrate before that monarch, paying homage to him as a vassal, and offering him gifts. "This monument," writes Parrot, "is extremely important for biblical archaeology. It is, moreover, the only example of a secular monument on which is depicted a historical personage from the Old Testament, whether Israelite or Judaean." The inscription reads: "The tribute of Jehu [*Ia-w-a*], son of Omri [*Hu-um-ri*]; I received from him silver, gold, a golden *saplu*-bowl, a golden vase with pointed bottom, golden tumblers, golden buckets, tin, a staff for a king, [and] wooden *puruhtu*." (ANET, 281; NAOT, 36, plate 3; WB, II, 269; BAR-2, 162)

2 Kings 12:3(4) —— *the high places were not taken away*   Several artificial mounds have been discovered to the east of Jerusalem. They are 98 feet in diameter and 19 feet high, and are formed of heaps of stones that cover a platform surrounded by a polygonal encirclement, with a paved pit in the center. No remains of any tomb have been found there, so one must presume that they were cultic places, probably the *bamoth* or high places which were built near Jerusalem in periods of apostasy. Potsherds found at the site make it possible to date them in the last century of the monarchy. (LTR, 36)

2 Kings 13:5 —— *the LORD gave Israel a savior*   Who was this savior to whom the people of Israel owed their being able to dwell "in their homes as formerly"? Some commentaries believe this to be a reference to Jeroboam II, who showed himself an active warrior and who "recovered for Israel Damascus and Hamath" (verse 28), overcoming the Syrians, the enemies and oppressors of Israel. Others consider that this statement is best interpreted as referring to the Assyrian king Adadnirari III, who victoriously fought against the Syrians, thus forcing them to leave Israel alone. A stele discovered at Saba shows Adadnirari's figure. The inscription narrates his campaign against Damascus and the defeat inflicted by him on the Aramean king Mari, the biblical Ben-hadad, son of Hazael. This occurred in the years 805–802 B.C., during the reign of Jehoahaz, the son of Jehu. (WB, II, 273)

2 Kings 14:7 —— *took Sela by storm* The name *Sela* means "Rock." It is identified with present-day Umm el-Bayyara (or Biyara), a rock formation facing Petra, southeast of the Dead Sea. Glueck found at this site ceramics of the ninth to seventh centuries B.C. (Iron Age II). This site must not, however, be confused with modern es-Sela, near Buseireh (the biblical Bosra), where a Nabatean city existed much later than the time of Amaziah, king of Judah. (BAR-2, 57)

2 Kings 14:21 —— *Azariah* [= Uzziah] Archaeology has found two seals belonging to officials of this king. They are not mentioned in the Bible. Their names are Shebaniah (*Shebanyau*) and Abijah (*Abiyau*), and in both cases the name is followed by the title or description as "the servant of Uzziyau" (Uzziah). (BAW, 161)

2 Kings 14:22 —— *He* [Azariah] *built Elath* Near the modern Israeli seaport of Eilat on the Gulf of Aqaba lies Tell el-Kheleifeh, where were found ruins of the city of Azariah's time, formerly called Ezion-geber. These ruins were discovered and excavated by Glueck. (See comment on 1 Kings 9:26.) (BAW, 161; OSJ, 106–37)

2 Kings 14:23 —— *Jeroboam* In the excavations of Megiddo (1903–5) under the direction of Schumacher, a jasper seal was found. It is beautifully carved with the figure of a raging lion and the inscription "Belonging to Shema, the servant of Jeroboam." It has been dated as belonging to the eighth century B.C., in the time of Jeroboam II. (APB, 30; ANEP, figure 276, p. 280)

2 Kings 15:5 —— *He lived in a separate house, relieved of all duties* (GNB; RSV does not have "relieved of all duties," which is explanatory.) The Hebrew expression *beth hahophshith* occurs only here and in the parallel passage of 2 Chronicles 26:21. It literally means "house of freedom" or "emancipation," a sense which does not seem applicable in the context, unless the expression is taken to mean "exemption from royal functions." This is GNB's understanding, and it is supported by the context. RSV and other versions translate simply "separate house," that is, in isolation because of his leprosy. A different version has been proposed, however, which identifies the Hebrew expression with the Ugaritic *bt hptt*, as Gordon does. He translates it as "the nether regions." This phrase occurs in two poems of Ras Shamra (Ugarit), the 51:VIII and the 67:V. Burrows mentions that the phrase may be understood as "the place to which Azariah was committed was a cave or cellar, perhaps a basement of the palace." (See *Revue Biblique*, 1937, p. 533.) This interpretation is possible and in a sense attractive, though it would be strange that such an important person as a king should be confined, even though a leper, to so indecent a place. On the other hand, the Israeli archaeologist Aharoni, in excavations started in 1956 at Ramat Rahel (some 2½ miles south of Jerusalem), discovered the ruins of a fortification, and, as part of it, a house or small palace, which he suggests is the one in which the leper king was secluded. Others believe this was the fortress palace of King Jehoiakim, at the end of the following century. Ramat Rahel probably is the ancient Beth-haccherem (Neh 3:14; Jer 6:1). (LTR, 15, 36; UT, 995, p. 404; WMTS, 261; BAW, 162; ADHL, 77–88; ABB, 166; EAE, 1003–6)

2 Kings 15:19 —— *Menahem gave Pul a thousand talents of silver*   In a stele of Pul (in Assyrian Pulu, another name of Teglath-Falasar or Tiglath-Pileser III), a list is given of tributary kings. Among them appears "Menahem of Samaria" (*Me-ni-hi-im-me al Sa-me-ri-na-a-a*). (NAOT, 40)

2 Kings 15:29 —— *and captured . . . Hazor*   The excavations at Hazor have uncovered the terrible traces of the capture and destruction of the city in 732 B.C. by the Assyrian monarch Tiglath-Pileser III. First of all, the excavators found evidences that, in the face of the growing threat of an Assyrian invasion, the defenses of Hazor were greatly strengthened, and preparations were made for a long seige. The Assyrian assault, however, was so overwhelming that the city was unable to resist for long. Concerning that destruction, Yadin concluded: "Tiglath-Pileser razed to the very ground the city of Hazor, once a key stronghold of the northern kingdom of Israel. The sight we encountered in area B [site of the citadel] is worse than any I can remember in archaeological excavations. The entire area was covered by a layer of ashes 1 meter thick and still black! Everything in sight was broken and scattered on the floors of the houses. We could visualize the Assyrian soldiers roaming about the houses, looting whatever they could and destroying the rest. The fire was so violent that even the stones were black, and numerous charred beams and pieces of burned plaster from the ceilings were strewn all over. The eastern side of the citadel, from which the fort had been attacked, was destroyed so thoroughly that in some places only the foundations below the floor level were visible." In spite of the sacking, the excavators found a multitude of household objects abandoned by the Assyrians, among them cosmetic pallets and other artifacts indicating the wealth of Hazor's people.

The degree to which heathen practices had contaminated Israelite worship may be judged by figurines pertaining to the rites of Baal and Astarte, the goddess of fertility, and by the extent of ceremonial prostitution practiced in the sanctuaries. The most interesting, and at the same time the most hideous of the finds, was a pig's skeleton which according to Yadin may have been left from a banquet, either by the Assyrian soldiers celebrating their victory or by the Israelite inhabitants of the town, whom the destruction took by surprise. If the latter was the case, it would indicate to what an extreme the intrusion of paganism had made the laws of Judaism of little consequence, for they strictly prohibited the eating of pork. Another interesting find was a potsherd belonging to a jar or pitcher with the inscription, "Belonging to Pekah. *Semadar*." Pekah was a common name, but it must be remembered that when the Assyrians took Hazor, it was a Pekah who reigned over Israel, so it is possible that this pitcher or jar belonged to the royal household. (On *Semadar*, compare comment on Song 2:15.) (HYY, 175–77)

2 Kings 15:30 —— *a conspiracy against Pekah* In Tiglath-Pileser's *Annals* it is said that it was "the people" of Israel who deposed Pekah, and that then he, Tiglath, appointed Hoshea as king. This seems to indicate that the conspiracy against Pekah was most likely plotted with Tiglath's connivance, for he had already invaded Israel and deported a large number of its inhabitants (verse 29). The Assyrian text reads: "The house of *Hu-um-ri-a* (Omri, i.e., Israel) . . . all his people, and their goods, I sent away to Assyria. They overthrew their king *Pa-qa-ha* (Pekah) and I made *A-u-si* (Hosheah) king over them. I received from them ten talents of gold, a thousand (?) talents of silver as tribute and I carried them away to Assyria." (NAOT, 42–43)

2 Kings 15:32 ── *Jotham the son of Uzziah* In the excavations at Ezion-geber (Eilat), Glueck found a seal with the figure of a ram and the inscription, "Belonging to Jotham." Strangely, the complete name is not given, that is, the usual *Ben* ("son of") followed by the father's name. By the location and time of this seal, it may have belonged to King Jotham, but the strange omission creates an element of doubt. (BAW, 161; UTB, 184)

2 Kings 16:1 ── *Ahaz the son of Jotham* Archaeologists have found a seal, evidently from the time of this king of Judah, which bears the inscription, "Belonging to Ashna, servant of Ahaz." "Servant" was often used to designate an important courtier. This seal bears symbols showing Egyptian influence: sun disk, horns, plants, and four serpents with raised heads (*ureus*). (SPA, 107; UTB, 184)

2 Kings 16:9 ── *hearkened to him* Ahaz requested help from the king of Assyria against the enemy alliance of the kings of Israel and Aram (Syria), and in exchange for that assistance Ahaz became his vassal. In the excavations at Calah, an inscription of Tiglath-Pileser was found which mentions among the kings who paid tribute to Assyria the name of *Ia-u-ha-zi* (Ahaz) of *Ia-u-da-a-a* (Judah). (ANET, 282; NAOT, 42)

2 Kings 16:10 ── *he saw the altar that was at Damascus.* The altar that Ahaz saw was in the temple of the god Hadad. Its ruins lie under the present mosque of the Ommayads at Damascus. A bas-relief was found there in which the god Hadad is represented by the figure of a sphinx (compare 5:18, where Naaman refers to this temple and to Hadad with his other name, Rimmon).

2 Kings 17:6 ── *the king of Assyria captured Samaria* It was Shalmaneser V who took Samaria, but it was his brother and successor Sargon II who completed Israel's subjugation and deported its inhabitants. In an Akkadian inscription on a stone slab of a doorway he calls himself "conqueror of Samaria (*Sa-mir-i-na*) and of all Israel" (literally "Omriland," *bit-Hu-um-ri-a*). In one of his prisms, which was uncovered in Nimrud (1952–53), he renders his own version of the event: "The man of Samaria and a king who was hostile to me, had joined together to refuse homage and tribute to me, and came out to fight with me; by the help of the great gods, my lords, I overthrew them: I captured 27,280 persons with chariots, their gods in whom they trusted, and took as my royal share of the booty 200 chariots. I gave orders that the rest should be settled in the midst of Assyria." Another version he gives is recorded in his *Annals*, which consist of inscriptions in steles and walls at Khorsabad. In them he says, "I besieged and conquered *Sa-me-ri-na* (Samaria)." Here he counts 27,290 prisoners and 50 chariots (see comment on verse 24). In the Turin Museum there is a magnificent relief depicting Sargon's head. (ANET 284–85; WB, II, 283; NAOT, 45–46; SCKI, 49–51)

2 Kings 17:24 —— *the king of Assyria brought people . . . and placed them in the cities of Samaria*   In his *Annals*, Sargon says: "I rebuilt the town (Samaria) better than what it was before and settled therein people from countries which I myself had conquered." On the other hand, in the excavations at Samaria letters have been found in which persons with Babylonian names are mentioned. (NAOT, 46)

2 Kings 18:11 —— *The king of Assyria carried the Israelites away*   Of this deportation an interesting graphic evidence is left in a great mural relief of Ashurbanipal. The Israelite captives are represented at the time when they were being carried in barges across a river. It is interesting to notice the Israelite garments of that time. (MTL, 61)

2 Kings 18:13 —— *Sennacherib . . . came up against all the fortified cities of Judah*   One of Sennacherib's inscribed prisms describes this campaign, which was carried out in 701 B.C. After telling of his military operations in Palestine up to the capture of Ekron, he goes on to say: "As to Hezekiah, the Jew, he did not submit to my yoke, I laid siege to 46 of his strong cities, walled forts and to the countless small villages in their vicinity, and conquered (them) by means of well-stamped (earth-)ramps, and battering-rams brought (thus) near (to the walls) (combined with) the attack by foot soldiers, (using) mines, breeches as well as sapper work. I drove out (of them) 200,150 people, young and old, male and female, horses, mules, donkeys, camels, big and small cattle beyond counting, and considered (them) booty. Himself I made a prisoner in Jerusalem, his royal residence, like a bird in a cage. I surrounded him with earthwork in order to molest those who were leaving his city's gate. His towns which I had plundered, I took away from his country and gave them (over) to Mitinti, king of Ashdod, Padi, king of Ekron, and Sillibel, king of Gaza. Thus I reduced his country, but I still increased the tribute and the *katru*-presents (due) to me (as his) overlord which I imposed (later) upon him beyond the former tribute, to be delivered annually. Hezekiah himself, whom the terror-inspiring splendor of my lordship had overwhelmed and whose irregular and elite troops which he had brought into Jerusalem, his royal residence, in order to strengthen (it), had deserted him, did send me, later, to Nineveh, my lordly city, together with 30 talents of gold, 800 talents of silver, precious stones, antimony, large cuts of red stone, couches (inlaid) with ivory, *nimedu*-chairs (inlaid) with ivory, elephant-hides, ebony-wood, boxwood (and) all kinds of valuable treasures, his (own) daughters, concubines, male and female musicians. In order to deliver the tribute and to do obeisance as a slave he sent his (personal) messenger." (ANET, 288)

2 Kings 18:14 —— *the king of Assyria at Lachish*   He was besieging the city, which finally fell into his hands. A great and famous stone mural, found in the ruins of Sennacherib's palace at Nineveh, represents in detail the assault and capture of Lachish, as well as the deportation of its survivors. Lachish, identified with present Tell ed-Duweir, has been partially excavated, particularly the city's gate and a section of the walls. In one of the gate's guardrooms were found the inscribed potsherds containing the famous Lachish letters, written during the Babylonian attack. (POTA, 85–90)

2 Kings 18:17 —— *the Tartan, the Rabsaris, and the Rabshakeh* These names were traditionally taken to be proper names of persons, and they are so treated in most translations until recent times. By means of cuneiform tablets we now know that they were titles of Assyrian officials. The Assyrian *tartanu* (or *tardennu*) was the second in military command. The *rabu-sha-reshi* (literally, "main eunuch") was someone like a first chamberlain. And *rab-shaqu* means "first officer." In Jeremiah 39:3, 13, a Rabmag (Assyrian *rab-mugi*) appears, but his function is uncertain. And in Jeremiah 51:27 a "marshal" is mentioned. The Hebrew word is *tiphsar* (Assyrian *tupsarru* or *dupsarru*), literally "scribe." He seems to have been a kind of recruiting officer or troop inspector (compare Nahum 3:17). (WMTS, 43, 44)

2 Kings 18:18 —— *Eliakim the son of Hilkiah* A seal from Hebron acquired by the Israel Museum in 1975, bears this inscription: "Belonging to Yehozarah, son of Hilkiyau, servant of Hezekiah." In this context "servant" means a royal official. The Bible mentions no one called Yehozarah. But in the present passage Eliakim a son of Hilkiah (or Hilkiyau) is mentioned as the palace steward ("over the household"). The reference may be to the same Hilkiyau, father of Yehozarah, the owner of the seal, who also may have been a royal official. Sometimes public positions passed from father to sons. (*Noticias de la semana* ["News of the Week"], a bulletin of the Press Office of the government of Israel, March 28, 1975.)

2 Kings 18:22 —— *whose . . . altars Hezekiah has removed* The dismantled altar found in Beersheba (see comment on Ex 19:12) could be an evidence of Hezekiah's religious reforms, the main purpose of which was to concentrate the worship of Yahweh in the temple at Jerusalem by suppressing worship places in other areas. (TBAR, 1, No. 1 [1975], 9)

2 Kings 18:26 —— *Shebnah* According to verses 18 and 37, he was the royal secretary, but neither in this passage nor in those in Isaiah where references are made to him is his father's name mentioned. In the excavations at Tell ed-Duweir was found a limestone seal in the shape of a button, inscribed "Shebnah, (son) of Ahab." A sure identification with the Shebnah in this passage is not possible, but there would be no difficulty in supposing it. (SPA, 107)

2 Kings 18:37 —— *Joah the son of Asaph* In the excavations at Megiddo was found a lapis lazuli seal which seems to be prior to the exile, possibly belonging to the seventh century B.C. It bears the inscription, "Belonging to Asaph." There is a figure of a lion and a stylized imitation of a cartouche like those in hieroglyphical Egyptian script. If its dating indicated is correct, it is not at all difficult to assume that it belonged to Joah, the herald or chronicler of King Hezekiah. The name Asaph recalls the name of the celebrated writer in the Psalms, but it does not seem probable that it was the same person. (SPA, 107)

2 Kings 19:9 —— *Tirhakah king of Ethiopia* At the ancient site of Thebes a granite head of Tirhakah was found, and in Palmyra a scarab seal with his Egyptian name *Taharka*. He was the last king of the Twenty-fifth Dynasty of Egypt. Thus he was a pharaoh, but the dynasty was of Ethiopian origin, so he is called in this passage "king of Ethiopia." (WB, II, 288)

2 Kings 20:7 —— *a cake of* (dry) *figs*. Among the texts from Ugarit there is a veterinarian's manual in which one of the medicines mentioned is "old fig-cakes." Dried or "old" figs seem to have been in common use for the treatment of ulcers or sores in general. They were also applied to the sores of animals. (BAR-2, 41; WMTS, 261)

2 Kings 20:11 —— *on the dial of Ahaz.* The reader will perhaps wonder why there should be "steps" on a "dial." (So also KJV.) Other traditional versions render "degrees" (on a dial). GNB translates "stairway." While the context does indicate a kind of sunclock, the Hebrew word used is literally "steps"; so it must have been some kind of "stairway." A model of a sunclock found in Egypt has finally clarified the sense of this passage. It consists of two series of steps, one toward the east, and the other toward the west. There is a wall in front of each series. As the sun rose higher in the east, the shadow of the eastern wall fell on the steps on the opposite side, literally "went back" or descended down the steps. Then, as the sun declined toward the west, the inverse phenomenon occurred on the eastern set of steps. There is a strong possibility that the sunclock of Ahaz was just of this kind. This theory is considerably strengthened by the fact that in the parallel passage of Isaiah 38:8, the Isaiah scroll from Qumran (IQIs[a]) inserts after "steps" the explanatory phrase "of the roof chamber." The Septuagint has "steps [*anabathmus*] of the house of your father [Ahaz]." Also in Josephus' version of this episode the sense is that of "steps" or "stairway" (*Antiquities*, X, II, 1) of Hezekiah's "house." The traditional rendering "dial" and "degrees" was due to the fact that translators had in mind the image of a Greek sunclock of the quadrant type. (WB, III, 67; ABB, 156)

2 Kings 20:12 —— *Merodach-baladan* The name is a Hebrew adaptation of the Babylonian *Marduk-apal-iddin*. In a stele which is kept at the Berlin Museum this monarch is seen as he receives an official's homage. (BOT, 74–75, plate 7)

2 Kings 20:20 —— *and the conduit* The aqueduct which Hezekiah ordered to be built in order to bring water into the city is an extraordinary work of ancient Israelite hydraulic engineering. The

Gihon spring, from which the water came, was and is still situated outside the city's wall. The aqueduct still exists under the southeastern hill upon which the City of David was located. It was cut into the solid rock and followed an irregular trajectory, including a wide curve (compare 2 Chron 32:30). It was made by two excavating teams, working simultaneously, starting from the two extremes and proceeding toward each other for a distance of some 1,750 feet, and at a depth which at some places is as much as 130 feet beneath the surface. At its southern end, the tunnel emerges in a pool now called "the pool of Siloam" (or Siloe). The two teams were able to meet with a difference of only 1 foot in the floor level and of less than 3 feet in the line of the side walls. This is all the more remarkable when we remember that the form of the tunnel resembles a huge letter "S." The means used for this underground orientation—certainly rudimentary compared to modern engineering methods—are now unknown. There are signs along the way that torches and oil lamps were used for lighting. As to ventilation, it must have been very poor. In the southern section a shaft has been discovered that served that purpose, but nothing similar has so far been discovered in the northern section.

The existence of the tunnel has been known for a long while. But in 1880, inside of the tunnel, some 20 feet from the southern end at the Siloam Pool, an inscription was found carved into the rock. Some inexperienced people tried to remove it, and in doing so they broke it in several pieces. Fortunately, the pieces could be put together, although the damage is evident. It was recovered by the Turkish authorities and is now in the Istanbul Museum. An exact replica of it can be seen at the Louvre Museum. In Albright's translation the inscription reads:

[. . . when] (the tunnel) was driven through. And this was the way in which it was cut through:—While [. . .] (were) still [. . .] axe(s), each man toward his fellow, and while there were still three cubits to be cut through, [there was heard] the voice of a man calling to his fellow, for there was *an overlap* in the rock on the right [and on the left]. And when the tunnel was driven through, the quarrymen hewed (the rock), each man toward his fellow, axe against axe; and the water flowed from the spring toward the reservoir for 1,200 cubits, and the height of the rock above the head(s) of the quarrymen was 100 cubits. (See the comment on 2 Chron 32:4.)

The book of Ecclesiasticus (or the Wisdom of Jesus, Son of Sirach), one of the deuterocanonical books, reads: "(Hezekiah) had a tunnel built through solid rock with iron tools and had cisterns built to hold the water" (48:17, GNB). (JAT, 269–79; JOT, 179–88; MTL, 175–76; ANET, 321)

2 Kings 21:1 —— *Manasseh . . . began to reign*   Avigad, who has made special studies of Hebrew seals, mentions among them one with the inscription "Manasseh son of the king." This probably belonged to Hezekiah's son while he was still the crown prince. (Quoted in BAH, 14)

2 Kings 21:18 —— *the garden of Uzza*   It seems that beginning with Manasseh the kings of Judah, their officials, and some members of aristocratic families were buried in the cemetery called at first "the garden of Uzza." It may have been in what is now the village of Siloam (or Silwan) on the western slope of the southern part of the Mount of Olives, facing the Kidron ravine. Some tombs of the epoch have been excavated in that area. (JR, 8, 63, et seqq.)

2 Kings 22:14 —— *in the Second Quarter*   In Hebrew, the *Mishneh*, literally "second, double." We know by this passage that it was a section of the city of Jerusalem. With this meaning the word appears in two other places: 2 Chronicles 34:22 and Zephaniah 1:10. There is no absolute certainty as to its location. Evidently it was a new quarter, created as the city increased in population. The only biblical reference to its location is given by Zephaniah, who mentions it along with the Fish Gate. Almost certainly this city gate was in the north, more or less where the present Damascus Gate is located. According to Simons, the Fish Gate would be precisely a *Mishneh* entrance on that side. If so, this quarter occupied the space west of the temple mount, extending up to the northern limit of the city of that period. On the south it would have included the site later occupied by the Jewish quarter of the present walled city. During excavations of this area in 1969 an impressive part of a wall was found, dated to the end of the eighth century or to the seventh century B.C. This may have been the wall which protected the Second Quarter on the western side. (JOT, 291–93; JR, 41–44; MTL, 55–56)

2 Kings 23:5 —— *the constellations*   (GNB, "the planets.") In Hebrew, *mazzaloth*, probably the same as *mazzaroth* in Job 38:32, where RSV simply transliterates the word. The reference may be to Venus, and the plural form (Hebrew ending -*oth*) may denote the morning and evening appearances of the planet. In Babylonian monuments of the twelfth century B.C., the symbols of the sun, the moon, and Venus are often shown together and in the same order as in this verse. Some lexicons, and therefore some versions, render the term "signs of the zodiac"; likewise the Vulgate *duodecim signis* "twelve signs." The Septuagint prefers to transliterate the word as *mazuroth*. It is doubtful, however, that the zodiac constellations were known as such in Josiah's time and that his Chaldean contemporaries worshiped them. It seems that the best translation is "the planets," perhaps involving an allusion to the brightest three: Venus, Jupiter, and Mars. The reference in Job 38:32 may be to Venus in particular. (AOT, 74–89)

2 Kings 23:8 —— *on one's left at the gate of the city.* This passage tells of Josiah's extensive religious reforms and how he demolished the pagan places of worship in several Judean cities, including Beersheba. In the excavations carried out in this city by the late Aharoni, the stones of an altar were found embedded in a wall. With these stones it was possible to reassemble the altar. But the remains of the temple to which the altar belonged were not found, nor were there any indications of the temple's site. Among the ruins of a building located "on one's left at the gate of the city," the excavators uncovered the remainder of a staircase at right angles. After rereading this passage and examining the plans of the excavations, Yadin came to believe that the altar was originally located in this place with the staircase as a sort of frame. If that is so, this may be the site of the Beersheba high place which Josiah commanded to be destroyed. But another archaeologist, A. F. Rainey, who also participated in the excavations, vigorously attacks Yadin's theory, on the basis of the layout and for certain other reasons. At the present time, the matter is still being debated. This scripture passage presents some problems which seem to militate against the identification proposed by Yadin. In the first place, the Hebrew text has the plural "high places," though this may be the so-called emphatic plural applied to a single object. This is Yadin's opinion, in support of which he cites Jeremiah 7:31 and 32:35 and Micah 1:5 as examples.

Furthermore, one cannot determine precisely which "city" is the one mentioned in this verse. Exegetes generally have taken it for granted that the city is Jerusalem, but Yadin argues that in Jerusalem there never was any "gate of Joshua." Moreover, there is no biblical or extrabiblical mention of a Joshua as governor of Jerusalem. Yadin believes that "the city" is Beersheba, previously named in this same verse. But only by some straining of the syntax can this text be said to apply to Beersheba. Another problem is that Aharoni, supported by Rainey, dates the stratum where the staircase was found to the eighth century B.C., the time of Hezekiah, but Josiah belongs to the seventh century B.C., a date which Yadin assigns to this stratum in support of his theory. Aharoni thought that the staircase at right angles led to the top of the wall. But this was so far away that Rainey believes that the staircase only served to give access to the roof of a building. He suggests that the altar was located in a temple upon which was constructed the building in the ruins marked as no. 32. (TBAR, 3, No. 1 [1977], 3–12; 3, No. 3 [1977], 18–21)

2 Kings 23:11 —— *the chariots of the sun* Under the name of *Shamash*, the sun was worshiped as a god in Mesopotamia. One can be almost certain that from that region came the mythological concept of the sun god riding across the sky in a war chariot. The Greeks took up this theme in their representation of the chariot of the sun god, Apollo. In Assyrian traditions, the chariot of the sun accompanied the king on a portable shrine in his military expeditions. A relief of Sennacherib in Nineveh shows a military encampment in which a chariot is depicted with two upright posts, each bearing the emblem of the god Shamash. In addition priests are pictured as burning incense, and also an offering table stands in front. This undoubtedly is "the chariot of the sun."

In her excavations of a cultic center near Jerusalem, Kenyon found some figurines of horses with sun disks on their foreheads. In her opinion these are probably miniatures of the life-size horses of the chariots of the sun that had been placed at the entrance to Yahweh's temple. (WB, II, 295; TBAR, 4, No. 2 [1978], 8–9)

2 Kings 23:29 —— *Pharaoh Neco . . . went up to the king of Assyria to the river Euphrates. King Josiah went to meet him* The Babylonian Chronicle, published by C. J. Gadd in 1923, gives information that throws light on the strange and tragic interference of the king of Judah in a conflict involving some of the great powers of that epoch. Medes and Babylonians were attacking Assyria. Nineveh had already fallen, but Assyrian resistance continued. Pharaoh Neco rushed to help the king of Assyria, not to fight against him, as some versions indicate. The Hebrew preposition *al* (used a second time with reference to the Euphrates River) denotes direction or purpose rather than opposition. It is not clear whether Josiah was siding with the Medes and Babylonians, or was simply acting in self-defense, since the passing of the Egyptian army through his territory was tantamount to an invasion. According to 2 Chronicles 35:20–22, Neco tried to dissuade him, but Josiah insisted on opposing the Egyptian march toward the north, with the result that he was killed in the battle and Judah became a vassal of Egypt. The pharaoh continued his advance, and at Carchemish, on the upper Euphrates, he suffered a decisive defeat at the hands of the Babylonians. Jeremiah refers to this defeat in 46:2. The Megiddo excavations (stratum II) clearly show that Neco destroyed the city to such an extent that it never recovered its importance. (WMTS, 252; BAW, 177)

2 Kings 23:31 —— *Jehoahaz . . . began to reign* Among the Hebrew seals studied by Avigad there is one that bears the inscription "Jehoahaz the son of the king." As in the case of Manasseh's seal (see comment on 21:1), this seal probably belonged to Josiah's son while he was still crown prince. (BAH, 14)

2 Kings 23:34 —— *and changed his name to Jehoiakim.* The former name of this king of Judah was Eliakim. The Babylonian Chronicle published in 1956 records the subsequent defeat of the Egyptians at Carchemish. Jeremiah (46:2) describes this event: "About Egypt: Concerning the army of Pharaoh Neco, king of Egypt, which was along the Euphrates River at Carchemish and which Nebuchadrezzar, king of Babylon, defeated in the fourth year of Jehoiakim the son of Josiah, king of Judah." (JBL, 93 [1974], 333)

2 Kings 24:1 —— *Nebuchadnezzar . . . came up* A letter in Aramaic found in 1942 at Saqqara, Egypt, was written by Adon, one king of a Palestinian city, probably Ashkelon. It reports that Babylonia's invading army had already reached Aphek. This place is identified as the present Tell el-Muhmar, near modern Ras el-Ain, northeast of Joppa. Adon, a vassal of Egypt, appeals for military aid because he will not be able to resist the invading army alone. Ashkelon was not saved (Jer 47:5). Jehoiakim chose to submit, at least for a period of three years. (BAW, 177–78; EB, I, 198)

2 Kings 24:8 —— *Jehoiachin* In the Palestine Archaeological Museum in Jerusalem there is a jar handle inscribed by a seal which reads "Belonging to Eliakim, servant of Joiachin" (Jehoiachin). The Hebrew word for "servant" is here *naar*, literally "boy." Perhaps in this case it means "steward." This impression is one of two found at Tell Beit Mirsim. A similar one was found at Tell er-Rumeila (Beth-shemesh). It is interesting that the three impressions were made with the same seal. (APB, 125; EAE, 252; ANEP, figure 278, p. 280)

2 Kings 24:12 —— *and Jehoiachin . . . gave himself up* Until 1956 the exact date of the first fall of Jerusalem at the hands of the Babylonians was unknown. But in that year a cuneiform tablet was finally deciphered giving the date as the second day of the month of Adar (the equivalent of March 15–16) in 597 B.C. This tablet of the Babylonian Chronicle reads: "In the seventh year, in the month of Kislev, the king of Accad gathered his troops and advanced towards the land of Hatti [Syria-Palestine]. He besieged the town of Judah, and on the second day of the month of Adar he took the town and made the king prisoner. He chose a king after his own heart, took much tribute from him and sent him to Babylon." (BAR-1, 119; BOT, 89–90)

2 Kings 24:20 —— *Zedekiah rebelled against the king of Babylon.* As Jehoiakim had done somewhat more than nine years before, Zedekiah tried to emancipate himself from Babylon. This brought about Nebuchadnezzar's two campaigns against Judah, which finally put an end to the southern kingdom. The first campaign occurred in 598 B.C., and the second in 589–87 B.C. The ruins of two of Judah's main cities, besides Jerusalem itself, show the severity with which Nebuchadnezzar put down the rebellion. These cities were Debir and Lachish. In Debir the adobe was turned red by the fire. In Lachish the conflagration was so intense that it reduced the walls to a sort of lava that flowed onto the ground. It was only by luck that the famous "Lachish letters" were preserved: twenty-one inscribed potsherds discovered in 1935. The majority of them are messages sent during the siege by one Hoshayahu, the commander of an advanced post, to Yaosh, the chief of the Lachish garrison. (See the comments on Jer 34:7; 38:4.) Some archaeologists (for example, Olga Tufnell, Aharoni, David Ushishkin, and Rainey) maintain that these traces point to the destruction of the city by Sennacherib (18:14). If so, what the Babylonians destroyed would have been the city as later reconstructed. Others (like Albright, Kenyon, and Wright) oppose that view. (ANET, 321–22; BAW, 181–82; TBAR, 3, No. 3 [1977], 56) ·

2 Kings 25:4 ——— *the gate between the two walls* In the southeastern excavations of the southeast part of Jerusalem, the remains of these two walls and the gate have been discovered. The eastern wall was built upon what had been left of the ancient Jebusite wall. The garden mentioned in this verse is still in the place where the valleys of Hinnom and Kidron meet, near the pool of Siloam, which supplies the water to irrigate it. In ancient times the garden was probably more extensive and more wooded than at present. (WB, III, 137)

2 Kings 25:9 ——— *And he burned . . . all the houses of Jerusalem* In excavations north of the Jewish quarter of Jerusalem, Avigad discovered toward the end of 1975 clear signs of the destruction of the city by the Babylonians. He found charred wood and ashes by the remains of one of the defense towers. These remains rise to a height of 23 feet. He also found four spearheads, one of iron and three of bronze, all of which belong to that period, judging by the pieces of ceramics and other objects found at the same site. (JPW, November 4, 1975)

2 Kings 25:22 ——— *Gedaliah* A seal impression found in the ruins of Lachish bears the inscription, "Belonging to Gedaliahu, steward of the palace" (literally "who is over the house"). According to most authorities the identification of the owner of the seal with Judah's governor is practically certain. The position of palace steward was very important in the court, so that Gedaliah would have simply been designated as governor by a disposition of the king of Babylon. (BAT, 105–7; BAW, 181)

2 Kings 25:23 ——— *Jaazaniah* At Tell en-Nasbeh (probably to be identified with Mizpah) archaeologists found a seal reading, "Belonging to Jaazaniah, servant of the king." Beneath it appears the figure of a rooster. There seems to be no doubt that this seal, which was found in an unopened tomb, belonged to the person mentioned in this passage. (BOT, 107–8; BAW, 181)

2 Kings 25:30 ——— *a regular allowance was given him by the king*   In the lists found in the excavations at Babylon and published in 1939, concerning the rations or allowances granted by Nebuchadnezzar, the phrase "Yaukin, king of Judah" appears several times. This is Jehoiachin. Five of his sons, probably born to him in Babylon, are also mentioned. Evidently he enjoyed special consideration, since he received 10 measures of oil for himself alone and 2.5 for each of his sons, whereas eight captives listed as coming from Gebal received only 11.5 measures for all of them together. After thirty-seven years in captivity Jehoiachin was released in 561 B.C. by Nebuchadnezzar's successor, Evil-merodach. (WB, III, 155; ABB, 177)

THE FIRST BOOK OF
THE CHRONICLES

1 Chron 4:23 —— *the potters . . . with the king for his work.* In diverse sites of Judea excavations have uncovered potsherds with handles of vessels bearing the inscription "Belonging to the king" or "For the king," followed by the name of a town. It is quite probable that these are ceramics from the royal potteries.

1 Chron 5:26 —— *and he carried them away, namely, the Reubenites* An Assyrian bas-relief of this epoch, found in Calah, represents this deportation. Several Hebrew captives, identified by their beards, their headgear, and their long tunics with fringes, are being driven by an Assyrian soldier as they march off with travel knapsacks on their backs. (WB, IV, 248)

1 Chron 17:19 —— *according to thy own heart* With a mere change of vowels, Hebrew *vehelibbekha* ("and according to your heart") may be emended to read *vehalebbekha* ("and your dog"). So, David would have said to the Lord in his prayer, "For the sake of your servant and dog, O Lord," etc., which is a quite probable alternative reading. In the Tell el-Amarna and the Lachish letters this superlative expression often occurs. Compare 2 Kings 8:13 in which "servant" and "dog" appear in apposition as synonyms with the same sense of humility. (WMTS, 40)

1 Chron 29:4 —— *of the gold of Ophir* A potsherd found at Tell Qasileh bears the inscription, "Gold of Ophir to Beth-horon, 30 shekels." On the identification of Ophir, the source of much gold and so often mentioned in the Bible, see the comment on 1 Kings 9:28. (WB, IV, 260)

1 Chron 29:7 —— *and ten thousand darics of gold*   The daric (some versions render "drachma") was already a minted coin, whereas other forms of money consisted rather of quantities of metal measured by weight. The minting of coins was a Greek invention, adopted later by the Persians. It was introduced in the fifth century B.C. The daric did not exist as yet in the time of David. Writing about the first half of the third century B.C., the Chronicler seems to employ this obvious anachronism in order that his contemporaries, who were well acquainted with the daric, might have an idea of the equivalent amount in terms of well-known minted money. On the other hand, the use of "daric" in Ezra 2:69 and 8:27, and Nehemiah 7:70–72 is appropriate for by then it was already widely used as currency. It was called daric in honor of King Darius. The daric's weight was just over ¼ ounce. Under Persian domination, Judah (Judea) was a province of the Empire, and its official name was *Yehud*. Coins from the second half of the fifth century B.C., as well as from the fourth century B.C., have been found bearing the name *Yehud* in Hebrew characters. This means that this province had been granted the privilege of producing its own coinage. Greek influence, however, is noticeable in its coins. On one of them an owl appears (an imitation of the Greek tetradrachma) and even an image of Zeus appears on another. (BAW, 206)

THE SECOND BOOK OF
THE CHRONICLES

2 Chron 4:1 —— *He made an altar of bronze* The altar was a very important cultic element, for the sacrifices were offered upon it. It is therefore strange that neither in 1 Kings nor in 2 Chronicles is there a description of the altar. In this passage only its dimensions are stated. In 1 Kings it is often mentioned but as something taken for granted (8:64; 9:25). Supposedly, it had the same shape, though not the same size, as the altar of the wilderness sanctuary (Ex 38:1, 2), except that in the latter the ascent was by a ramp (Ex 20:26), while the temple's altar apparently had steps (Ezek 43:17, assuming that the prophet's description was based on Solomon's altar and not on that of Ahaz). Archaeology has uncovered altars of Canaanite temples which have various forms and dimensions. But evidently the type of altar most closely resembling Solomon's is the altar found in Beersheba (see comment on 2 Kings 23:8). (MTL, 98; TOJ, 43)

2 Chron 12:2, 7 —— *In the fifth year of King Rehoboam . . . my wrath shall not be poured out upon Jerusalem* The date here indicated is the first that permits the synchronizing of biblical and Egyptian chronologies. In a wall of Ammon's temple at Karnak the conquests of the Pharaoh Sheshonq (Shishak) in Palestine are recorded. There is a list of the 180 cities conquered by him. Jerusalem is not included, although we know by the biblical narrative that Shishak presented himself before this city. Undoubtedly the city escaped from being attacked and captured because of the large tribute it paid to Shishak from the treasures of the temple and the royal palace (verse 9; compare 1 Kings 14:21–31). But certain biblical cities, including

Beth-horon, Beth-shan, Gibeon, Megiddo, and Taanach, are mentioned in the list. (WB, II, 232; UTB, 148)

2 Chron 26:15 —— *engines, invented by skilful men*　These probably were war machines similar to the ones represented in the bas-relief showing the capture of Lachish by Sennacherib's army, using bows and slings. Or the weapons may have been new types, such as crossbows and small catapults for stone throwing.

2 Chron 26:23 —— *And Uzziah slept with his fathers*　A stone plaque in the Russian church of St. Mary Magdalene, situated on the western slope of the Mount of Olives, bears the Aramaic inscription, "Hither were brought the bones of Uzziah King of Judah. Do not open." The place where the plaque was originally found is not known, so there is no way of knowing where the secondary burial of the monarch took place. The plaque was discovered in its present location in 1931, and it seems to date from the first century B.C. That would have been the time when the bones were transferred from the place of their first interment to some other location. The original tomb would have been in the new royal cemetery, which evidently was situated on the eastern slope of the western hill, facing the temple. This, in fact, is the place where Mazar uncovered a cemetery which was apparently so important that it could well have been a royal cemetery. "It may be inferred," Mazar writes, "that the tomb of King Uzziah was originally located here." As a result of urban expansion on that side of the city in the days of Manasseh, the cemetery was transferred to the place called "the Garden of Uzza" (see comment on 2 Kings 21:18). In the extreme southwest of the place now called Mount Zion, two tombs were found which seem to have belonged to families of high rank. They date from the eighth century B.C. This indicates the probability of a cemetery on this site, although not specifically a royal one (see comment also on Jer 26:23). (JR, 8; MTL, 183–89)

2 Chron 30:2 —— *his officials*　(GNB; RSV: "princes.") There exists a seal impression which reads "Belonging to Jehozeriah, son of Hilquiyahu, servant of Hezekiah." As previously noted, in such a context "servant" (Hebrew *ebed*) refers to an official. This Jehozeriah is not mentioned in the Bible, but he may have been one of the officials who cooperated with King Hezekiah in the celebration of the passover. (MTL, 179)

2 Chron 32:4 —— *the brook that flowed through the land* This could also be translated ". . . through the earth." According to R. Amiran, this is how the phrase should be understood. She believes that it refers to "the former existence of a natural subterranean stream which ran from the spring (of Gihon) through the hill, emerging at the bottom of the valley on the west of the Mount Zion spur" (JR, 77). In Amiran's view, this answers the question about ventilation for the construction of Hezekiah's tunnel (see comment on 2 Kings 20:20), and it explains the amazing fact that the two teams of excavators working from the opposite ends could have met in the middle with such accuracy. She believes they simply followed the course of the subterranean stream.

2 Chron 32:5 —— *and outside it he built another wall* In the excavations carried out in 1969–71 in the old Jewish quarter of the walled city of Jerusalem, located in the western hill and facing the Temple Mount, a segment of a wall was uncovered, which dates from the eighth or the seventh century B.C. It is 23 feet thick and runs northeast and southwest at a distance of some 900 feet from the Western Wall. This recently found wall supposedly first turned westward for a stretch, then southward, and again toward the southeast in the direction of the City of David, where it joined the wall of the City of David at its southern extreme. This left the pool of Siloam on the inside. According to Avigad, "there are reasonable grounds for ascribing the building of this wall to Hezekiah." Mazar writes more cautiously, "We cannot be sure that Hezekiah's 'other wall' is the same as the wall uncovered by Avigad, but it is a plausible equation." The westward growth of the city required the building of this wall "outside" the City of David. Zephaniah (1:10, 11) mentions the Second Quarter, *Mishneh*, where the Jewish quarter stands today, and the Mortar, *Makhtesh*, another new quarter. (JR, 41–44; MTL, 176–77)

2 Chron 32:30 —— *Hezekiah closed the upper outlet of the waters of Gihon* Parker found this outlet in his explorations of 1910–11. It was closed up with stones and sand.

2 Chron 32:33 —— *they buried him in the ascent of the tombs* It seems that this rather obscure detail about the place of Hezekiah's burial has been definitively solved by Mazar's discovery of a cemetery situated on the eastern slope of the western hill, in front

of the western wall of the Temple Mount (see comment on 26:23).
The Hebrew word means literally "ascent," "rise," or "slope." But
the meaning of "ascent of the tombs" is not clear. The Septuagint
retained the literal sense and rendered *anabasis* ("ascent," "climb").
The Vulgate translated *supra* ("above," "upon"). Some modern
versions have "the upper section," "the uppermost," or "the upper
part." Some versions in other languages have taken the meaning to
be "the most prominent place" or have interpreted "ascent" as the
way leading *up to* the cemetery. Actually the cemetery was situated
on an "ascent" or "slope," that is to say, on the eastern slope of the
western hill facing the Central Valley (the Tyropoeon). (MTL,
183–87)

2 Chron 33:11 —— *took Manasseh with hooks* This was a very
common Assyrian practice in dealing with their prisoners of war. A
relief from Zenjirli, in northern Syria, depicts an Assyrian king
holding two of his defeated enemies, who are represented as very
small in order to depict by contrast their conqueror's greatness. He
holds them with ropes passed through rings in their noses, the
customary manner of leading oxen. The "hook" referred to in this
passage was circular like a ring. In the so-called prism B of
Esarhaddon, king of Assyria, mention is made of "Manasseh (*Me-na-si-i*)* king of Judah (*Ia-u-di*)," in a long list of vassal kings who
were forced to transport to Nineveh, "under terrible difficulties,"
material for the construction of the royal palace. Manasseh also
appears in cylinder C of Ashurbanipal, in the list of kings this
monarch called "servants who belong to me." The name is written
with a slightly different spelling, *Mi-in-si-e.* It is interesting that in
both these lists, Manasseh's name occurs in the second place,
following the name of the king of Tyre. According to Wright, this
detail indicates the important place he held among the kings of Syria
and Palestine. (WB, IV, 288; ANET, 291, 294; BAW, 175–76)

2 Chron 33:14 —— *an outer wall* To the west of a very ancient wall
on the western slope of the City of David (southeastern hill), Kenyon
discovered the remains of another wall. In the opinion of Mazar,
this may be the wall built by Manasseh when the city had expanded
considerably toward the west. On the eastern slope of the western
hill, Mazar uncovered an extensive cemetery which apparently
ceased to be used in the time of Manasseh (beginning of the seventh

century B.C.). This was probably due to the city's expansion in that area of the Tyropoeon. (MTL, 57)

2 Chron 33:18 —— *Manasseh, . . . his prayer to his God* The apocryphal writing in Greek called "Prayer of Manasseh" was found by Christians of the second or third century A.D. in Egypt. According to some scholars it was translated from a Hebrew text of the first century B.C. or the first century A.D. It appears in a Syriac version in the *Didascalia* (third century A.D.). It was later incorporated into the *Apostolic Constitutions* (II, 22), fourth century A.D. (TAL, 67–69)

EZRA

Ezra 1:2 —— *The LORD, . . . has given me all the kingdoms of the earth* In a clay cylinder containing a proclamation from Cyrus, it is the god Marduk who "pronounced the name of Cyrus . . . (and) declared him . . . the ruler of all the world" and who ordered him to march against Babylon and capture it. Marduk would be "going at his side like a real friend." Further on Cyrus says: "I am Cyrus, king of the world, great king, legitimate king, king of Babylon, king of Sumer and Akkad, king of the four rims (of the earth) . . . whose rule Bel and Nebo love, whom they want as king to please their hearts." He adds that he entered Babylon "as a friend," that his "numerous troops walked around . . . in peace," not terrorizing anyone, and that he "strove for peace" and liberated the people of Babylon from servitude. "Marduk, the great lord," Cyrus continues, "was well pleased with my deeds." Finally, he explains his policy of returning to certain sacred cities (including Ashur, Susa, Agade, and others he has previously enumerated) "the sanctuaries of which have been ruins for a long time, the images which (used) to live therein, and established for them permanent sanctuaries. I (also) gathered all their (former) inhabitants and returned (to them) their habitations. Furthermore, I resettled, upon the command of Marduk, the great lord, all the gods of Sumer and Akkad whom Nabonidus has brought into Babylon to the anger of the lord of the gods, unharmed, in their (former) chapels, the places which make them happy."

As may be seen, Cyrus' attitude toward the Jews in leaving them free to return to their fatherland and even in helping them to rebuild the temple of "The LORD, the God of heaven" in Jerusalem, was in accord with his magnanimous policy toward the peoples under his domain. The religious tolerance of this policy may point to his having considered the gods of these various peoples, including the God of Israel, as diverse manifestations of the same supreme Divine Being. He seems to have been a distant supporter of a primitive, vague kind of pantheism. Burrows, however, regards it rather as an example of "the shrewd Oriental diplomacy of the conqueror . . . who evidently represented himself to other peoples also as their deliverer and the champion and servant of their gods." (ANET, 315–16; WMTS, 267; ABB, 220, 222)

Ezra 4:1 —— *the returned exiles were building a temple* This second temple was built under the direction of Zerubbabel and Joshua with the authorization of King Cyrus of Persia. Very little information about the temple is found in the books of Ezra and Nehemiah. Undoubtedly, it was much less imposing than Solomon's temple, but it was not, for that reason, without importance. There is information about it in the books of the Maccabees, the writings of Josephus, and the Letter of Aristeas (third century B.C.). It was the temple that Herod the Great enlarged and rebuilt with a magnificence surpassing that of Solomon's temple, and which the Jews still think of as the Second Temple. No remains of it have been found by archaeologists. This is understandable in view of the utter destruction of Herod's Temple by the Romans in A.D. 70 (TOJ, 68–75; MTL, 104–5)

Ezra 4:7 —— *written in Aramaic* The passages in Ezra 4:8–6:18 and 7:12–26 are not in Hebrew but in Aramaic in the original text. The Elephantine documents (see comment on Neh 12:22), also written in Aramaic, show that this was the official language of the Persian Empire and that it was spoken from Babylon to Egypt. These documents, moreover, support the view that the Aramaic of the book of Ezra is precisely the form of the language spoken at that time. From literary evidence recovered in Mesopotamia, we know that even official Persian documents were drawn up in Aramaic. (BAW, 211)

Ezra 4:10 —— *the great and noble Osnappar* No Assyrian king bearing this name is known. It seems that *Osnappar*, rather than being an adaptation into Aramaic, is really a corruption of the name *Ashurbanipal*, concerning whom there exist numerous inscriptions and written records. The problem is that not one of them refers to the deportation mentioned in this passage. In the so-called Warka Cylinder, this king describes himself as "the great king, the legitimate king, the king of the world, king of Assyria, king of (all) the four rims (of the earth), king of kings, prince without rival, who rules from the Upper Sea to the Lower Sea and has made bow to his feet all the (other) rulers and who has laid the yoke of his overlordship (upon them). . . ." (ANET, 297; EB, I, 881–82, 907–10)

Ezra 5:8 —— *the province of Judah* In Aramaic the name of this new province of the Persian Empire was *Yehud*. Coins, potsherds, and seals of the Persian period (approximately 538–331 B.C.) have been found bearing the inscription *Yhd* (the same name without vowels). (WB, IV, 224)

"Tomb of Herod's Family," in the modern sector of Jerusalem, west of the walled Old City. The huge round stone, which was rolled down to close the tomb, is partially visible to the left (Mt 27:60).

Ancient alabaster flasks discovered in the Holy Land. They were ideal containers for the very costly perfumes of the New Testament period (Mk 14:3).

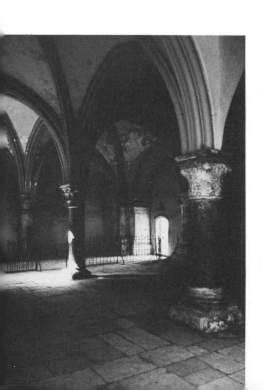

Medieval chapel built on the traditional site of the Upper Room or Cenacle. The present structure was built in the fourteenth century A.D. (Mk 14:15).

Qumran caves where most of the Dead Sea scrolls were found, especially in Cave 4, in the

center of the picture. The Isaiah scroll was discovered in Cave 1, not seen here (Lk 4:17).

Near modern Jericho, the ruins of the Jericho of Jesus' time have been excavated. It is located some 17 miles from Jerusalem. Jesus visited Jericho on his way to Jerusalem at the end of his ministry. The Jericho of the Old Testament was at a different location (Lk 19:1).

Colonnade along Gerasa's main street, as seen today after the excavations. Gerasa was one of ten cities, east and southeast of Galilee, which formed the Decapolis (a federation of Greek towns), one of the provinces or districts into which Palestine was organized by Rome after its conquest in 63 B.C. (Mk 7:31).

Above: The pool of Siloam (Jn 9:7).   Below: Steps of the "Holy Thursday Stairway" (Jn 18:1).

Present state of the Bethzatha pool (Jn 5:2).

The crypt over the traditional "Jacob's Well" near Nablus, Samaria. Water may still be drawn from it (Jn 4:6).

Roman games carved on the pavement of the Antonia Tower (Jn 19:13).

Pavement on the site of the Antonia Tower from the time of Jesus (Jn 19:13).

NEHEMIAH

Neh 2:8 —— *the fortress of the temple* This is a reference to the fortified enclosure or citadel called in Hebrew *Birah*. It stood in the northwestern angle of the Temple Mount and protected the temple on that side. It is mentioned in the Letter of Aristeas, an Alexandrian writer, who recounts his journey from Alexandria to Jerusalem as an official and envoy of Ptolemy II Philadelphus (285–246 B.C.). Aristeas says that the fortress had a garrison of 500 men. It is the fortress which Josephus calls *Baris* (*Antiquities* XV, 11, 4) and which Herod transformed into a more imposing structure. Herod called it Antonia, in honor of the Roman Mark Anthony. On this site the Arab Omariya school now stands, and it is the starting point of the traditional Via Dolorosa. (See also Josephus in *Wars*, V, 5, 8.) (MTL, 65, 80)

Neh 2:10 —— *Sanballat . . . Tobiah* In 1962, in a cave of the Wadi Daliyeh north of Jericho, was found a seal from the fourth century B.C. in which is mentioned a "son of Sanballat, governor of Samaria." A papyrus fragment was also found there in which the name of Sanballat appears. Judging by the date, this Sanballat probably was the grandson of the Sanballat of the book of Nehemiah. Sanballat could have been a family name, or the position, sometimes preserving the same name, might have been hereditary. "Ammonite," the adjective here applied to Tobiah, seems in this case to be not an identification of national origin, but rather a title belonging to a high position in Ammon, perhaps that of a provincial governor in the Persian domain. According to Nehemiah 6:18, 13:4, it seems that

Tobiah was a Jew. In Iraq el-Amir in Transjordan, close to the ruins of a palace, a tomb was excavated which bears the name *Tobiyah* carved in the rock in Aramaic characters. According to some scholars, both the palace and the tomb may be dated to the time of Nehemiah. It is attractive to think that perhaps this Tobiah is the same as the one mentioned here in Nehemiah. Other scholars disagree. A letter has been found, dated in the early third century B.C. and written by an Ammonite governor named Tobiah. This fact has led to the conclusion that, as in the case of Sanballat, Tobiah may have been a family name. Some scholars, in fact, now speak of the Tobiyads as a sort of dynasty. The name Sanballat also appears in the Jewish papyri of Elephantine as a governor of Samaria who was of Jewish religion. (APB, 170; NDBA, 59–63; BAW, 207)

Neh 2:13 —— *the Dung Gate* (In Hebrew, literally "the gate of the ash heaps.") It is located at the southern end of the southeastern hill (City of David), facing the point of intersection of the Hinnom and Kidron valleys. No remains of it have so far been found by archaeologists. Its proposed location is an inference from the fact that Nehemiah mentions it immediately after the Valley Gate in his listing of various locations from north to south (see comment on 3:13). (MTL, 193–94)

Neh 2:17 —— *let us build the wall of Jerusalem* Kenyon's excavations (1961–67) at the Ophel (southeastern hill of the city) have made it clear that the stretch of wall discovered by Macalister and J. G. Duncan (1923–25) in this area and attributed by them to the Jebusite city really belongs to the wall rebuilt by Nehemiah. According to Mazar the recent excavations indicate that Nehemiah's wall enclosed only the temple area and the southeastern hill (City of David). No traces of it have been found on the western hill. This limited circumscription explains, in Mazar's view, why the reconstruction could be completed within fifty-two days (6:15). (JR, 9; MTL, 192–98)

Neh 2:19 —— *Geshem* This Arab, who was a contemporary of Nehemiah, is called in 6:6 Gashmu, the form in which this name appears in a Nabatean inscription. He is identified as the king of Qedar, a region in the north of Arabia, east of Transjordan. In the Tell el-Maskhutah near Ismailia, Egypt, a silver dish was found which, according to the inscription it bears, was the one "which Qainu, the son of Geshem the king of Qedar, brought as an offering to Han-Ilat." (WB, IV, 236)

Neh 3:13 —— *the Valley Gate* What are evidently the remains of this gate have been uncovered not far from the gate discovered by J. Crowfoot (1927–28) among the ruins of the City of David's western wall, looking down on the Tyropoeon, or Central Valley. (JR, 6; MTL, 193–94)

Neh 3:15 —— *the stairs that go down from the City of David.* In the southeastern end of the Ophel hill (the one which the City of David occupied) remains of stairs have been discovered. The whole flight is 43 feet long and approximately 6 feet wide. It is very steep, and is partly hewn out of the rock itself. These stairs lead down as far as a gate in the wall, which could have been "the gate between the two walls" mentioned in 2 Kings 25:4 (see comment on that verse). According to some authorities the upper section of these stairs dates from Nehemiah's time. (WB, IV. 234; MTL. 195)

Neh 3:26 —— *the Water Gate on the east* No evident remains of this gate have been found in the excavations carried out on the eastern slope of the hill on which the City of David was situated; on the other hand, traces of the wall existing during several periods of the monarchy have been discovered. One may conclude, therefore, that this gate mentioned by Nehemiah must have been in the area of the Gihon spring, and that it received its name because it gave access to the spring. It may have been the gate implied in the incident of Solomon's being proclaimed king (1 Kings 1:38–40), but it doubtless became less important after the construction of Hezekiah's tunnel. (MTL, 174, 195)

Neh 3:27 —— *the great projecting tower* It is not clear whether or not the tower mentioned in this and the previous verse is the same as the one referred to in verse 25. Remains of towers have been located in the excavations of the City of David. One of them may have belonged to either the Hellenistic or the Persian period. If the latter is the case, it may be identified as the tower mentioned here. (MTL, 198)

Neh 12:22 —— *Johanan* In 1893 and 1903–11 some papyri of the fifth century B.C. were obtained in Egypt. They are called the Elephantine papyri because they were found on the Elephantine Island in the Nile River. They are written in Aramaic and come from a Jewish colony which was established there. These documents were evidently part of the archives of the colony. In one of them a letter is mentioned as having been sent to Johanan, the high priest at Jerusalem. If this Johanan is the person mentioned in this passage, which is later than Nehemiah, and also the one mentioned in Ezra 10:6, then such an identification can throw considerable light on the difficult problems of chronology between Ezra and Nehemiah. According to the Chronicler, Ezra preceded Nehemiah, but if the identification in the Elephantine papyrus is correct, Ezra would have gone to Jerusalem after Nehemiah. The Artaxerxes of Ezra 7:1 would then have been Artaxerxes II (405–358 B.C.) and not Artaxerxes I (464–424 B.C.). Ezra would have arrived in Jerusalem, not by the middle of the fifth century but at the beginning of the fourth century B.C., and chapters 7–10 of the book of Ezra should be placed at the end of the book of Nehemiah. (BAW, 209–11)

ESTHER

Esther 1:1 —— *who reigned from India to Ethiopia* This king is identified as the Xerxes of Greek history, the son of Darius I Histaspes and father of Artaxerxes. His domain actually did extend from the River Indus (India) to Ethiopia (Nubia). With the exception of Greece, this was practically the whole known world of that time. Xerxes finally attacked Greece in the hope of establishing a universal empire equivalent in extent to the world of his time. One of the titles which he bestowed upon himself and which appears in his inscriptions is "king of the whole world." In the set of bas-reliefs in the palace of Darius and Xerxes at Persepolis, both Indian and Ethiopian deputations are portrayed among those bringing tribute from various regions of the empire. In one of these reliefs, Xerxes himself is depicted standing behind Darius, who is seated on his throne. (WB, IV, 181)

Esther 1:3 —— *he gave a banquet* In the Louvre Museum one may see part of a wall covered with many-colored mosaics from the great banquet hall built by Darius in Susa. This was the place in which, according to the book of Esther, this sumptuous banquet took place. (MLB, 128–30)

Esther 1:5 —— *for all the people . . . a banquet lasting for seven days* The immense multitude of guests may well be imagined. Such manifestations of grandeur and liberality were not uncommon on the part of oriental monarchs. In 1951 M. E. L. Mallowan discovered in Nimrud a stele of Ashurnazirpal in which it is recorded that this

Assyrian king gave a banquet in his palace at Kalakh in which he entertained 69,574 guests! (MLB, 127)

Esther 2:3 —— *to gather all the beautiful young virgins* They were concentrated in Susa, but the ruins of the palace built at Persepolis by Xerxes for his queen Amestris, which included a "women's house," may give an idea of the harem in Susa where Esther and the other girls were confined to prepare themselves to be presented to the king. The house at Susa consisted of two sections, each with a vestibule whose roof was supported by four pillars. (WB, IV, 185)

Esther 2:16 —— *Esther was taken to King Ahasuerus into his royal palace* The ruins of this magnificent palace have been uncovered at Persepolis. Its throne room had seventy-two gigantic pillars and a capacity for some ten thousand people. This palace was detached from the queen's quarters and the harem but was not far from it. Several well-preserved reliefs of the palace have been found. (WB, IV, 187)

Esther 5:2 —— *he held out to Esther the golden scepter* This gesture meant that Esther was being welcomed, and by touching the end of the scepter she indicated her gratitude and obeisance. In the ruins at Persepolis there is a bas-relief in which Darius is represented as sitting on his throne with a scepter in his right hand. The scepter is of wood covered with gold and is as long as a staff. This length made it possible to extend the scepter to the person on whom favor was being bestowed. This person could thus touch it, as Esther did, but always at a respectful distance from the monarch. Xerxes' scepter was undoubtedly identical to the one depicted in the bas-relief of Darius. And Xerxes would have been sitting on his throne in the same way. (WB, IV, 191)

Esther 8:8 —— *and seal it with the king's ring* Among the objects found at Persepolis is a gold signet ring, engraved with the figure of an antelope. A similar ring, although surely with a different engraving, was the one belonging to Xerxes. It was used to make his edict in favor of the Jews valid and irrevocable. The impression of another of Xerxes' seals has also been found. This is in the shape of a cylinder, and the monarch is pictured between two winged bulls, with the winged emblem of Ahura-mazda, the sun god, above his head. (WB, IV, 194)

Esther 8:15 —— *Mordecai . . . the city of Susa* In a cuneiform tablet discovered in Borsippa a person named Marduka is mentioned. He was a financial official of King Xerxes I at Susa. The name is the Akkadian equivalent of Mordecai. It cannot be proved, however, that this official was the tutor and cousin of Esther, but the coincidence, if only that, is very interesting. Actually, Mordecai (Hebrew *Mordokhai*) is a name of Babylonian origin, and it probably means "Belonging to Marduk," one of the principal Babylonian gods.

JOB

Job 1:1 —— *that man was blameless and upright*   Some tablets found at Nippur in Mesopotamia and dated to the eighteenth century B.C. contain fragments of a poem which its author calls "lamentation to a man's god" and which scholars refer to as "The Sumerian Job." Its date corresponds to the Third Dynasty of Ur. The poem tells of a man who, being rich, wise, and righteous, finds himself plagued by sickness and suffering that he deems undeserved. Even his friends have turned against him. He complains to his god about his misfortune. "For me," he says, "the day is black. . . . Suffering overwhelms me. . . . How long will you neglect me . . . ?" He would like to be able to present himself before his god personally to speak to him. Nevertheless, he trusts in his god. He pleads, "You who are my father, [lift up] my face." Finally, he confesses his sins, which his god has caused him to recognize, and his god comes to his assistance. Sickness leaves him, and his sufferings are transformed into joy. His god assigns him a "spirit, (as a) watch (and) guardian," a kind of guardian "genie" to look after him. (ANES, 589–91; WB, IV, 101)

Job 26:10 —— *He has described a circle upon the face of the waters*   Ancient peoples conceived of the earth as a flat disk, supported by submarine pillars and totally surrounded by the water of the oceans. God had placed around it fixed and unsurpassable limits. All the peoples of the ancient Middle East shared this concept. In a clay tablet found in southern Babylonia there is engraved a *mapamundi* ("map of the world"). This tablet is dated from the

138

seventh century B.C., but it seems to be only a copy of a much more ancient original, for in it are recounted the conquests of Sargon I, a king of Akkad in the twenty-fourth century B.C. This almost complete drawing represents the earth as a disk at whose center stands the city of Babylon. Surrounding the disk is a wide belt, inscribed as "Bitter River," beyond which the dominion of eternal darkness was understood to extend. According to the rest of this verse, the circle is drawn "at the boundary between light and darkness." (WB, IV, 118)

Job 37:18 —— *the skies, hard as a molten mirror*   The ancient image of the sky as a solid metal plate is found as far back as in Genesis, where the word *raquia* is used to designate the dome of the sky. This word comes from a verb meaning "to pound metal" (with a wooden hammer) in order to spread or roll it into sheets. In this manner copper was and is still worked to produce certain articles. This concept is reiterated in the verse by means of the strong analogy of a "molten mirror." Mirrors were usually made of bronze, and many specimens of them have been found in the excavations. The mirror was a bronze disk, so well polished that it would reflect the person looking into it. It had a wooden handle, sometimes inlaid with a precious metal such as silver or gold. Mirrors of this type have turned up in Egyptian tombs and other archaeological sites.

Job 38:36 —— *or who tells the rooster that the rain will fall?*   (GNB; RSV: "Who has . . . given understanding to the mists?") The whole verse in the Hebrew text is obscure. This accounts for the different renderings in various versions. According to the Lexicon of Ludwig Koehler and Walter Baumgartner, the Hebrew word *skhevi* used here means "cock." The Vulgate renders it *gallus* ("rooster"). Domestic fowls entered Palestine probably in the fifth century B.C., and unless this rendering is correct, the cock or rooster is never mentioned in the Old Testament. In Proverbs 30:31 some versions also render as "rooster" the Hebrew word *zarzir*, which is of very obscure meaning (RSV, "strutting cock"). The context indicates that it is some kind of animal, but it could as well be a horse or a greyhound (Koehler and Baumgartner). At any rate it seems strange (and this could be a real exception) that a rooster appears in the seal of Jaazaniah, dated to the end of the seventh century B.C. (see comment on 2 Kings 25:23). It is the oldest known representation of the rooster. On the other hand, the final editing of Job's book probably dates to the beginning of the third century B.C., when the rooster would have already been known in Palestine. The rooster on the seal still must be explained, but the fact must not be forgotten that already in Solomon's time specimens of exotic fauna had been imported into Israel as curios or exceptional luxuries. Perhaps because it was something exotic in his time, Jaazaniah chose it as his blazon; or he had perhaps seen a rare specimen in a "zoo." In any case, the fact remains that at least the breeding of domestic fowl was of a rather late date. It must have been started in the Hellenistic or at the earliest in the Persian period. (BAW, 187; FFB, 16–17)

THE PSALMS

Ps 1:3 —— *He is like a tree*   Compare Jeremiah 17:7, 8. In chapter 4 of *The Instruction of Amen-em-opet*, one may read:

> The truly silent man holds himself apart.
> He is like a tree growing in a *garden*.
> It flourishes and doubles its yield;
> It (stands) before its lord.
> Its fruit is sweet; its shade is pleasant;
> And its end is reached in the garden. . . .

[ANET, 422]

Ps 6:6 —— *I flood my bed with tears*   This same literary figure appears in the Ugaritic poem called *The Legend of King Keret*, in which it is said of the protagonist: "His bed *is soaked* by his weeping." (ANET, 143)

Ps 15:1, 2 —— An Israeli archaeological expedition led by Yadin found in a cave near En-gedi, close to the Dead Sea, a manuscript fragment probably dated in the first century B.C., in which is found verse 1 and the first half of verse 2.

Ps 29:1 —— *Ascribe to the* LORD   This expression occurs three times in verses 1–2. The form of parallelism called repetitious is characteristic of Canaanite poetry, as shown in Ugaritic poems. In Hebrew poetry this form came to be less frequent as time passed, and other forms of parallelism, such as the synonymous, the antithetic, and the synthetic, became common. In view of this fact and because of the vigorous images used to describe Yahweh as lord of the storm,

141

this psalm is considered to be one of the two earliest of the Psalms. The other is Psalm 68. There is much resemblance between these psalms and the descriptions in Canaanite poems of Baal-hadad, the god of thunder, rain, and fertility of the land (see comment on Ps 68:4[5]).

Ps 29:8 —— *the wilderness of Kadesh.* This namc does not occur in any other place in the Bible in the same form, although several times Kadesh or Kadesh-barnea is mentioned. It is an oasis situated between the wilderness of Zin and the wilderness of Paran. It was one of the stations of the exodus and is identified with the present Ain Kedeish. In one of the ritual texts of Ugarit the same expression ("the wilderness of Kadesh") appears. This cannot refer to Kadesh-barnea nor to any biblical Kadesh mentioned in other passages. Its mention in this psalm, which is so full of echoes of Canaanite poetry, seems to refer to the Ugaritic Kadesh. The context suggests one of the Mediterranean storms that pour inland, striking first the Lebanon and then spilling over into "the wilderness of Kadesh." This Kadesh, therefore, should be identified with the wilderness east of the Lebanon range. (BAR-2, 45–46)

Ps 37:7 —— *Be still* From verses 7 to 40, except verse 27, this psalm is quoted in a commentary found among the Qumran manuscripts (Dead Sea scrolls). The text is similar to the Masoretic text, except in verse 20b, where it reads literally "those who hate Yahweh," while the Qumran text has "those who love Yahweh." The ancient versions support the Masoretic text. The change is typical of some deliberate changes from the original made by copyists or editors when it seemed to them that the text contained a blasphemy, even though the resulting reading would be obscure or even contradictory, as in this case. In the whole Qumran text, the name *Yahweh* is written in archaic or Phoenician script in order to make more difficult any accidental attempt to pronounce the unutterable Name. (DSSE, 243–45; LRQ, 315–19)

Ps 49:10(11) —— *even wise men die, as well as foolish and stupid men* (GNB). See also Ecclesiastes 1:11; 2:14–16; 6:8; 9:1–6, et seqq., and Job 21:26. In an Akkadian text, called *A Pessimistic Dialogue Between Master and Servant*, the servant says to his master, "Climb the mounds of ancient ruins and walk about: look at the skulls of late and early (men); who (among them) is an evildoer, who a public benefactor?" (ANET, 438)

Ps 68:4(5) —— *to him who rides upon the clouds* Some versions translate "upon the skies." The Hebrew word literally means "wilderness," and this is how it is rendered in the Septuagint (LXX). In the Ras Shamra (Ugarit) texts, the god Hadad is so described. He was called "the lord of the storms," a title which the Hebrews appropriated and gave to Yahweh. Albright is of the opinion that this psalm is a catalog of the first lines of several primitive Israelite hymns. He dates them between 1300 and 900 B.C., thus refuting some critics who assigned this psalm to the second century B.C. (LC, 9, 12)

Ps 68:22(23) —— *depths of the sea* In Hebrew "sea" is *yam*. In the cuneiform tablets uncovered in Ras Shamra (Ugarit) frequent reference is made to Yam, Tanin, Leviathan, and the "Twisting Serpent" (Is 27:1) as cosmic powers opposed to the Creator. They were conceived and represented as mythological monsters. Some of them appear in cylindrical seals found in Mesopotamia.

Ps 74:14 —— *Thou didst crush the heads of Leviathan* This allusion to Leviathan is a reflection or survival in Hebrew literature of ancient Canaanite mythological symbols, as the Ugaritic tablets from Ras Shamra give us to understand. (Compare Job 41:1; Ps 104:26; Is 27:1. See comment on the last.)

Ps 81–85, 150 —— In the excavations of the Masada fortress, carried out between 1963 and 1965 under the direction of Yadin, fragments of a leather scroll containing these psalms were found.

Ps 86:16 —— *the son of thy handmaid.* This expression of humility, by calling oneself "son of a handmaid" (or "son of a slave"), must not always be taken literally. It is a characteristic idiom, not only in Hebrew but in other related languages (for example, the Ugaritic). In this language, for instance, it occurs in *The Legend of King Keret*, in which the king, addressing the god El, describes himself as "a handmaid's son." (ANET, 143)

Ps 104 —— Some of the literary forms in this psalm resemble those in *The Hymn to the Aton* (the Sun) of Pharaoh Amen-hotep IV (Akhen-Aton, fourteenth century B.C.). This poem was found in the tomb of Eye at Tell el-Amarna. Some of the resemblances, not so much in words as in the sense, include the following:

Darkness *is a shroud*, and the earth is in stillness. [verse 20]
All the world, they do their work. [verse 23]
The fish in the river dart before thy face;
Thy rays are in the midst of the great green sea. [verse 25]
Thou suppliest their necessities:
Everyone has his food. . . . [verse 27]
For thou has set a Nile in heaven,
That it may descend for them and make waves
upon the mountains. . . . [verses 6, 10]

As may be seen at once, it is not possible to regard Psalm 104 as an imitation or a borrowing. The formal likeness is remote. Whether there exists any direct relationship between the psalm and the Egyptian hymn is a debatable question, but some persons may still cling to this view. (ANET, 369–71)

Ps 110:1 —— *till I make your enemies your footstool.* It was the custom of ancient sovereigns to dramatize in this way the utter defeat and submission of their enemies. A fresco in the tomb of Kenamon at Thebes represents Pharaoh Amen-hotep II with his feet resting upon Nubian and Semite captives. In a cylinder found in Larsa the god Nergal tramples under his feet a man lying upon a mountain. Similar scenes appear on other monuments. To make oneself another's footstool, in a figurative sense, was to declare oneself his vassal. In one of the Tell el-Amarna tablets, the king of Tyre writes to the pharaoh: "I am my lord the king's footstool." The same image also appears as an ornament in an armchair found in Tut-ankh-amen's tomb. (WB, IV, 50; MLB, 17)

Ps 137:3 —— *Sing us one of the songs of Zion!* In Sennacherib's palace in Nineveh there is a bas-relief showing three singers, apparently Jews, playing their instruments beside a river. They probably were captives, for an Assyrian guard armed with club and bow is seen watching them. (WB, IV, 58)

Ps 145:13 —— *Thy kingdom is an everlasting kingdom* There is a notable parallel to this verse in a Ugaritic text dedicated to Baal. It says:

Thou wilt win thy Kingdom of eternity,
Thy dominion of all generations.

These are poetic forms common to oriental inspiration or which the psalmist adopted from Canaanite poetry, while stripping them of their pagan and idolatrous meaning and dedicating them to the one and only God of Hebrew monotheism (compare comment on Ps 29:1). (BAR-2, 47–48)

Ps 150:3 —— *Praise him with trumpet sound* We are indebted principally to the Haifa Museum of Music for the most important study of ancient Jewish music and musical instruments based on archaeological evidence. Not only has the museum collected objects of musical use, figurines of musicians with their instruments, and representations in frescoes, bas-reliefs, and coins, but it has also made reconstructions of the instruments based on such finds. The horn (*shofar*) of a ram or an antelope was the ritual trumpet, and it is still employed today in the religious and national celebrations of Israel. The most remarkable picture of the zither (*kinor*) occurs in a bas-relief of Nineveh (seventh century B.C.), which shows three Hebrew captives playing this instrument and guarded by an Assyrian soldier (see comment on 137:3). The tambourine (*toph*) is best illustrated by the figurines of a youth and a woman, dated in the Iron Age II (900–600 B.C.) and found in Ahzib. There is another bas-relief of a woman of the same period found in Megiddo, and one of a man, dating from about the fifth century B.C., discovered at Nir David. In this last mentioned, the tambourine is square, rather than round. A rare specimen, found at Kabara, is a flute (*halil* or *ugab*) made of a bird's bone and having four holes. It dates back to the prehistoric period. Some specimens of bronze cymbals or castanets (*tsiltselim*) have been found in Hazor and Megiddo (fourteenth century B.C.), and others, from the Roman period, were discovered near Nablus. The shape of the harp or lyre (*nebel*) has not been determined with certainty, for in spite of its being the instrument most commonly used in biblical times, its only known representations are those found on coins of later times, such as those of Ben Cosiba (Bar Kokhba, first half of the second century A.D.). Other specimens of musical instruments collected by the Haifa Museum include timbrels, rattles, sistrums, bells, whistles, shell trumpets, syringes, and lutes, either the actual objects or in figurines and in pictures. (MAW)

THE PROVERBS

Prov 4:22 —— *and healing to all his flesh.* This seems to have been a common expression to commend the good effect of wise words (compare 16:24). An Aramaic proverb from *The Words of Ahiqar*, a text found in Elephantine, Egypt, says, "Treat not lightly the word of a king: let it be healing for thy [flesh]." (ANET, 428)

Prov 5:15 —— *cistern . . . well.* The figure of woman as a cistern or well seems to have been a favorite one in oriental literature. In this passage a woman is also compared with a fountain (verse 18). (See also Song 4:15.) In an Akkadian text known as *A Pessimistic Dialogue Between Master and Servant*, it is said that "Woman is a well," but in this case the meaning is that she is a mortal danger, for the text goes on to say that "woman is an iron dagger—a sharp one!—which cuts a man's neck." This sense is the very opposite of the sense in the biblical passages mentioned. The Akkadian word means either "cistern" or "well," but the Hebrew has distinct terms for these. (ANET, 438)

Prov 12:23 —— *but fools proclaim their folly.* Compare *The Instruction of Amen-em-opet*, xxii, 15:

> Better is a man whose talk (remains) in his belly
> Than he who speaks it out injuriously.
>
> [ANET, 424]

Prov 13:3 —— *he who opens wide his lips comes to ruin.* A text of Babylonian wisdom, dated before 700 B.C., offers this parallel:

146

Let your mouth be restrained, guarded your speech.
Like a man's wealth, let your lips be precious.

Also the text called *The Words of Ahiqar* (see comment on 4:22) says, "[My s]on, ch[at]ter not overmuch. . . . More than all watchfulness watch thy mouth. . . ." (ANET, 426, 428)

Prov 13:4 —— *The soul of the sluggard craves, and gets nothing* Compare 10:4, 12:11, et seqq. An Akkadian text from about 1800–1600 B.C. contains this parallel:

As long as a man does not exert himself,
he will gain nothing.

[ANET, 425]

Prov 15:16 —— *than great treasure and trouble with it.* Compare *The Instruction of Amen-em-opet*, ix, 5:

Better is poverty in the hand of the god
Than riches in a storehouse;
Better is bread, when the heart is happy,
Than riches with sorrow.

[ANET, 422]

Prov 16:1 —— *the answer of the tongue is from the LORD.* A proverb of Aramaic wisdom, from *The Words of Ahiqar*, says: "If a man be small and grow great, his words *soar* above him. For the opening of his mouth is an *Utte[ra]nce* of gods, and if he be beloved of gods they will put something good in his mouth to say." (ANET, 429)

Prov 19:21 —— *Many are the plans in the mind of a man* Compare *The Instruction of Amen-em-opet*, xix, 16:

One thing are the words which men say,
Another is that which the god does.

[ANET, 423]

Prov 20:19 —— *do not associate with one who speaks foolishly.* Compare *The Instruction of Amen-em-opet*, xxii, 14:

. . . Nor associate to thyself one [too] outgoing
of heart [outspoken].

[ANET, 424]

Prov 20:20 —— *his lamp will be put out* In *The Words of Ahiqar* this parallel occurs: "[Whosoever] *takes no pride* in the names of his father and mother, may the s[un] not shine [upon him]." (ANET, 429)

Prov 20:23 —— *and false scales are not good.* Compare *The Instruction of Amen-em-opet*, xvi, 16:

Do not *lean on* the scales nor falsify the weights,
Nor damage the fractions of the measure.

[ANET, 423]

Prov 22:17 —— *Incline your ear, and hear the words of the wise* Compare verses 17, 18a with the following three verses of the "First Chapter" of *The Instruction of Amen-em-opet* (see comment on verse 20):

Give thy ears, hear what is said,
Give thy heart [mind] to understand them.
To put them in thy heart [inner self] is worth while.

[ANET, 421]

Prov 22:20 —— *Have I not written for you thirty sayings* The Hebrew word rightly translated here "thirty" (with "sayings" implicit) appears with a rather strange spelling. For this reason several different sets of vowels for the early consonantal text have been proposed. These would make the word read "day before yesterday," or "three times," or "thirty." The last is adopted by some modern versions. The other alternatives do not seem to suit the context. But this is not the only reason for the preference. There is a striking resemblance between Proverbs 22:17–24:22 and a document from ancient Egypt, namely, *The Instruction of Amen-em-opet*, which consists of thirty brief chapters. Papyrus 10474 of the British Museum, seemingly from Thebes but of uncertain date (though probably between the tenth and the sixth centuries B.C.), was published in 1923. Biblical scholars differ as to whether there is a direct or indirect literary dependence of Proverbs upon this interesting treatise of ancient Egyptian wisdom. Even if such a dependence could be proved, the book of Proverbs is still free from every allusion and sense peculiar to the cultural, geographic, political, and religious environment of Egypt. There is only a resemblance, or at most an influence; there is not a literal echo or a servile imitation. This will be seen at once when the two documents are compared. The author of the Proverbs may have taken from the Egyptian text the idea of composing thirty maxims, which can be easily discerned in his text. But then one must remember that symbolic numbers such as 30 (3 × 10) were common in the culture of the Middle East. On the other hand, some biblical exegetes think that the Egyptian book is a translation of a text which is larger than the canonical book of Proverbs and which must have existed earlier. They base their theory upon a careful linguistic comparison of the two writings, with particular attention to their respective semantics. The French orientalist E. Drioton comes to the conclusion that Amen-em-opet's book is an Egyptian adaptation (adding the local color of which there is abundant evidence) "of an old Israelite writing which the refugees carried with themselves." These would have been refugees who fled to Egypt from the Northern Kingdom after its fall at the hands of the Assyrians (721 B.C.). In all probability the Egyptian book can be dated between the seventh and the sixth centuries B.C. It is therefore later than the early form of Proverbs. The parallel of this verse in *The Instruction of Amen-em-opet*, xxvi, 15, is:

> See thou these thirty chapters:
> They entertain; they instruct. . . .

[ANET, 421–24; ETB, 115–31; LTR, 81–91]

Prov 22:21 —— *that you may give a true answer* Compare *The Instruction of Amen-em-opet*, Introduction, ". . . to know how to return an answer to him who said it. . . ." (ANET, 421)

Prov 22:22 —— *Do not rob the poor* Compare *The Instruction of Amen-em-opet*, iv, 4:

> Guard thyself against robbing the oppressed
> And against overbearing the disabled.

[ANET, 422]

Prov 22:24 —— *Make no friendship with a man given to anger* Compare *The Instruction of Amen-em-opet*, x, 16:

> Do not associate to thyself the heated man,
> Nor visit him for conversation.

[ANET, 423]

Prov 22:29 —— *a man skilful in his work* Compare *The Instruction of Amen-em-opet*, xxvii, 16:

As for the scribe who is experienced in his office,
He will find himself worthy (to be) a courtier.

[ANET, 424]

Prov 23:1 ff. —— *When you sit down to eat with a ruler* Compare
The Instruction of Amen-em-opet, xxii, 19; xxiii, 17:

Do not eat bread before a noble,
Nor lay on thy mouth at first. . . .
Look at the cup which is before thee,
And let it serve thy needs.

[ANET, 424]

Prov 23:5 —— *flying like an eagle toward heaven.* Compare *The
Instruction of Amen-em-opet*, ix, 10; x, 4:

Cast not thy heart in pursuit of riches. . . .
. . . they have made themselves wings like geese
And are flown away to the heavens.

[ANET, 422]

Prov 23:8 —— *You will vomit up the morsels which you have
eaten* Compare *The Instruction of Amen-em-opet*, xiv, 11:

The mouthful of bread (too) great thou swallowest
    and vomitest up,
And art emptied of thy good.

[ANET, 423]

Prov 23:9 —— *Do not speak in the hearing of a fool* Compare *The
Instruction of Amen-em-opet*, xxii, 13:

Spread not thy words to the common people. . . .

[ANET, 424]

Prov 23:10 —— *Do not remove an ancient landmark or enter the field
of the fatherless* (See 22:28.) Compare *The Instruction of Amen-
em-opet*, vi, 13:

Do not carry off the landmark at the boundaries
    of the arable land. . . .
Be not greedy after a cubit of land
Nor encroach upon the boundaries of a widow. . . .
Guard against encroaching upon the boundaries
    of the fields. . . .

[ANET, 422]

Prov 25:9 —— *and do not disclose another's secret* A parallel in *The Words of Ahiqar* is, "Reveal not thy [secrets] before thy [fri]ends, lest thy name become despised of them." In this case the secrets not to be disclosed are one's own. (ANET, 429)

Prov 25:21 —— *give him bread to eat* Compare verses 21, 22 with *The Instruction of Amen-em-opet*, v, 3:

Lift him up, give him thy hand;
Leave him (in) the arms of the god;
Fill his belly with bread of thine,
So that he may be sated and may *be ashamed.*

[ANET, 422]

Prov 27:3 —— *A stone is heavy* The Words of Ahiqar (Aramaic proverbs) offers the following parallel: "I have lifted sand, and I have carried salt; but there is naught which is heavier than [rage]." (ANET, 429)

Prov 27:7 —— *to one who is hungry everything bitter is sweet.* Compare *The Words of Ahiqar:* "Hunger makes bitterness sweet, and thirst [sourness]." (ANET, 430)

ECCLESIASTES

Eccles 2:6 —— *I made myself pools.* If the writer of the book is presenting himself as Solomon, the allusion here would be to the pools built by that king. They are not mentioned explicitly in 1 Kings 9 or in 2 Chronicles 8, nor has archaeology ever found their remains. The allusion may simply be based by implication on the Song of Solomon 4:12. A little over 3 miles south of Bethlehem, near the village of Urtas, there are three pools traditionally called "of Solomon." They get their water supply from four springs in the vicinity, and in the Roman period they were connected with aqueducts that carried their water to Jerusalem. Since 1919 they have again formed part of the water-supply system for that city. In the course of time they have undergone repairs and modifications. They have really had nothing to do with Solomon. If he did build pools, they would have been only small ponds located in one or another of his palace gardens. (THL, 96, 280)

Eccles 2:14 —— *The wise man . . . the fool . . . one fate comes to all of them.* The impartiality of death, which sweeps away all without distinction, is a favorite theme in oriental wisdom literature and one which is repeated in other passages of Ecclesiastes. It also gives rise to various types of contrast, such as between poor and rich, powerful and weak, good and evil. See the quotation from *A Pessimistic Dialogue Between Master and Servant* in the comment on Psalm 49:10(11).

Eccles 5:2(1) —— *Be not rash with your mouth* To this counsel to be

152

cautious when speaking, and above all in worship, there is an interesting parallel in a cuneiform tablet dating from before 700 B.C.:

Do not slander, speak what is fine.
Speak no evil, tell what is good. . . .
Open not wide your mouth, guard your lips;
The words of your inner self do not speak (even) when alone.
What you now speak hastily you will later take back,
And you should cause your mind to refrain by its efforts from speech.

Concerning the sparseness of words in prayer, the following parallel is found in the Egyptian maxims of Ani, dated considerably before the eighth century B.C.: "Do not talk a lot. Be silent, and thou wilt be happy. Do not be garrulous. The dwelling of god, its abomination is clamor. Pray thou with a loving heart, all the words of which are hidden, and he will do what thou needest, he will hear what thou sayest, and he will accept thy offering. . . ." (ANET, 427, 420)

Eccles 5:15(14) —— *and shall take nothing . . . which he may carry away in his hand.* In the Egyptian poem called *A Song of the Harper* (Papyrus Harris 500), from about 1300 B.C., the refrain is:

Make holiday, and weary not therein!
Behold, it is not given to a man to take his property with him.

[ANET, 467]

Eccles 8:2 —— *Keep the king's command* On the theme of obedience to the king, with which this passage deals (verses 2–5), there are two interesting ancient parallels. One is found among the Aramaic proverbs of Ahiqar: "Treat not lightly the word of a king. . . . Soft is the utterance of a king; (yet) it is sharper and stronger than a [two]-edged knife . . . a hard look [on the f]ace of a k[ing] (means) 'Delay not!' . . . [The wr]ath of a king, if thou be commanded, is a burning fire. Obey [it] at once. . . . Why should wood strive with fire, flesh with a knife, a man with [*a king*]?" The other parallel appears in the stele of Sehetep-ib-Re (about 1840–1790 B.C.), discovered at Abydos, Egypt. It deals with the pharaoh's authority:

Fight on behalf of his name,
And be scrupulous in the oath to him,
(That) ye may be free from a taint of *disloyalty*.

He whom the king has loved will be a revered one,
(But) there is no tomb for a rebel against his majesty,
And his corpse is cast into the water.

[ANET, 428, 431]

Eccles 8:15 —— *And I commend enjoyment*   In *The Epic of Gilga-mesh*, the hero is told:

Make thou merry by day and by night.
Of each day make thou a feast of rejoicing,
Day and night dance thou and play! . . .
For this is the task of [mankind]!

And in *A Song of the Harper*, already quoted, one finds:

Follow thy desire, as long as thou shalt live.
Put myrrh upon thy dead and clothing of fine linen upon
    thee . . .
Let not thy heart flag.
Follow thy desire and thy good.
Fulfill thy needs upon earth, after the command of thy heart,
Until there come for thee that day of mourning.

[ANET, 90, 467]

Eccles 10:11 —— *If the serpent bites before it is charmed*   Here are some formulas for neutralizing or charming serpents, taken from the pyramid at Saggara, Egypt (twenty-fifth to twenty-fourth centuries B.C.):

"Words to be spoken: 'A face has fallen against a face; a face has seen a face. The mottled knife, black and green, goes forth against it. It has swallowed for itself that which it tasted.'

"Words to be spoken: 'This is the fingernail of Atum, which was on the backbone of *Nehebu-kau* and which brought to an end the strife in Hermopolis. Fall, roll up!'

"Words to be spoken: 'Back with thee, hidden snake! Hide thyself! Thou shalt not make King Unis see thee. Back with thee, hidden snake! Hide thyself! Thou shalt not come to the place where King Unis is, lest he tell that name of thine against thee: *Nemi*, the son of *Nemit*. The *servant of the Ennead* fell into the Nile. Turn about, turn about! O monster, lie down!' " (ANET, 326)

Eccles 12:1 —— *before the evil days come*   In the Egyptian manuscript called *The Instruction of the Vizier Ptah-hotep* (Papyrus Prisse, about 2450 B.C.), there is a parallel to this famous passage concerning old age: "Oldness has come; old age has descended. Feebleness has arrived; dotage is coming anew. The heart sleeps wearily every day. The eyes are weak, the ears are deaf, the strength is disappearing because of weariness of heart, and the mouth is silent and cannot speak. The heart is forgetful and cannot recall yesterday. The bone suffers old age. Good is become evil. All taste is gone. What old age does to men is evil in every respect. The nose is stopped up and cannot breathe. (Simply) to stand up or to sit down is difficult." (ANET, 412)

Eccles 12:9 ⸺ *and arranging proverbs* Proverbs form only parts of the book of Ecclesiastes. The book is attributed by tradition to Solomon, due in part to the author's pseudonym, "the Preacher" (Hebrew *Koheleth*). The proverbs were probably introduced by later editions, for they seem to differ from the subject and purpose of the book. They are found primarily in 5:1–12; 7:1–22; and 10:1–11:6. There is a Babylonian poem which is called by some scholars a "Babylonian Koheleth," but which does not seem to be sufficiently like Ecclesiastes to justify such a designation. It sounds more like the book of Lamentations, though the motive for the biblical laments is the destruction of Jerusalem, while the Babylonian text is more personal. The title given to this document by other scholars seems more adequate: *A Dialogue About Human Misery.* (ANET, 438–40)

SONG OF SONGS

(GNB TITLE)
(RSV TITLE, THE SONG OF SOLOMON)

Song 1:14 —— *a cluster of henna blossoms . . . of Engedi.* Excavations at Tell el-Jurn, conducted by Mazar and I. Dunayevsky, show that from antiquity this area was famous for its aromatic plants and perfumes. Ruins of houses were found which contained storage jars for the preservation of liquids, metal utensils, various kinds of vessels, and clay "barrels" for elaboration of perfumes. All of this gives clear evidence of an active perfume industry in this place. (ABB, 205)

Song 2:15 —— *our vineyards are in blossom.* The Hebrew word usually translated "blossom" is *semadar.* Potsherds consisting of jar handles with engraved inscriptions almost always give the owner's name. In the ruins of Hazor in Upper Galilee, one of these potsherds was found with the inscription, "Belonging to Pekah. Semadar." This could very well mean that *semadar* was the name of a special kind of grapevine and therefore of a wine. It could also have been the name of the locality where this particular type of vine was grown, although there is no mention of it in the Bible. If this suggestion is correct, the translation would be "our vineyards are of *semadar*" (that is, of a very fine quality). The meaning of the term is somewhat uncertain, but according to Yadin it has to do either with the blossoming of the vines or with tender grapes. In that case the jar may have contained wine made from the latter. Yadin says, "This meaning of *semadar* is, by the way, preserved in the Mishnah (*Orlah* 1:17)." (HYY, 183)

Song 3:9, 10 —— *King Solomon made himself a palanquin* The description in this passage of a sumptuous palanquin accords with the palanquins or litters belonging to kings or wealthy magnates. Some of those found in Egyptian tombs are made of fine wood and have silver or gold ornamentation. A good example is the one belonging to Queen Hetepheres, the mother of Khufu (the Cheops of the pyramid), dating to the third millennium B.C. (WB, IV, 145)

Song 5:14 —— *ivory work, encrusted with sapphires.* (Or, more likely, "with lapis lazuli.") Inlaying lapis lazuli on ivory was a technique of ancient jewelers. It is confirmed not only by allusions in an inscription of Adadnirari III but also by the finding of ivories with such work in the excavations at Nimrud, Samaria, and Ugarit (Ras Shamra). This type of ornamentation is mentioned in a tablet containing the inventory of Queen Ahatmilku's wedding apparel. (SCKI, 63–65)

Song 6:4 —— *You are beautiful as Tirzah, my love,* Tirzah was the capital of Israel (the Northern Kingdom) during the reigns of Baasha, Elah, and Zimri, and for a short time of Omri (ninth century B.C.). This must have been the epoch of Israel's greatest splendor, so much so that Tirzah could be compared with Jerusalem, the capital of the Southern Kingdom of Judah. Omri founded the new capital of Samaria and moved his court there. Accordingly, after that time Tirzah began to decay. In 1930 Albright identified the site of Tirzah at Tell el-Farah, northeast of Shechem. Formal excavations began there under de Vaux in 1947. Tirzah's first settlement dates from the fourth millennium B.C. It reached its height during the Bronze Age (3000–1200 B.C.), but it was destroyed toward the end of the tenth century or the beginning of the ninth century B.C. It was rebuilt by the kings listed above and recovered its importance and beauty. The most notable ruins found at the site are those of a great building of this second epoch, which shows signs of having been left unfinished. According to de Vaux, it was Omri's palace which was left uncompleted when he moved to his new capital, Samaria. The reference to Tirzah in the Song of Songs must, however, not be taken as a sure indication of the poem's composition in the ninth century B.C. Its style and language reveal too much influence by the Aramaic language, which became the common form of language in the fifth century B.C. The occurrence in the Hebrew text of the

Persian word *pardes* ("park," "garden," sometimes translated "paradise") would suggest a time of considerable Aramaic influence, but this is not decisive evidence. All the evidence, however, does point to a relatively late date. At least the final redaction and editing occurred probably in the fifth century B.C. In that case, the reference to Tirzah could be interpreted as a retrospective literary allusion. (BAW, 152; IDB, IV, 421)

Song 8:7 —— *neither can floods drown it.* In an Egyptian poem from between 1300 and 1100 B.C., the same figure appears to express the irresistible force of love. The bridegroom says:

> The love of my sister is on yonder side,
> A stream lies between us,
> And a crocodile waits in the shallows.
> But when I go down into the water,
> I wade the current,
> My heart is great upon the stream,
> And the waves are like land unto my feet.
> It is the love of her that makes me steady,
> For it makes a water-charm for me!

In this and other Egyptian love poems, the bridegroom and the bride treat each other as "brother" and "sister," as in the Song of Songs. (ANET, 468)

ISAIAH

Is 1:1 —— *The vision of Isaiah* The best preserved and most important manuscript found in 1947 in Cave 1 of Qumran (a "Dead Sea scroll") contains almost the entire book of Isaiah. Another copy, but incomplete, was also found there later. The former dates from about 100 B.C. According to Burrows and John C. Trever the text is substantially that of the Masoretic text, although it shows a number of differences in orthography and grammar and some rather meaningful variants. This beautiful manuscript, together with the others found in Qumran and nearby, is now kept in the Shrine of the Book in Jerusalem, a place built especially for that purpose by the Israeli government. In Cave 4 a commentary on Isaiah was found, fragments of which preserve quotations of 1:1, 2a; 5:5, 6a, 11–14, 25, 29, 30; 8:7, 8; 10:12, 13b; 10:20–11:5; 14:8, 26–30; 30:15–21; and 54:11, 12. (DSS, 73–119; DSM, xiii–xvii; PQI, 70–138; LRQ, 320–23)

A seal of unknown origin has surfaced in Cairo. It is probably of Egyptian origin, but some scholars consider it to be Aramean. In any case its inscription, "Amoz, the scribe," is in Hebrew. In spite of this fact, its owner evidently did not adhere to the Israelite religion, for it represents two persons in Persian dress standing at either side of an altar, above which appears the winged disk of the sun god. The owner of the seal could not, of course, have been the father of Isaiah. However, the seal serves to verify the importance of the office of scribe, for only a person of some importance would possess and use a seal. (SPA, 106)

Is 3:16 —— *the daughters of Zion are haughty* In verses 16–24 the

159

prophet makes a detailed and curious list of the ornaments, jewels, and other finery of the women of Zion. Actually, these were not exclusive with them but were at that time commonly used by women of high social status throughout the Middle East. Some of these articles are now difficult to identify. But in excavations at various sites a considerable assortment of jewels, amulets, and other items for personal adornment have been found. In Egyptian frescoes and Mesopotamian reliefs, as well as on a number of statues and figurines, adornments and vestments may be seen. Sometimes there are very elaborate hairstyles, worn by women or female deities.

Is 6:2 —— *the seraphim; each had six wings*   This is the only passage where the Hebrew word *saraph* (from a root meaning "to burn" or "to set on fire") refers to a supernatural being, who, together with angels and cherubim, forms part of the heavenly court. In all the other cases in which this term occurs, it means "serpent." The Hebrew plural is *seraphim*. According to the description in this passage, the seraphim differ from the cherubim, which are usually described as having two wings. Very rarely, in extrabiblical references, they are said to have four wings. If the "living creatures" of Ezekiel 1:6 are cherubim, this would be a biblical exception. Mythological beings of this kind often appear in Middle Eastern art. For example, a relief from Tell Halaf (Gozan) depicts a being with human face and body and six wings. The two for flying are at the shoulders, while the other four come out from the waist. Two of them spread out, and two more cover the legs but leave the feet uncovered. This figure holds a staff in either hand, and its diadem with four long horns seems to indicate that it is a god. Some scholars see an older antecedent of the seraph in the winged serpent or four-winged *uraeus*, the symbol of the pharaoh's universal dominion in Egypt. This symbol occurs on Tut-ankh-amen's throne (fourteenth century B.C.). It is also shown in numerous scarabs found in Megiddo, Gaza, Beth-shemesh, Lachish, and other places, as well as in some carved ivories of Ahab's palace in Samaria. (WB, III, 27; ABB, 150)

Is 7:6 —— *the son of Tabe-el*   The Masoretic text gives this name as *Tabe-al* ("not good" or "good, not at all"), a mocking or contemptuous parody of *Tabe-el*, which means "God is good." Nothing more is known about this person. In an Assyrian letter discovered at Calah (modern Nimrud), reference is made to a "land of Tabel," situated on the eastern side of the Jordan River and facing Jericho. It may have some relation to the "son of Tabe-el." (WB, III, 30)

Is 7:14 —— *a young woman shall conceive* In a cuneiform tablet uncovered at Ras Shamra (Ugarit) there is a poem about the goddess Nikkal and the Katirat. Speaking of Nikkal, the poem says: "Behold, the young woman conceives a son." The Ugaritic word for "young woman" is *glmt*, cognate with Hebrew *almah*, the term used in this famous verse. Ugaritic was a language akin to Hebrew. (UT, text 77:7; ABB, 152)

Is 9:4 —— *the yoke . . . the staff* It was very common in the ancient Near East to make captives and slaves work like beasts, tied to yokes for the dragging of heavy loads. They are pictured this way in an Assyrian bas-relief from Dur-Sharrukin, modern Khorsabad. The curved staff which was the part of the yoke laid on the shoulders can be clearly seen. (WB, III, 33)

Is 11:6 —— *The wolf shall dwell with the lamb* The concept of beasts of prey living together with tame domestic ones as a symbol of reconciliation and peace in an ideal future kingdom seems to have been relatively common in the East. This is represented in the inlay of the sound box of a lyre coming from the middle of the third millennium B.C. and found in Ur. A lion and a dog (or wolf) are shown together laying a table for a banquet; an ass is plucking a lyre whose box is shaped like a bull; a jackal is playing a sistrum and a drum, and a bear is dancing. (WB, III, 36)

Is 21:9 —— *Fallen, fallen is Babylon* The so-called *Nabonidus Chronicle*, one of the main texts of Babylonian history, tells of the fall of the city in 539 B.C. According to this document, the last Babylonian king, Nabonidus, had for some years been absent from his capital. He stayed in Teima (or Tema) in Arabia. From there he ruled through his son Belshazzar (Akkadian *Bel-sar-usur* or *Bel-sharra-utsur*, Aramaic *Belshatsar*, Hebrew *Beltshatsar*). When Cyrus marched against Babylon, Nabonidus had already returned from Arabia and tried to confront him at Sippar, but this city fell to the Persians without a struggle. Nabonidus evidently fled to Babylon, where he was reportedly "arrested." Cyrus entered the city and was received with "green twigs." "The state of 'Peace' was imposed upon the city [and] Cyrus sent greetings to all Babylon." The

Babylonians seemingly welcomed him as an ally or liberator, although the historian Berossus, quoted by Josephus, says that it "cost him [Cyrus] a great deal of pains to take it [Babylon]." According to this same chronicler, Nabonidus withdrew to Borsippus, where he was afterward besieged by Cyrus. Nabonidus then delivered himself into Cyrus' hands. Cyrus treated him with benevolence and gave him Carmania, where, according to Berossus, he died. The *Nabonidus Chronicle* does not say where this king fled to, nor what became of Belshazzar. Daniel 5:30 says the latter died the same night the city fell. Josephus gives his readers to understand that he died later.

The *Nabonidus Chronicle*, as well as ancient historians (Berossus, Herodotus, Xenophon), raises a problem concerning this narrative in the book of Daniel, which attributes the capture of Babylon to "Darius the Mede." There seems to have been some confusion in the minds of writers of that epoch concerning the Medes and the Persians for they are sometimes referred to as being the same nation. In addition there was confusion concerning the names of their kings. Josephus, for instance, on the basis of Berossus, takes Nabonidus (Nabonnedus or Nabonadius) and Naboandelus as being the same person, whom he then identifies with Belshazzar. Concerning Belshazzar he says that "the Babylonians called him Naboandelus." The consensus of opinion among present-day biblical scholars is that the book of Daniel belongs to Haggadic literature (narratives with moral and religious intent by way of parables and with no claim to be literal history) and that it was written about 166 B.C. This last proposal is made on the basis of linguistic and other internal evidences. If all this is true, it can easily be understood how there were differences in names and details about events that occurred nearly four centuries earlier.

From other sources one learns that Nabonidus evidently had serious conflicts with the traditional Babylonian priesthood. Nabonidus did not give up his devotion to Marduk, the official Babylonian god, but his favorite deity was Sin, the moon goddess, who with Shamash and Ishtar formed an astral trinity. This may explain his prolonged absence from Babylon and the welcome the city accorded Cyrus. It would also explain the rumor, perhaps originating with the priests, that Nabonidus was mentally unbalanced. Some commentators consider this rumor the basis for the story of Nebuchadrezzar's madness related in the book of Daniel. Witness to the bitterness of this struggle between the priesthood and the throne is found in tablet No. 38,299 in the British Museum. This tablet contains a poem reviling Nabonidus. It says that "[. . . against the will of the g]ods he performed an unholy action" by introducing an unknown deity. He is also criticized for having "entrusted the kingship" to his son and for having moved to Tema. On the other hand, Cyrus "king of the world" is praised for his good treatment of Babylon. For the inhabitants of Babylon now "the prisons are opened" after having been "surrounded by oppression." In an inscription concerning his seizure of Babylon, Cyrus says: "When I entered Babylon as a friend and (when) I established the seat of the government in the palace of the ruler under jubilation and rejoicing, Marduk . . . [induced] the magnanimous inhabitants of Babylon [to love me]. . . . My numerous troops walked around in Babylon in peace, I did not allow anybody to terrorize. . . . I strove for peace in Babylon and in all his (other) sacred cities." He adds that he abolished the yoke of the Babylonians and put an end to their complaints. (ANET, 305–7, 312–16; WFJ, 317–18, 868; EB, I, 1302–3, V, 407–9; IDB, I, 764–67, III, 493–95)

Is 22:13 —— *Let us eat and drink, for tomorrow we die.* This seems to be a very old saying which had become a proverb. A Babylonian text from between 1800 and 1600 B.C. has it as follows: "Very soon he will be dead; (so he says), 'Let me eat up (all I have)!' " (ANET, 425)

Is 22:15, 16 —— *Shebna, . . . you who hew a tomb on the height* In 1870 a tomb hewn in the rock was discovered in the village of Siloam to the southeast of Jerusalem. It had a scarcely legible inscription in archaic Hebrew characters, which was dismantled and taken to the British Museum. Avigad succeeded in deciphering it in 1954. It assigns the tomb to one "who is over the house" (a palace superintendent). His partly blurred name ends in -*yahu*. The inscription reads, "This [is the burial of . . .]-yahu, who is over the house. There is no silver and no gold here but [his bones] and the bones of his handmaiden [slave wife] with him. Cursed is the one who opens this [tomb]!" Avigad and Yadin suggest that the reference is to Shebna, for his complete name could very well have been *Shebnayahu*. This identification cannot be completely certain, but the probability is great. (MTL, 188; EB, II, 251)

Is 27:1 —— *Leviathan the twisting serpent* In one of the Ugaritic tablets of the series of poems about Baal and his sister Anat (a text designated by some scholars with the code letters I*AB), the god Mot gives Gapn and Ugar, messengers of Baal, a message for him. He sends them to say:

> If thou smite Lotan, the serpent slant,
> Destroy the serpent tortuous,
> Shalyat of the seven heads. . . .

These three lines are repeated further on. Lotan is the Canaanite Leviathan. (Another interpretation is: "For she (Anat) smites . . . destroys. . . .") (See the comment on Ps 74:14.) (UT, text 67:I, 1–3, 27–30; ANET, 138; WB, III, 53)

Is 29:11 —— *Read this, . . . I cannot, for it is sealed.* Important or confidential letters or legal documents which had to be kept private were sealed. Those written on papyrus (and later on vellum or parchment) were rolled and tied, and a seal was affixed to the knot. The seal had to be broken before the scroll could be unrolled. When the writing was on a clay tablet or potsherd, it was encased in a sort of clay envelope. If the writing was a contract or other legal document, a summary of its contents was sometimes inscribed on the envelope. A separate copy of a document might be kept in another place (compare Jer 32:14). Letters and other documents inscribed and sealed in this manner have been uncovered in several excavated sites. In No. 3 of the famous Lachish Letters, written on potsherds, Hoshayahu assures Yaosh under oath that he has not read or had read to him a certain secret letter sent by the king of Judah to Yaosh, of which he (Hoshayahu) was the bearer. (WB, III, 55, 130)

Is 30:22 —— *silver-covered . . . gold-plated* Figurines of gods made of bronze and covered with silver or gold have been found in excavations. Sometimes the same image is covered partly with silver and partly with gold. This is true of a tiny idol from Minet el-Beida (now in the Louvre), of which the crown and the face are covered with gold while the rest of the body is covered with silver. It represents Baal-hadad and dates from the second millennium B.C. (MLB, 48)

Is 42:6 —— *I have taken you by the hand* In Ugarit (Ras Shamra) a

seal was found belonging to a Hittite king of the thirteenth century
B.C. It represents the god Mutawali holding the king's right hand,
which in turn holds a club. This means that the god gives the king
his full support. (WB, III, 70)

Is 44:13 —— *stretches a line, he marks it out . . . fashions . . .
shapes* In this verse the prophet vividly describes the carver of
idols at work. He undoubtedly had personally watched such activity.
Some paintings discovered in Egypt are a striking illustration of this
process. In one of them the design of a human figure appears drawn
upon a squared background to facilitate the designing. In another
the carver is shown giving a wooden statue the final touches with a
chisel and a club used as a mallet. (WB, III, 73)

Is 46:1 —— *Bel . . . Nebo* It was not by chance that the prophet
mentioned these two Babylonian gods together. A cylinder in the
Louvre Museum shows Bel (Marduk) and Nebo (Nabu) together.
They are easily identified by their respective emblems, for the first
a triangular spade, and for the second a scribe's stylus because he
was the god of script and writing. From this cylinder and other
evidence we know these gods were worshiped together. Bel was
Nebo's father. (BOT, 56–58)

Is 46:7 —— *They lift it upon their shoulders, they carry it* The context
shows that the prophet is referring to an idol. A bas-relief in the
palace of Tiglath-Pileser III at Calah depicts a line of Assyrian
soldiers carrying on litters placed on their shoulders four idols
captured in a conquered city. (WB, III, 77)

Is 52:9 —— *the LORD has comforted his people, he has redeemed
Jerusalem.* On a recently found tomb at Khirbet-Beit-Lei, some
5½ miles east of Lachish, there is a sixth-century B.C. inscription in
Hebrew which is an interesting parallel to this passage. It reads, "I
am Yahweh thy God, I will protect the cities of Judah and will
redeem Jerusalem." (MTL, 60)

Is 65:4 —— *and spend the night in secret places* The Hebrew word
translated here as "secret places" and in other instances as "caves"
is *netsur* (plural *netsurim*). In a personal communication to the
present writer Henry S. Gehman pointed out that the term appears
in an inscription on an ancient tomb at Siloam (southeast of
Jerusalem) with the evident meaning of "burial chamber."

Is 66:14 —— *You shall see, and your heart shall rejoice* "One of the most sensational discoveries," writes Mazar, "made while uncovering the Western Wall," was this verse inscribed in one of its huge stones. The inscription dates from the time when the emperor Julian "the Apostate" allowed the Jews to resettle in Jerusalem and to start to rebuild the temple. It seems that whoever inscribed the verse understood the comfort promised in verse 13, "in Jerusalem," as the building of what would have been the Third Temple. It is "the written evidence," Mazar comments, "of the people's devotion to the holy place through centuries of hope and disappointment." (MTL, 94)

JEREMIAH

Jer 1:1 —— *who were in Anathoth* The city of the prophet Jeremiah has been identified as Tell Ras el-Kharubeh in the modern Arab village of Anata, some 4 miles northeast of Jerusalem. In the excavations carried out in this site ruins have been found which date from the time of the kingdom of Judah.

Jer 4:11 —— *A hot wind* The translation could also be "a summer wind." The Hebrew word is *tsah*. But in the excavations at Arad (1962) the word appears to be the name of a month, probably equivalent to the beginning of summer. No month of that name, however, is known in the usual Hebrew calendar. Postexilic names of summer months are Tamuz, Ab, and Elul. In order to compensate for the difference between the solar and the lunar years an additional month was inserted every two or three years, but this occurred in winter, after Adar. It was called "Second Adar."

Jer 7:18 —— *cakes for the queen of heaven* Papyri found at Hermopolis in 1945 (and published in 1966) refer to the worship of the "Queen of Heaven," a title given to the Mesopotamic goddess Ishtar (the Phoenician Astarte). She is identified with the planet Venus, and her symbol is an eight-pointed star. Cakes made for her were probably in the shape of her image or of a star. Compare 44:19. (See comment on Judg 2:13.) (DDB, 1667; BAH, 12, 13)

Jer 9:23(22) —— *let not the rich man glory in his riches* Compare *The Words of Ahiqar*, "Let not the rich man say, 'In my riches I am glorious.'" (ANET, 430)

Jer 20:1 —— *Pashhur the priest, the son of Immer* In the environs of Jerusalem a seal was found from the sixth century B.C. with the following inscription, "Belonging to Pashhur, son of Adayahu." In the priestly genealogies of 1 Chronicles 9:10–17 and the parallel in Nehemiah 11:10–24, there is mention of one Adaiah (another form of Adayahu) with a Pashhur among his ancestors and of several priests who descended from Immer. The Pashhur of the seal, if he is the son of the Adayahu mentioned in these other passages, would not be the same person, but he would belong to the same priestly family. The position of "chief officer in the house of the Lord," also mentioned in other cases, was a very important one. (WB, III, 117)

Jer 26:6 —— *I will make this house like Shiloh* (Compare 7:12–14.) From the biblical account we know that the ark of the covenant remained for a time at Shiloh, where a temple came into existence (1 Sam 4:3). The excavations begun in 1926 and 1929 at Khirbet Seilun, where this city was located, have not revealed remains of the temple itself, but they do indicate that the town was a flourishing center in the twelfth and eleventh centuries B.C., the time of the chieftains (judges). Archaeology shows that from the tenth to the sixth centuries B.C. the place was practically deserted and in ruins. This suggests that the Philistines completely destroyed Shiloh after defeating Israel at Ebenezer (toward 1050 B.C.) and seizing the ark of the covenant. (APB, 57; BAW, 89; WMTS, 251)

Jer 26:23 —— *the burial place of the common people.* (Or "the common burial pit.") This was different from the places for the burial of kings and aristocrats. It was simply a cemetery for ordinary people, called in Hebrew "tombs of the sons of the people." Mazar believes it was located in the Kidron Valley or ravine. There is also a reference to this place in 31:40 as "all the fields as far as the brook Kidron." Some interpret the Hebrew *shdemoth* (literally "terraces") in an emended form as *sde-mavet* (literally "fields of death" or "fields of the dead"). But no archaeological remains of these burial grounds have been found so far. (MTL, 188)

Jer 29:5 —— *Build houses and live in them* Evidence that many Jews did follow the prophet's advice appears in the 700 inscribed tablets known as the Murashu Archives, uncovered at Nippur, southeast of Babylon, in 1889, 1900, and 1948. They record contracts, loan certificates, receipts of payments, and other documents belonging to a Jewish family of the fifth century B.C. Both Hebrew and non-Hebrew names are mentioned in them. This is undoubtedly an indication that the family tried to integrate itself into the Babylonian community. An important Jewish colony existed at Nippur, as in other cities in Mesopotamia, including Babylon itself, a city where the so-called Babylonian Talmud was produced. Obviously, not all of the exiled Jews returned from the captivity. Some ceramics uncovered at Nippur show that Jews continued to live there for many centuries. (BAW, 209; ABB, 180)

Jer 32:11 —— *the sealed deed of purchase, . . . the open copy* This purchase was made in accord with the legal stipulations of that time. The original purchase contract and a copy were written on papyrus, vellum, or parchment. The original was then folded, tied, and sealed. The copy was left open, and it was the one consulted when necessary. In this way damage to the original by handling or fraudulent alteration was prevented. In the case recorded in this passage, both the original and the copy were deposited in an earthen jar. Yadin found some of these sealed contracts in caves in the Judean desert. In Mesopotamia the inscribed clay tablets and the original deed were kept in a case or closed "envelope" made of clay (see comment on Is 29:11). (ABB, 168)

Jer 34:7 —— *when the army of the king of Babylon was fighting . . . against . . . Lachish and Azekah* The excavations at Lachish (1935) offer impressive evidences of the fury of the Babylonian onslaught and the pitiless destruction that followed. At the city gateway a layer of burned debris 8 feet high was found. The palace-citadel was completely destroyed, and there were heaps of burned bricks lying on its stone foundations. The most pathetic find was an old tomb outside the city. It was full of human bones, which, according to calculations, belonged to some 2,000 bodies that had been thrown into it through a hole in the roof. According to Starkey these remains were gathered and thrown there during the process of clearing up the city after the fierce slaughter by the Babylonians. Among these bones were found three skulls of special interest for the history of medical science. They represent primitive cases of surgery performed on the skull, no doubt in a desperate effort to save the lives of men injured in battle. In two of them a square of bone appears to have been coarsely cut by a saw. Evidently the men operated on in this way did not survive. In the third case, the skull surgery involved scraping, and it seems that the patient may have lived for a while after this crude operation, for the bone had mended.

Several letters written on potsherds or pieces of ceramics were also discovered there. They were published in 1938 and for reference purposes they were given ordinal numbers. Letter No. 4 probably refers to the last phases of the brave resistance of the defenders of Lachish and Azekah against the Babylonian besiegers. The writer was probably the same Hoshayahu mentioned in Letter No. 3, and the addressee was probably the same Yaosh or Yaush mentioned in it. Among other things Hoshayahu reports to Yaush that from his watch post he can clearly see the signals sent out from Lachish by fire or smoke, but none from Azekah. This seems to indicate that this city had already fallen into the hands of the enemy. It is known that Lachish was the last city of Judah taken by the Babylonians. More than a hundred years before, the Assyrian troops of Sennacherib had also captured it, as may be seen in the famous bas-relief of this king found in Mesopotamia. In it the final assault and capture of the city is depicted (see comment on 2 Kings 25:1). (AHL, 293–95)

Jer 36:4 —— *Baruch the son of Neriah* Somewhere in Judea (at a place as yet unknown) a seal-impression (*bulla*) was found. It was made with an oval seal in cursive script from the seventh century B.C. The inscription reads, "Belonging to Berekhyahu son of Neryahu the scribe" (or secretary). According to Avigad the owner of the seal is to be identified with Baruch, Jeremiah's secretary, who would previously have been a scribe or secretary at the court. In Avigad's opinion *Barukh* (so in Hebrew) is a shortened form of *Berekhyahu* or *Berekhyah*. In Hebrew his father's name *Neriyah* is a slight shortening of *Neriyahu*. (IEJ, 28 [1978] 52–56; BAH, 14)

Jer 36:26 —— *Jerahmeel the king's son* Along with the impression of Baruch's seal (see comment on verse 4), another seal impression was found with the inscription, "Belonging to Yerahmeel the king's son." Avigad feels certain that the owner of this seal is to be identified as the Jerahmeel of this verse. (IEJ, 28 [1978] 52–56)

Jer 37:5 —— *The army of Pharaoh had come out of Egypt* This time it was to assist the king of Judah (verse 7) who had asked for

Pharaoh's help against the Babylonians. He was not the only monarch of Palestine who appealed to Egypt for such help. A papyrus found in Saggara, Egypt, written in Aramaic and probably from the same period, requests the Pharoah's urgent assistance against an invading Babylonian army. Its author has not been identified, but he could have been a Philistine governor, perhaps of Ashkelon, who had also rebelled against Babylon. Ashkelon was seized and sacked by Nebuchadrezzar in 704 B.C. according to the Babylonian Chronicles.

Jer 38:4 —— *he is weakening the hands of the soldiers* In Lachish Letter No. 4 the last part of a prophet's name (*-yahu*) appears. The rest of the name is illegible. The letter says that the king and his officials are enraged against the prophet because he weakens the morale (literally "the hands") of the people before the enemy. The Hebrew name of Jeremiah is *Yirmeyah* or *Yirmeyahu*. Since the Lachish Letters are precisely from the time of King Zedekiah (see 28:1), the reference could perhaps be to Jeremiah. Some scholars, however, suggest that the letter alludes rather to Uriah (Hebrew *Uriyahu*, see 26:20–23), but the story concerning this other prophet takes place under Jehoiakim. The identification of the incident and the prophet in the Lachish Letter is not completely certain, but the similarity is striking. At least this document recovered by archaeology is evidence of the similarities in the biblical accounts about Jeremiah. (BOT, 101–5)

Jer 43:11 —— *He [Nebuchadrezzar] shall come and smite the land of Egypt* An inscription was found in Babylon according to which this invasion can be dated as occurring in 568–67 B.C., when the Pharaoh Amasis ruled in Egypt. Josephus (*Antiquities, X, 9, 7*) alludes to a similar campaign by the Babylonian monarch.

Jer 44:15 —— *had offered incense to other gods* The inroads of paganism among the Israelites are very well attested to by plain references in the historical books and the prophets' flaming denunciations. Pagan practices continued to appear among the exiles in Egypt. This is confirmed by archaeology. Precisely in Tell Daphna, the site of ancient Tahpanhes, a stele from the sixth century B.C. was found in which the worship of a Babylonian god, probably Marduk, is depicted. This confirms that devotion to Semitic gods was widespread in that region, where exiled Jews had a colony.

Also a letter was found which had been sent to Memphis by a woman who swears an oath by several gods, including the Semitic Baal Zaphon. More striking still are an inscription and drawing found on a storage jar at Kuntillet Ajrud, southwest of Kadesh-Barnea in the Sinai. The inscription above two of the figures contains the word *asherah*, the name of the god El's consort in west Semitic mythology. This leads Zeev Meshel to suggest that the figures "may represent Yahweh and his consort." If that is true, it would be another strong evidence of the extent to which pagan concepts and cults had been mixed with Jewish monotheism. (WB, III, 143; TBAR, 5, No. 2 [1979] 24–35)

Jer 44:30 —— *Behold, I will give Pharaoh Hophra . . . into the hand of his enemies*   Pharaoh Hophra (Apries) (588–560 or 568 B.C.), who is pictured in a bas-relief at Abydos, had tried to rush to the assistance of Zedekiah, the king of Judah, who was being attacked by the Babylonians. But he was defeated and had to withdraw. After having suffered a further defeat in Cyrene, he was forced to share the throne with his army's commander in chief, Amasis. Finally, Amasis revolted against Hophra, and in an armed clash between the two the pharaoh was killed. Amasis then took the throne with the name of Ahmosis II. (WB, III, 144)

Jer 47:5 —— *Ashkelon has perished.*   The prophet describes, by means of the poetic figure of a sweeping torrent, the invasion of the Babylonian armies. He refers especially to the Philistine coastline and mentions the city of Ashkelon. A letter in Aramaic found in Egypt was addressed to the pharaoh by the king of Ashkelon. It contains an anguished plea for help in order to curb the onslaught of Nebuchadrezzar's troops. But they captured and destroyed Ashkelon in 604 B.C. Too late to rescue the city, the Egyptians nevertheless defeated the Babylonians and stopped their advance southward in 601 B.C. (ABB, 172–73)

Jer 49:35 —— *I will break the bow of Elam*   Outside the Bible there is no record of this war against Elam, but in the excavations of Mesopotamia a narrative was discovered about an attack by Nebuchadrezzar against the country of Elam precisely at this time (596 B.C.). "The bow of Elam" was the symbol of this nation's power. From bas-reliefs of Ashurbanipal at Nineveh one can see how the

Elamite army was composed mainly of bowmen. Their prowess
became proverbial. (WB, III, 150)

Jer 51:59 —— *Seraiah the son of Neriah, son of Mahseiah* A seal
bearing the inscription "Belonging to Serayahu [Ben] Neriyahu" or
"Seraiah the son of Neriah" is similar to the impression made by
the seal of Baruch (see comment on 36:4) in that the source of this
seal is unknown. "It seems highly probable," says Avigad, "although
not absolutely certain, that the owner . . . is the person mentioned
in the Bible." Seraiah was "the quartermaster" or "chief chamberlain"
at the court of Zedekiah. According to Avigad he was Baruch's
brother. If so, the complete name of Jeremiah's secretary would be
Baruch the son of Neriah, son of Mahseiah. (IEJ, 28 [1978], 56)

LAMENTATIONS

Lam 1:1 —— *How lonely sits the city*   A distant, but very interesting, predecessor of the book of Lamentations is preserved in the cuneiform tablets (most of them uncovered at Nippur) which contain the so-called Lamentation over the Destruction of Ur. They date from the first half of the second millennium B.C. Ur was destroyed by the Elamites and Subarians. The find consists of twenty-two tablets and fragments. The poem has eleven songs or stanzas of diverse length, and they differ much from the biblical book in their structure. The following is one sample of the poem:

> O thou city *of name*, thou hast been destroyed;
> O thou city *of high walls*, thy land has perished.
> O my city, like an innocent ewe thy lamb has been torn away
>   from thee;
> O Ur, like an innocent goat thy kid has perished.

As can be noted, the literary genre of "lamentations" may be considered, from its antiquity, as classic in the ancient Near East. (ANET, 455–63)

Lam 2:5 —— *he has destroyed all its palaces, laid in ruins its strongholds*   For the author, in accord with the traditional Hebrew concept, it was really God who destroyed the land by the hand of the Babylonians in order to punish his people. Not only in Jerusalem, but also in such places as Lachish, Eglon, Beth-shemesh, Gibeah, Ramat Rahel, Arad, and Beth-zur, the excavations have uncovered dramatic evidence of the terrible destruction wreaked by the victors. In many places the destruction was total (see comment on 2 Kings 25:9).

174

EZEKIEL

Ezek 1:10 —— *the face of a man . . . the face of a lion . . . the face of an ox . . . the face of an eagle* The human-headed winged oxen and the winged lions so common in Sumerian and Assyrian statues and bas-reliefs may have influenced the vision described by the prophet. The conjunction of these four beings, supreme in their respective dominions, would represent an ideal combination of intelligence, strength, and sexual fertility. At a very early time the Christian community saw in these the symbols of the four Gospels: Matthew, the man; Mark, the lion; Luke, the ox; and John, the eagle. This explanation of the symbolism is obviously strained. (AAS, 32, 207)

Ezek 4:1 —— *take a brick . . . and portray upon it a city, even Jerusalem* Since Ezekiel dwelt in Mesopotamia, the plan of the city which he was commanded to make had to be drawn upon a brick, for this was the material which served in that region for writing and also for building. Papyrus was as foreign to the region as stone. Excavations carried out in Mesopotamia have found such maps of cities as well as diagrams of buildings and plots of land, incised on baked clay tablets (bricks). (WB, III, 162)

Ezek 8:10 —— *all kinds of creeping things, and loathsome beasts* Among the ruins of the temple of Gozan (Tell Halaf), on the river Habur in Mesopotamia, two stone panels from the tenth or the ninth century B.C. were found. These have fantastic creatures engraved on them. One of the creatures is part man and part fish, holding a frame in the shape of a snake. The other is a winged creature with

175

a human face and a scorpion's tail. Other finds show that figures of
this kind were common in pagan temples. The animal figures in the
famous Ishtar gate of Babylon should be recalled. One of them is
an ox, symbol of the god Adad, and the other is a dragon, symbol
of Tiamat, the mythological god who is the incarnation of the
primeval chaos and also of Marduk. It has the body of a quadruped,
with its forelegs like those of a lion and its hind legs like the legs of
an eagle. Half of its body is covered with snake scales, including
the tail and the long neck, which ends in a snake's head with a
pointed horn. (WB, III, 165; BOT, 31–33)

Ezek 9:2 ——— *a writing case*   The scribe's case, which some versions
translate as "inkstand," was a small case in which the scribe carried
his reed pens. Inside it had some receptacles where at the time of
writing the ink was mixed. This case or small box was generally
carried hanging from the belt. Sometimes the ink-mixer had the
shape of a palette, with two circular hollows for two colors of ink,
and was carried hanging from a cord. In bas-reliefs found in Sakkara
and Gizeh, Egypt, scribes are pictured using such equipment. Palettes
or receptacles for mixing ink have also been found. (ANEP, 231–
34; BAW, 200)

Ezek 14:14 ——— *Daniel*   This Daniel is not the one associated with
the Daniel of the book of Daniel. He would have been later than
Ezekiel. This Daniel is a person of Canaanite tradition, also called
Danel. He is recorded in Ugaritic texts as a judge whose wisdom
and righteousness became proverbial, so much so that in this passage
he is ranked along with Noah and Job. (WB, III, 168; BAR-2, 42,
43)

Ezek 16:24 ——— *a couch and . . . high-stools*   (NEB; RSV: "a vaulted
chamber, and . . . a lofty place.") The respective Hebrew words
translated in these two versions are *gab* (literally "elevation") and
ramah (literally "height"). Some scholars propose for the latter the
reading *bamah* (literally "high place," a pagan shrine). These could
be technical terms to designate the places devoted to the practice
of ritual prostitution. They could also be translated "a platform" or
"a high couch." In some bas-reliefs of Assyrian monuments, structures may be seen which are associated with the ritual prostitution
practiced in pagan temples as a part of fertility cult worship.

Ezek 19:9 —— *they put him in a cage, and brought him to the king of Babylon* A king of Judah is here compared by the prophet to a lion cub. In a bas-relief from Nineveh I, King Ashurbanipal is pictured in a hunting scene shooting with his bow and arrow a lion that has been brought to him in a cage, then released for him to kill it. The wild beast hurls itself against the king, but he is protected by a shield held by his personal guard. (WB, III, 174)

Ezek 20:28 —— *they poured out their drink offerings.* During the 1978 and 1979 excavations at Tell Dan, an installation was found which seems to have been connected with water libations or drink offerings practiced at pagan high places. It consists of a sunken plastered basin with basalt slabs on either side sloping toward a sunken jar. This structure dates from the tenth or ninth century B.C. (TBAR, 7, No. 5 [1981], 34–36)

Ezek 21:21 —— *he looks at the liver.* One of the most common forms of soothsaying in antiquity was hepatoscopy, the observation of an animal's liver, usually that of a lamb sacrificed for the purpose. This method was probably based on the elementary knowledge which ancient peoples had concerning the importance of the liver in the functions of the body. As a sort of guide or code, soothsayers often used a clay model of a liver. Its several sections were marked with code symbols denoting various predictions. So general was the use of these models that specimens have been found not only in Palestine (for instance, at Hazor) and Mesopotamia but in Asia Minor and in Italy (Etruria) as well. Some of them date from the second millennium B.C. (WB, III, 176–77)

Ezek 23:14 —— *she saw . . . upon the wall, the images of the Chaldeans portrayed in vermilion* In several museums there are extraordinary mosaic bas-reliefs in enameled colors which embellished temples and palaces in Babylon. The most famous are the ones recovered from the ruins of the monumental Ishtar gate, with its figures of lions and mythological beasts. There were also some decorated with human figures. In other cases, the figures were carved in stone and then painted in colors such as vermilion. This art was also common in Assyria and remains of this kind of wall decorations in residences have been uncovered in places such as Khorsabad. (ANEP, 237; WB, III, 179)

Ezek 28:2 —— *the seat of the gods, in the heart of the seas* In the epic poems of Ugarit (Ras Shamra) the dwelling of the Canaanite god El is described as "at the source of the rivers, in the channels of the two deeps." (WB, III, 185; ANET, 129)

Ezek 28:14 —— *With an anointed . . . cherub I placed you; . . . in the midst of the stones of fire* (See the comments on Isaiah 6:2 and Exodus 25:18.) The king of Tyre identified himself with Melkart, the patron god of the city, whose emblem was a winged sphinx bedecked with jewels. (ABB, 182)

Ezek 32:24 —— *Elam is there, . . . all of them slain* Bas-reliefs uncovered at Ashurbanipal's palace in Nineveh represent with terrifying realism the defeat of the Elamite army at the hands of the Assyrians, who are shown cruelly slaughtering their enemies. The Elamites are fleeing in disorder, only to throw themselves into a river and drown. The ground is covered with Elamites slain with spears, swords, and arrows. (WB, III, 192–93)

Ezek 37:4 —— *dry bones* A manuscript of the book of Ezekiel was found at the Jewish fortress of Masada. Its best-preserved fragments contained this famous passage of the dry bones.

Ezek 38:6 —— *Gomer and all his hordes* Among the battalions forming Gog's powerful army are the troops of Gomer, the *gimirai* of the Assyrian chronicles and the Cymmerians of the Greek records. In a sarcophagus painting from Clazomenae, a Greek town in Asia Minor, Cymmerian horsemen are pictured with fierce dogs of prey, fighting the Greeks. The Cymmerians came from the Caucasus, and from the eighth to the sixth centuries B.C. they were the terror of Armenia and Asia Minor. This sarcophagus dates from the sixth century B.C., Ezekiel's time. (WB, III, 198)

Ezek 39:9 —— *handpikes* The Hebrew expression *maqqel yad* (literally "handstaff" or "handstick"), sometimes translated "throwing stick," is probably a boomerang. It was a very common weapon in the Near East, as may be seen from the collection of boomerangs of various sizes found in the tomb of Tut-ankh-amen, a pharaoh of the fourteenth century B.C. Boomerangs were used especially in hunting, but they may also have served as weapons of war. (WB, III, 199)

A rock formation overlooking the Bay of Tabgha on the Sea of Galilee. Nearby is the Church of Primacy containing a rock called *Mensa Christi* ("Christ's Table") where, according to tradition, Jesus ate breakfast with his disciples and said to Peter: "Feed my sheep." (Jn 21:15).

Small chapel on the Mount of Olives, built upon the traditional site of Jesus' ascension (Acts 1:9).

Ruins of ancient Perga, visited by Paul during his first missionary journey. Pictured here is the main street leading up to the acropolis (Acts 13:13).

A main street in the ancient city of Corinth. Paul probably walked it many times, since he lived in that city for almost two years (Acts 18:1).

Ruins of the great temple of Apollo in Corinth. The fact that the meat sold in the markets had often been offered to idols presented a serious problem of conscience for the Christians in Corinth and in many other pagan centers (Acts 18:1).

Reproduction of a statue of Diana or Artemis found in the excavations at Ephesus. The statue is carved of white marble, was originally gilded and painted, and is 5½ feet high. "Artemis [or Diana] of the Ephesians" was a goddess of fertility and was worshiped throughout Asia Minor (Acts 19:28).

The great theater at Ephesus, with a seating capacity of some 25,000, was one of the largest in the ancient world. This seems to have been the place to which Paul was taken by the mob during the tumult in that city (Acts 19:29).

Ruins of the Temple of Artemis in Sardis. The worship of this goddess was widespread throughout the Roman Empire (Acts 19:27; Rev 3:1).

Ezek 41:18, 19 —— *Every cherub had two faces: the face of a man . . . and the face of a young lion* In a carved tile from Carchemish, dating from the ninth century B.C., there appears a cherub with two faces, one of a man and the other of a lion. The figure is shown in profile, with the lion's head under the man's—a naïve way in which the sculptor solved a problem of perspective so as not to hide the man's head behind the lion's. In fact, both heads are supposed to be at the same height and side by side. Although this sculpture antedates the time of Ezekiel by three centuries, it demonstrates that such a way of representing a supernatural being had been well known in Mesopotamia for several centuries. (BOT, 137)

Ezek 43:7 —— *defile my holy name, . . . by the dead bodies of their kings* The reference to the dead bodies of kings as a cause of defilement seems to have been clarified by the discovery of a probable royal cemetery belonging to the time of the First Temple. These excavations were carried out at the foot of the Temple Mount starting in February 1968. West of the western stretch of the Herodian wall ("Wall of Lamentations," but now better known as the Western Wall) archaeologists found tombs from this period carved out of solid rock at the foot of the eastern slope of the hill facing the Temple Mount, with only the Central Valley (Tyropoeon) in between. The foundations of the wall lie right on the entrance to two of these tombs. The cemetery stood so close to the temple that it may have been considered a profanation of the holy precinct. Mazar, who discovered this cemetery, said, "Ezekiel heaped his wrath upon the royal tombs close-by the holy precincts of the temple, and called for their removal." (JR, 40)

Ezek 43:14 —— *from the base on the ground* The Hebrew word for this part of the altar literally means "lap of the earth" (in verse 13 it is only "lap"). It seems to be a technical architectural term from the Akkadian phrase *irat ertsiti*, the name for the platform upon which a *ziggurat* (stepped pyramid) or a temple was built. Apparently this platform was considered to be a representation of the earth's bosom or lap on which the foundations of the sacred building rested.

DANIEL

Dan 5:30, 31 —— *Belshazzar . . . was slain. And Darius the Mede received the kingdom* See the comment on Isaiah 21:9. According to secular history, Babylon's last king was Nabonidus, so that there seemed to be a serious divergence from the biblical account. The problem continued until new archaeological evidence showed that the two reports could be reconciled by the fact that, in the last stage of his reign, Nabonidus withdrew to Arabia and left the regency or administration of the kingdom in the hands of his son Belshazzar. There is, however, another problem, namely, the fact that the conqueror of Babylon was Cyrus. Darius came later. So far no solution to this problem has been found, but the suggestions mentioned in connection with Isaiah 21:9 may be worth considering. (WMTS, 276–77; BOT, 116–19)

HOSEA

Hos 1:1 —— *The word of the LORD that came to Hosea* Fragments of a commentary of Hosea found at Qumran (near the Dead Sea) contain quotations of 2:6(8), 7(9)b–12(14); 5:13c–15, as well as of other portions of which only a few letters are legible. Some differences from the Masoretic text can be noted, but the textual tradition seems to be the same. (DSSE, 230; LRQ, 313–14)

Hos 12:1 —— *and oil is carried to Egypt.* A potsherd found at Tell Qasileh bears the following inscription in the cursive Hebrew script of the eighth century B.C.: "For the king, one thousand . . . and one hundred (logs of) oil [100 logs = 25 quarts] . . . (A)hijahu." It is no doubt a fragment of an entry in a record of remittances sent by a royal steward, perhaps to Egypt. (WB, III, 218)

AMOS

Amos 1:1 —— *Tekoa* The ruins of Tekoa are identified as the present Khirbet Taqua, about 5 miles south of Bethlehem.

two years before the earthquake. In the excavations led by Yadin at Hazor traces of an earthquake were found in stratum VI corresponding to the prophet's time. There are cracked walls (some of them tilted), remains of fallen roofs, and materials fallen at the side of pillars which supported the roof of a building. The damage shown by a tomb found in Dothan was also probably caused by the same earthquake. (EB, III, 1084, illustration; WB, III, 230–31; LTR, 13; HYY, 150–53)

Amos 5:5 —— *do not . . . cross over to Beer-sheba* Compare 8:14. The prophet seems to refer to Beersheba as a seat of pagan worship. The finding of the great altar of sacrifices by Aharoni (see comment on 2 Kings 23:8) appears to confirm the fact that a schismatic sanctuary did exist at one time in Beersheba. (BAH, 27)

Amos 6:1 —— *those who feel secure on the mountain of Samaria* The prophet probably refers not only to the false security of wealth and material prosperity, but also to the security offered by the city's system of fortifications, remains of which have been found in the extensive archaeological excavations at the site. The extensive walls from the time of the northern kingdom of Israel deserve special attention.

Amos 6:4 —— *those who lie upon beds of ivory* In the National Museum in Damascus one may see ivory carved plaques found at

182

Ugarit (Ras Shamra). They belonged to a royal couch. These plaques are from a period much earlier than the time of Amos, but they constitute an excellent illustration of the luxurious beds and couches of Samaria's wealthy elite to whom the prophet refers.

Amos 8:1, 2 —— *summer fruit. . . . The end* As RSV's marginal notes indicate, the Hebrew word translated "summer fruit" is *qayits* (literally, simply "summer"), and the word for "end" is *qets*. In Hebrew, the play upon words is evident. The same pun also occurs in the famous tablet called the *Gezer Calendar*, found by Macalister in 1908 at this city's former site. In the last line of the tablet appear the consonants *qts*, which could be vocalized as *qets*, or they could be considered an abbreviation of *qayits*, with the *y* omitted and different vowels employed. This line, then, could be read "month of the end" or "month of the summer fruit." The latter has been the most common translation.

Amos 8:9 —— *I will . . . darken the earth in broad daylight.* What is described is an eclipse of the sun. In Nineveh some tablets were found containing a list of personal names associated with particular events. It amounts to a year-by-year chronicle of Assyria's history. For each person in the list the main event of the respective year is recorded. One of the entries says, "In the year of the eponym Buru-Sagale, the governor of Gozan: an uprising in the city of Ashur. In the month of Sivan there was an eclipse of the sun." By astronomical calculations it has been possible to fix the exact date of this eclipse, namely, June 15, 763 B.C. This is precisely the time of Amos. The eclipse was accompanied by an earthquake (see verse 8, and also comment on 1:1). (WB, III, 242)

Amos 8:14 —— *who swear . . . As the way of Beer-sheba lives* It seems most probable that here we have an allusion to the title "the Way" of a pagan god worshiped in Beersheba, the parallelism being with "Ashimah of Samaria." (See the comments on 5:5 and 2 Kings 23:8.)

JONAH

Jon 1:3 —— *He went down to Joppa* This port, one of the most important in Palestine, was also called Joppe and is now known as Yafo or Jafa. It is often mentioned in Egyptian and Assyrian chronicles. During the time of the Israelite monarchy it was under Philistine dominion, but it was constantly coveted by the great neighboring empires of the time. It did not become a Jewish port until the Hasmonean period. In recent excavations remains of the wall and gates of the Canaanite period have been uncovered. (WB, III, 251)

Jon 3:3 —— *Nineveh . . . three days' journey in breadth.* The book of Jonah assigns to Nineveh a seemingly much exaggerated size. For that reason some commentators have regarded the book as belonging to a relatively late period when Nineveh had become legendary. Excavations have shown that the widest diameter of the city, from the gate of Ashur to the gate of Nergal, was only some 3 miles, at most a walk of an hour and a half. Parrot, however, considers that the dimensions in the book of Jonah refer rather to what may be called "the greater Nineveh," that is, metropolitan Nineveh plus the neighboring cities of Khorsabad to the north and Nimrud to the south, joined by a suburban ring of inhabited places with almost no space between. It is the urban aggregate usually called today "the Assyrian triangle" which adds up to a length of some 24 miles, almost three one-day marches at a moderate pace, and even more if loaded beasts and families were taken along, as was usual in ancient travel. (NAOT, 85–86)

Jon 4:11 —— *more than a hundred and twenty thousand persons who do not know their right hand from their left* This expression, translated literally from the Hebrew, usually refers to minors, that is, persons in a state of innocence or immaturity. It could be used in a figurative sense to mean "simple" or "innocent" people, meaning that they had repented (3:6–9). If understood in this sense, then the number, which at first sight seems so exaggerated, might really mean the entire population of Nineveh. In comparison with what we at present call a "city," ancient cities were rather small. But in the excavations carried out by Mallowan, a stele was uncovered belonging to Ashurbanipal. It records a banquet given by this king to 69,574 guests. Mallowan estimated a population of 65,000 for Nimrud. Felix Jones estimated that Nineveh could have had a population of 174,000. (See the comment on 3:3 about "greater Nineveh.") Parrot is of the opinion that "the figure mentioned in Jonah 4:11 finds an indirect but precious confirmation." (NAOT, 86)

MICAH

Mic 1:1 —— *The word of the LORD that came to Micah* Finds at Qumran (near the Dead Sea) included fragments of a commentary of this book, in which there are quotations of verses 2–7a, 9b, and 6:15–16a in a text practically the same as the Masoretic text. (PQI, 55–63; LRQ, 307–8)

Mic 3:12 —— *Zion shall be plowed as a field* After his last visit to Jerusalem (A.D. 130), the emperor Hadrian decided to build a temple to Jupiter Capitolinus in the area where the Second Temple had stood. His obvious purpose was to prevent once and for all any attempt to reconstruct it. He wanted to change the Holy City into a Roman colony. With this end in view, one of the first tasks of the legate Tinus Rufus was literally to plow up the areas near the walls. This deed precipitated the general Jewish uprising of A.D. 132. (MTL, 235)

NAHUM

Nahum 1:1 —— *The book of the vision of Nahum*   In Qumran (near
the Dead Sea) four fragments were found of a commentary on the
book of Nahum, in which verses 1:3b–6a; 2:11(12)b–3:12a are quoted.
As in the case of other Qumran commentaries, the text of the
quotations coincides in almost all details with the Masoretic text.
(DSSE, 231–35; LRQ, 309–12)

Nahum 3:1 —— *Woe to the bloody city*   The capture and destruction
of Nineveh announced by the prophet is described in a Babylonian
tablet which tells of Nabopolassar's wars (625–605 B.C.). This
narrative is known as the Gadd Chronicle, named after the English
archaeologist who published it in 1923. It tells about the military
action of the Median allies of the king of Babylon who threw
themselves against Nineveh: "They advanced up the bank of the
Tigris . . . (encamped) against Nineveh . . . launched a powerful
attack on the city, and in the month Abu the city was taken. They
made great (slaughter) of the princes. . . . They took a heavy weight
of booty from the city and the temple, (and turned) the city into a
mound and a ruin. . . ." (WB, III, 264)

Nahum 3:8, 10 —— *Thebes . . . she was carried away*   The allusion
is no doubt to the capture of this city by Ashurbanipal in 663 B.C.
This Assyrian monarch left a chronicle containing the following
statement: "From Thebes I carried away booty heavy and beyond
counting. . . . I pulled two high obelisks, cast of shining bronze, the
weight of which was 2,500 talents, standing at the door of the temple,
out of their bases and took (them) to Assyria." (WB, III, 266)

HABAKKUK

Hab 1:1 —— *The oracle . . . which Habakkuk . . . saw* Among the manuscripts found in 1947 in Cave 1 at Qumran (near the Dead Sea) there is a commentary (Hebrew *pesher*) on the book of Habakkuk. The commentary attempts to find in the prophecy specific allusions to persons and historic situations at the time when the commentator was writing. He was particularly concerned to find reference to the antecedents of the religious community of the Qumranites, who were related to the sect of the Essenes. From this commentary it has been possible to determine most of the text of Habakkuk which they used, and it has turned out to be almost identical with the Masoretic text. (DSS, 123–42; DSM, plates XIX–XXIII; LRQ, 297–306)

Hab 1:15 —— *he drags them out with his net* This figurative expression about a conqueror who hauls the vanquished into captivity as a fisherman encloses many fish in his net was common in Mesopotamia. It is even seen in some bas-reliefs of steles uncovered there. On one of them, coming from the end of the third millennium B.C. and found in Susa, the capital of Elam, an unidentified god or king is pictured as holding a net full of enemy prisoners. (WB, III, 272; MLB, 14–15)

Hab 2:19 —— *overlaid with gold and silver* In the excavations at Megiddo a statuette was found of a Canaanite god, perhaps El. It is of bronze, overlaid with gold leaf and dating from approximately the thirteenth century B.C. Similar figurines have been discovered at other excavated sites. Sometimes they are of copper with a coating of precious metal. (See the comment on Is 30:22.) The coating probably represents vestments or garments. These idols, both large and small, are also described in other prophetic passages, but they have not been found in the ruins of Israelite towns. (BAW, 107, 116)

Hab 3:5 —— *and plague followed* The Hebrew word translated "plague" could also be the proper name Resheph, the Canaanite god of recurring fever, or the Ugaritic god of war. Resheph was also considered to be a god of fertility. The worship of Resheph was introduced into Egypt, for it is depicted in a funeral stele from about 1250 B.C. discovered in a tomb. It bears the pointed beard with which the Egyptians normally characterized (almost caricatured) the Canaanites and Semites in general. According to Albright the name is equivalent to Makal, called "god of Beth-shan" in inscriptions on a stele found at this site. (WB, III, 274; APB, 41)

ZEPHANIAH

Zeph 1:1 —— *The word of the* LORD *which came to Zephaniah* A fragment of a commentary on the book of Zephaniah found at Qumran (near the Dead Sea) quotes most of verse 8 of this first chapter in a text like the Masoretic text. (MDQ, 544)

Zeph 1:11 —— *inhabitants of the Mortar!* The name in Hebrew is *Makhtesh*, also meaning "hollow." It was given to a new quarter of Jerusalem which was evidently populated in the time of Hezekiah. Its location is not certain, but in all probability it was situated in a depression shaped like a bowl (hence the name), which existed in the Central Valley (the Tyropoeon mentioned by Josephus). This glen was afterward filled up and is at present occupied by ancient constructions. Its original existence is known only by the general geological formation. It ran from north to south and crossed the Transversal Valley, which ran eastward from the place where the Jaffa Gate now stands. It seems that "the Mortar" was located at the intersection of these two valleys, a zone where recent excavations have been carried out. (MTL, 55; ABB, 187)

Zeph 2:4 —— *and Ekron shall be uprooted.* In a bas-relief from the palace of Sargon II the capture of Ekron is depicted. The Assyrian form of the name is *Amqaruna*. (ABB, 187)

ZECHARIAH

Zech 1:11 —— *all the earth remains at rest.* This is probably an allusion to the pacification of the Persian Empire after the rebels who had risen against Darius had surrendered. The date of this event appears in the inscription on the Behistun Rock. It coincides with "the twenty-fourth day of the eleventh month . . . in the second year of Darius" (verse 7), the equivalent of February 15, 519 B.C. (WB, III, 287)

Zech 9:6 —— *a mongrel people shall dwell in Ashdod* The calamity that descended upon this and other cities mentioned by the prophet in this passage (9:1–8) seems to be an allusion in retrospect to the campaign of Sargon II in Palestine. His *Annals* contain the names of several places mentioned by Zechariah. (ANET, 284–85)

MALACHI

Mal 4:2(3:20) —— *the sun of righteousness* This could be a poetic figure taken from nature, but it could also have a Messianic sense. Accordingly, some versions print *Sun of Righteousness* as a title. Archaeology has offered many examples from Egypt and Mesopotamia in which a king was given the title or epithet of "the Sun." This is the title, for example, in a Sumero-Akkadian hymn to the sun god Shamash, where the literal designation "the enemy of the sun" means "the enemy of the king," according to the translator, F. J. Stephens. (ANET, 389)

THE NEW TESTAMENT

MATTHEW

Mt 2:1 —— *in the days of Herod the king* Several kings belonging to the same family bore the name Herod. The Herod in this verse, later called "the Great," was the founder of that royal house. His father was an Idumean and his mother an Arab. He was a great builder, and archaeologists have uncovered, both in Jerusalem and in other parts of Palestine, numerous and impressive remains of his constructions, in addition to those that had already been known for centuries. He lived from approximately 73 to 4 B.C.

Herod's most famous construction was the temple in Jerusalem, but he also built the Antonia fortress, a royal palace, a theater, and an amphitheater in the city. He strengthened its walled defenses with several towers, such as the tower of Phasael, the foundations of which have been excavated. No ruins of the temple proper are left, but there still exist parts of the enormous retaining wall built to expand the esplanade upon which the Solomonic temple had stood. The most famous section of this wall is the western one, in former times called the Wailing Wall and now simply the Western Wall. For Jews this is the city's most sacred place. The modern state of Israel has built in front of it a large square for major religious ceremonies held there. Very important excavations have been carried out at the southwestern corner and the southern side of the wall, under the direction of Mazar, beginning in February 1968. The discoveries made there have radically changed the traditional idea about the access to the temple in that area. Herod's style of construction is typical and is identified by, among other characteristics, enormous, carefully worked stone blocks.

Herod also carried out important works in Samaria. He founded the city of Caesarea and gave it a magnificent artificial harbor and a great aqueduct. He built the imposing palace-stronghold of Masada, and constructed for himself as a funeral monument a palace called the Herodium. It was located on the top of a conical artificial hill southeast of Bethlehem. He also built the renowned fortress-palace of Machaerus, east of the Dead Sea. The synagogues which he had built at the Herodium and at Masada are the oldest so far discovered. His winter palace at Jericho is another example of Herod's magnificence as a builder. For this building he used parts of an already existing Hasmonean winter palace, and he erected his own palace on both sides of the Wadi el-Qelt, which runs down from Jerusalem. This palace had spacious halls, luxurious baths, a great pool, and an ample sunken garden. The excavations at this site were begun by J. L. Kelso and D. C. Baramki in 1950, followed by James B. Pritchard in 1951, but the main excavations are those carried out by Ehud Netzer since 1973. They have all confirmed Herod's fame as one of the most sumptuous builders of antiquity. (MTL; TBAR, 3, No. 2 [1976], 1, 6–17)

Mt 2:11 —— *gold and frankincense and myrrh.* One can easily understand that gold would be a proper gift for a king, but why should this be so of vegetable resins, frankincense and myrrh? As a matter of fact, these were costly substances at that time. They were produced in the region of the Gulf of Aden in southern Arabia and along the African coast on the other side of the Red Sea. Those were limited and remote areas, and it was difficult to transport their products to markets where the demand for them was great, that is, India, the Middle East, and the Roman world. (BAR-2, 99–126)

Mt 2:23 —— *a city called Nazareth*   Modern Nazareth lies north of the Plain of Esdraelon and at an elevation of some 1,150 feet above sea level. It doubtlessly occupies the same location as the town in which, according to the Gospels, Jesus lived until the beginning of his ministry. Archaeological remains of human settlement in Nazareth date from the ninth to the sixth centuries B.C., but the town was of little importance in the time when Jesus lived there. It is not mentioned in the Old Testament or by Josephus or in rabbinic literature. Contemporaries of Jesus thought little of it (Jn 1:46). The earliest known mention of Nazareth outside of the Bible occurs in fragments of an inscription found at a site in Caesarea where a synagogue stood in the third or fourth century A.D. These fragments were part of the Twenty-four Priestly Courses and their places of residence. This is also the earliest occurrence of the name Nazareth in Hebrew.

Archaeology has not so far revealed with certainty any place directly relating to Jesus and his family. It seems that in the time of Constantine a person named Joseph of Tiberias, who was a great builder of Christian churches, erected at least one church in Nazareth, but the actual location of it is not known. A pilgrim called Anonymous of Piacenza, who wrote toward the end of the sixth century A.D., says, "St. Mary's house is a basilica." Remains of the church built by Joseph of Tiberias have not been found, but remains of another, probably dating from the fifth century A.D. and clearly identified as Byzantine, may belong to the basilica mentioned by Anonymous. It was probably built on the site of an earlier structure. The crusaders raised a new structure in the same place, and in 1730 yet another building was started, but it was never finished. This unfinished building was demolished in 1955 to make room for the modern and sumptuous Church of the Annunciation. Like the former buildings, it supposedly stands over the place where Mary was visited by the angel Gabriel (Lk 1:26–38).

At another location in Nazareth stands the Church of St. Joseph, completed in 1914 and built upon ruins dating from the time of the Crusades. Beneath it is a cave which, according to tradition, was where the family of Jesus lived and where Joseph had his carpenter shop.

At yet another site stands the Church of St. Gabriel. Nearby is the town's only spring of drinkable water. According to another old tradition, the angel Gabriel met Mary here when she went to draw water. The so-called Fountain of the Virgin or Mary's Well, on the road to Tiberias, is the outlet given to the spring's water in 1862, when a pipeline was laid from the spring, some 500 feet up the hill. Water from this spring has been piped to the crypt of the Church of St. Gabriel. (TANT, 27–33; EB, V, 464–70)

Mt 3:3 —— *The voice of one crying in the wilderness* The Essene sect of Qumran (to which belonged the famous Qumran or Dead Sea scrolls) also considered themselves as being called to "prepare the way of the Lord." They quoted this passage in Isaiah as their motto. This fact has led to the supposition that John belonged to that sect. Since he lived in the wilderness of Judea, where the sect had its center, it is very likely that he knew them; but it is very doubtful that he was ever one of their members. From the Gospel account, it is evident that he lived and acted on his own. In spite of certain similarities, such as the ascetic simplicity of his way of life, the differences are much greater. His ideal was not monastic, and he did not profess the strict legalism of the Qumran sect. These formed a select, hermetical group of initiates, who withdrew from the world to prepare themselves to receive the Messianic era. John, on the contrary, called all the social classes of the entire nation to prepare themselves for it through repentance and newness of life. (SNT, 33–53; DSS, 328–29; LRQ, 100–3)

Mt 3:6 —— *were baptized by him in the river Jordan*   According to Luke 3:3, John "went into all the region about the Jordan" preaching and baptizing. This would mean that there was no single fixed place in the river where he baptized. Various sites suitable for baptism were probably used. They would no doubt have been some of the fords which even today can be found at various points along the Jordan. In John 1:28 mention is made of one of these places, "Bethany beyond the Jordan." (Some Greek manuscripts of lesser authority call it Bethabara.) This location has not been identified. Origen and Eusebius mention it. The famous mosaic map of Madaba (a place in Transjordan east of the Dead Sea), discovered in 1884, locates Bethabara close to the point where the Jordan flows into the Dead Sea, but it is on the western side. An ancient tradition, perhaps dating from the third century A.D., indicates the place of Jesus' baptism in this region about 5 miles north from where the Jordan enters the Dead Sea, that is, in the area of Wadi el-Charrar. Some 700 yards from the river and facing west stands the Monastery of St. John, built in accordance with that tradition. It is this part of the river which is shown to tourists as the supposed site of Jesus' baptism. John 3:22–23 says that "John also was baptizing at Aenon near Salim" and that this was in "the land of Judea," that is, west of the Jordan. According to Eusebius, Aenon was situated some 7½ miles south of Bet-shan, which would have been considerably upstream. The Madaba Map has two places called Aenon. One is east of the Jordan, facing Bethabara, and the other is in the region indicated by Eusebius. It is marked as "Aenon, the one which is near Salim." Five springs are there, which is what the name in Aramaic suggests. (TANT, 8–13; EB, III, 37–38)

Mt 3:11 —— *I baptize you with water* The baptism instituted by John was something new and different in both form and meaning from the ablutions and ritual bathings of Judaism. Some scholars have regarded John's baptism as being derived directly from the practices of the Essene sect of Qumran. The only resemblance, however, consists in the use of water with a figurative or symbolic value, but this usage was already old and common in Judaism. John's baptism and the ablutions of the Qumran community represent distinct developments. In spite of a common tradition, they are radically different. John called all Jews to be baptized as a token of repentance; it was he who administered the baptism, and this was received just once. The ablutions at Qumran were rites of purification for which several pools had been built in the community. Only the initiates took the ablutions, and they were self-administered and frequent, because they were intended for purification from all possible accidental ritual or ceremonial defilement. (MLD, 59–60; SNT, 36–37; LRQ, 101–2; DSSE, 45)

Mt 4:1 —— *into the wilderness to be tempted by the devil.* West from Jericho there is a craggy mount called Quarantal (literally "of the Forty Days"). It is pointed out as the traditional site of the Lord's temptation. Ruins on its top seem to be those of a Maccabean stronghold. There are also many caves, in some of which Christian hermits lived beginning with the fourth century. Halfway up its slope is a Greek monastery, said to occupy the place of the first temptation. The third temptation is traditionally located on the summit of the mountain. Obviously, no archaeological evidence can confirm this identification. (TANT, 82)

Mt 4:5 —— *the pinnacle of the temple* The Greek word translated "temple" refers to the whole area occupied by the sanctuary. And the pinnacle (literally "small wing") could designate a corner or extreme point. It is therefore probable that the reference in this passage is to the southeastern corner of the Herodian wall, which has been preserved up to some 20 feet from what would have been the top of the wall. In recent years the base of this corner has been excavated, where in the course of centuries the level has risen considerably by the accumulation of debris. According to archaeological calculations, this corner may have reached a height in Jesus' time of no less than 295 feet above the bottom of the Kidron Valley, although the wall itself would have had an imposing height of about 140 feet. One can understand why Josephus wrote that since the Kidron Valley was so deep, if one looked from above into the ravine, "he would become dizzy and his vision would be unable to reach the end of so measureless a depth" (*Antiquities*, XV, XI, 5). Eusebius (*Ecclesiastical History*, chapter 23) draws from Hegesippus' *Commentaries* the story of the death of James, the brother of the Lord, who was reportedly cast down from this height. (TOJ, 79, 86; TANT, 125–26; LOC, 16)

Mt 4:23 —— *teaching in their synagogues* No ruins of synagogues in which Jesus may have taught have been discovered except for a few basalt blocks of the foundation of the synagogue at Capernaum (see comment on Lk 7:5). Remains of three synagogues from the first century A.D. have been excavated, but that none of these was visited by Jesus is evident from their locations and the Gospel records concerning his travels. One of them was in the Masada, the Jewish fortress in the wilderness of Judea; another was in the Herodium, the palace built by Herod the Great southeast of Bethlehem; and the third was at Gamla in the Golan Heights. At the southeastern extremity of the eastern hill of Jerusalem an inscribed stone was discovered. It belonged to a synagogue which once stood in that place, but no remains of the synagogue were found. Furthermore, it appears that this synagogue was built in A.D. 65, which was after the time of Jesus. (MTL, 87)

Mt 5:3 —— *the poor in spirit* This is the literal translation preserved in traditional versions. The same expression is found in the Qumran scroll called *War of the Sons of Light Against the Sons of Darkness*, 14.7 (the Hebrew *aneve ruakh* is the equivalent of Greek *ptochoi toi pneumati*). The fact that in both the New Testament and the Qumran scrolls the expression appears only once makes it impossible to determine its meaning with any certainty. Moreover, this precise expression appears nowhere in the Old Testament. The closest parallel is in Isaiah 66:2, where the Hebrew *ani unekhe ruah* means literally "the poor and contrite in spirit." The expression in 5:3 does not mean "poorly spirited," "spiritless," or "pusillanimous," as some might vulgarly suppose. It refers rather to persons who are conscious of their own inner need and the insufficiency of their own resources and who therefore look up to God for help (GNB, "those who know they are spiritually poor"; NEB, "those who know their need of God"). Some have proposed the meaning of "voluntary poor," in the sense of having no attachment to earthly riches—the inwardly poor. The expression may have been relatively common in the time of Jesus, so that both he and the people of Qumran used it independently. More likely, however, the two uses of the expression were coincidental. (SNT, 121–22; LRQ, 104, 227; DSSE, 142)

Mt 6:9 —— *Our Father*   A very curious and cryptic anagram was discovered at two places in Pompeii, a city in Italy destroyed by an eruption of Mount Vesuvius in A.D. 79. The form of the anagram is:

ROTAS
OPERA
TENET
AREPO
SATOR

Another example of the same anagram, dating from the third century A.D., appears in the ruins of Dura-Europos on the Euphrates River. And a third, dating from the fourth century A.D., turned up in faraway Cirencester, England. Other examples of the anagram, dating from the Middle Ages, have been found in various places in Europe. In some cases the order of the lines from top to bottom is reversed, but in any case the lines are the same, whether read vertically or horizontally. Several interpretations of the anagram have been proposed, but it has been observed that these same letters can be rearranged in the form of a cross. In that case they form the first two words of the Lord's Prayer in Latin, both horizontally and vertically preceded by the letter *A* and followed by the letter *O*, which correspond to the letters alpha and omega (the first and the last) of the Greek alphabet. If this interpretation of the anagram is correct, its discovery in Pompeii would indicate that there was a Christian congregation in that Roman city before A.D. 79. It would also show that the form in which the Lord's Prayer appears in Matthew is probably the earliest. According to Papyrus 75, from the beginning of the third century A.D., and the Sinaitic and Vatican codices, both from the fourth century A.D., the Lord's Prayer in the

Gospel of Luke has simply "Father." Some versions, which are supported by Greek manuscripts of lesser authority, have adopted for Luke the same reading as that which occurs in Matthew. (WMTS, 33–34)

```
            A
            P
            A
            T
            E
            R
  A PATERNOSTER O
            O
            S
            T
            E
            R
            O
```

Mt 8:14 —— *Jesus entered Peter's house* Close to the remains of the Capernaum synagogue, some ruins have been excavated at the traditional site of Peter's house. These ruins date from the first century A.D. and consist of two parts: a square structure next to the synagogue, and a church of octagonal shape, dating from the fifth century A.D. From inscriptions on the wall of the house, it is possible to conclude that by the second half of the second century this was already a place of worship and that the identification of this place as Peter's house is a very old tradition. The remains of the shrine are under the church, and in fact they do seem to be those of a fisherman's home. The pilgrim Aetheria (A.D. 385) wrote, "In Capernaum, out of the house of the first of the apostles a church was made. . . ." And in A.D. 570 Anonymous of Piacenza says, "We came to Capernaum into the house of St. Peter, which is a basilica." Kenyon says, however, "Claims that the house of Peter has been found at Capernaum, based on the find in it of a fish-hook, must be regarded with some scepticism." (TANT, 56; ABB, 280; BRA, 95–96)

Mt 14:19 —— *the five loaves and the two fish* On the north side of the Plain of Gennesaret (today Ginosar), at a place called by the

Arabs et-Tabgha (an adaptation from the Greek *Heptapegon*), are the remains of a small church excavated and restored in 1932. The claim is made that it stands on the place where the feeding of the five thousand took place. This is a very old tradition for the pilgrim Aetheria refers to it (A.D. 385). She mentions that "the stone on which the Lord put the bread" was made into an altar. Under the present small altar a piece of limestone is seen, which may be the stone mentioned by Aetheria. The church was paved with mosaic, of which considerable fragments are preserved. The most beautiful of them pictures a basket full of loaves, with a fish on either side. Under the present floor the remains of an earlier chapel were found in 1936. It probably dates from the middle of the fourth century A.D. and is surely the one visited by Aetheria. It seems that the stone which was considered sacred was at the apse, the same place as in the present church. The mosaic dates from the end of the fourth or the beginning of the fifth century A.D.

In spite of the antiquity of this tradition, the narratives of the four Evangelists locate the feeding of the five thousand on the eastern or northeastern shore of the lake. It is clearly said that after the miracle Jesus returned with his disciples to the western shore. Eutychius of Alexandria says that there was a church at Kursi, east of the lake, which commemorated the feeding of the four thousand and the healing of the Gadarene demoniac. It seems that the feeding of the four thousand took place in the same region as the feeding of the five thousand. Jack Finegan suggests that because in the course of time it became more difficult for pilgrims to visit the east side of the lake, the traditional site of the miraculous feedings "was transferred" to the west side, namely, to the Seven Springs (Tabgha). (TANT, 48–49)

Mt 21:1 —— *and came to Bethphage* The location of this village, mentioned only here and in the parallel passages, has not been identified by archaeological evidence. Apparently it completely disappeared. The biblical account implies that when Jesus came up from Jericho, he first arrived at or in front of Bethphage. This would locate the village on the eastern slope of the Mount of Olives. Mark and Luke associate it with Bethany, so it must have been close to this town, but they seem to suggest that it would be the one reached first when coming from Jericho. This has given rise to the proposal that Bethphage is to be located at Abu Dis, an Arab village southeast of Bethany. The Talmud mentions a Beth-Page, understood to be a suburb of Jerusalem, that for ritual purposes would mark the limits of the city. Rather late traditions, such as those of the monk Epiphanius (end of the eighth century A.D.), locate it halfway between Bethany and the summit of the Mount of Olives. Some frescoes from the time of the Crusades indicate that this location was then accepted. A Franciscan chapel now marks the supposed site. It stands in the area known as Ras esh-Shiyah, north of the modern road coming from Jericho and passing by Bethany. The identification of Bethany as the present Arab village el-Azariyeh (the name seems to preserve the old Latin name *Lazarium*) is considered certain by biblical authorities. Literary evidence for this comes from as far back as the *Onomasticon* of Eusebius, fourth century A.D. (TANT, 90–91; IDB, I, 396; EB, I, 1177–78)

Mt 21:12 —— *And Jesus entered the temple* The exact place occupied by the ancient gate through which Jesus entered the temple has not yet been located. Coming from the Mount of Olives and across the Kidron Valley, it had to be a gate situated more or less directly on the east, and would not be one of the southern or western gates giving access to the Temple Mount. A historic gate on the east side was the one through which the High Priest went out to sacrifice the red heifer on the Mount of Olives, as prescribed in Numbers 19. The exact site where this gate stood has not been identified. It would probably have also been the one through which Jesus entered. Some 1,023 feet north from the southeastern corner of the walls, a great gate may be seen today, popularly called the Golden Gate, and by Jews and Moslems the Gate of Mercy. It dates either from the Byzantine or from the Ommayad period, but one cannot be certain that it was built exactly on the site occupied by the former gate, although most probably it was close to it. As all photographs of this gate show, the outer face of it is walled up, but there is access to it from the platform of the esplanade on the inner side. Inside the gate there are three huge pillars which support the vault and which belonged to the porticoes of Herod's temple. According to an ancient legend, when the Messiah comes, he will enter through this gate, and not until then will it be opened from the exterior. (MTL, 148–51; TOJ, 80–82)

Mt 23:2 —— *Moses' seat*   Originally called "chair" or "bench" (Greek *kathedras*), this was a seat reserved in the synagogue for an important teacher of the Law or for one whom the synagogue leaders wished to honor. It generally had a tall back and arms and was usually made of stone. Remains of chairs of this kind have been found among the ruins of several synagogues. The remains of one of them found among the ruins of the synagogue at Chorazin bears a carved inscription in remembrance of a certain Yudan the son of Ishmael who had given to the synagogue the portico and the steps of the gate. (WB, V, 63; TANT, 58)

Mt 23:15 —— *you traverse sea and land to make a single proselyte*   In contrast with its attitude of today, there was a time when Judaism was a religion with great missionary zeal that sometimes degenerated into proselytism. This was especially true when paganism was declining in the Greco-Roman world. Greek and Roman inscriptions have been discovered with names of such proselytes who were more or less formally incorporated into Judaism. In a tombstone of a Jewish catacomb along the Via Appia in Rome, an inscription indicates that a certain Chrysis, whose brother Mannacius dedicated to her this epitaph, was a "proselyte." (WB, V, 64)

Mt 24:15 —— *the desolating sacrilege*   The Greek *bdelugma tes eremoseos* is the literal translation of Hebrew *shiquts shomem* or *shiquts meshomem* (Dan 9:27; 11:31; 12:11), which is literally "abomination of desolation" (KJV) or "desolating abomination." *Shiquts* ("abomination") was a term used to refer to a pagan god, particularly Baal, while avoiding the use of the god's name. In the use of *shomem* or *meshomem* there seems to be a play on words with the name and title given to this god, *Baal Shomem* ("Lord of Heaven"). Some think that the reference of the prophet was used in the Gospel to apply to the desecration of the temple in Jerusalem by bringing into it Roman standards which bore images of pagan gods or of the emperor or by the celebration of idolatrous rites in its sacred precincts. A bas-relief, originally honoring Marcus Aurelius but later used with necessary alterations in the triumphal arch of Constantine I, represents the sacrifice of an ox, a sheep, and a pig. A company of Roman soldiers with their standards and banners is also pictured. Some have suggested that the historical reference in Daniel could have been to the pagan altar and image of Zeus which

Antiochus IV Epiphanes is said to have erected in the temple. In A.D. 39 the emperor Caligula ordered that an image of himself be placed in the Jewish sanctuary. Others suggest that in both cases the reference may be to a stele (Hebrew *matsebah*) or small stone altar representing the deity and placed upon the great altar of sacrifices in the temple court. (WB, V, 67; WMTS, 263)

Mt 26:27 —— *he took a cup* A great sensation was created in 1931 by the exhibition in Paris of a vessel which had been found in the hands of some antiquarians in Antioch. It was promptly named the Chalice of Antioch and is now kept in the Metropolitan Museum of Art in New York. It is made of silver and is beautifully decorated. Its reliefs include two depictions of Christ, as well as of ten other persons of uncertain identity. All of them are surrounded by vines, clusters of grapes, and various symbols: sheep, doves, an eagle, a basket, and other symbols. Inside, there is a plain cup, also of silver, but perhaps older than the container, which is considered to be from the fourth or fifth century A.D. Some claim that the cup inside could well be the very one which was used by Christ in the Last Supper and the institution of the Eucharist. This claim caused understandable excitement the world over. According to its proponents, the cup would have been recovered and perhaps miraculously transported from Jerusalem to Antioch, where it would have been preserved in the chalice richly made for it. But other ancient pieces of religious silverwork from old Syria exhibit similar elaborate decoration, so that the Chalice of Antioch does not seem, after all, quite so extraordinary. At present no serious archaeologist considers the inner cup of the chalice to be the legendary and much sought, but never found, Holy Grail. (LOC, 111–12; BAW, 251–52)

Mt 26:36 —— *a place called Gethsemane* References in the Gospels indicate that this memorable place was a garden or orchard across the Kidron Valley on the slope of the Mount of Olives. From the circumstances of Jesus' arrest one may infer that it was located at the foot of the mount. Its site was undoubtedly more or less in the area where the garden of this name may be seen today. The biblical references coincide with its location. The present garden contains large and very old olive trees, lawns, and flowerpots. Everything is looked after with painstaking care by the Franciscans who own the place. Their church and annex monastery adjoin the garden. The church, dedicated in 1924, is a type of basilica of modern architecture. It is called the Church of the Agony, the Church of All Nations, and more popularly the Church of Gethsemane. Previous excavations on the site uncovered the remains of a basilica from the fourth century A.D., when Emperor Theodosius ruled. From the *Onomasticon* of Eusebius we know that before such a church existed there, Christians frequented the place for prayer, so that the tradition about it seems to date at least from the third century A.D. The Persians destroyed this basilica in 614, and it remained in ruins until the crusaders built another church there in the twelfth century A.D. The remains of this church have also been identified. The present basilica was built along the same lines as the Byzantine structure, but with some enlargement. The so-called Rock of the Agony, upon which tradition supposes that the Lord prayed, has been preserved in the apse before the altar. Across the main road leading to the summit of the Mount of Olives and near a chapel which is said to contain the tomb of the Virgin Mary, there is a place called Grotto of the Agony. It is supposedly the place which gave shelter to the rest of the apostles while Jesus and the three withdrew to pray. It was in front of this grotto that Jesus is said to have been arrested. On the same rock where this cave is found, archaeologists found the remains of an oil press with a cistern and channels for water. Gethsemane, a name derived from the Aramaic *gat shemani*, refers to a press used for the extraction of olive oil. The Greek word used by Matthew and Mark to designate the place literally means "farm" and not specifically a garden for beauty or recreation. John 18:1 says that Jesus and his disciples "entered" the garden. This may indicate that it was enclosed by a wall. If so, Jesus no doubt had the owner's permission (could he have been a secret disciple?) to go there with his disciples.

When Titus besieged Jerusalem, he undoubtedly destroyed all the trees, including those in Gethsemane and on the entire slope of the mount. The eight olive trees found at present in the garden may be close to a thousand years old, and it is possible that they sprouted from the roots of the ones which were growing there at the time of the Lord's agony. (TANT, 104–8; EB, I, 224–28; III, 871–76; IDB, II, 387; LOC, 114; IFJ, 176–78, illustrations)

Mt 26:74 —— *And immediately the cock crowed.* East of the site where according to tradition the Upper Room was located, and some 820 feet from it down the slope of the so-called Mount Zion, stands a beautiful modern church of the Assumptionist Fathers. It was dedicated in 1931 and is known as the Church of St. Peter in Gallicantu (*in galli cantu* is Latin for "when the cock crowed"). The excavations carried out at the site in 1888 and 1911 uncovered the ruins of a church of the fifth century A.D., judging by coins found among the ruins. The monk Epiphanius (eighth century A.D.) mentions the existence of another church at the site "where Peter, when he went out, wept bitterly" (verse 75). Other visitors, such as the monk Bernard (A.D. 870), Saewulf (A.D. 1102), Daniel (A.D. 1107), and the so-called Anonymous VII (A.D. 1145), mentioned the same place. On the other hand, the Pilgrim of Bordeaux (A.D. 333) was shown another place on Mount Zion as "the house of Caiaphas." It was already in ruins, as indicated by Cyril some years afterward. Theodosius (A.D. 530) talks about a "Church of St. Peter" in what had been "the house of Caiaphas," and he says that this house was "50 paces more or less" from the Church of Holy Zion. This place has been recently excavated (see comment on Lk 22:54). Does the tradition contradict itself by pointing out two different places for the incident of Peter? It seems the difference is clarified by distinguishing between the place of Peter's denial, which according to the Gospels did occur in the court of Caiaphas' house, and the place "outside," where he withdrew to weep over his denial. This could have been in the area of the present Church of St. Peter in Gallicantu. (TANT, 152–54; LOC, 117)

Mt 27:2 —— *delivered him to Pilate the governor.* In the 1961 excavations in the ruins of the Roman theater at Caesarea, a slab was found with a badly damaged inscription. (The stone had been used in a landing for a flight of steps.) The legible remaining part of the inscription reads in part, *Tiberieum . . . [Pon]tius Pilatus . . . [Praef]ectus Iuda[ea]e.* This is the only inscription bearing Pilate's name which so far has been discovered. From the traces left by the marred letters, it seems that the complete inscription was "Pontius Pilate, the Prefect of Judea, has dedicated to the people of Caesarea a temple in honor of Tiberius." Pilate is here not called "Procurator," as historians refer to him, for Roman governors assumed this title only after the time of the emperor Claudius. Thus Pilate is called "Procurator" only in retrospect. (TANT, 80; MTL, 81–82)

Mt 27:24 —— *he took water and washed his hands* In 1960 the caves in the ravines near the Dead Sea were explored. In some of them the last freedom fighters of the second Jewish revolt under the leadership of Bar Kokhba took refuge from the Romans. A bronze basin and pitcher (or jug) used for personal cleaning were found among the objects taken by the rebels from the Romans. The utensils used by Pilate for his famous symbolic washing of hands must have been very similar. (WB, V, 75)

Mt 27:33 —— *a place called Golgotha* Archaeologists have not been able to identify with complete certainty the precise site of the crucifixion of Jesus. The place is not mentioned outside of the Gospels, and the only reference given for its location is that it was "near the city" (Jn 19:20). The author of the letter to the Hebrews says that Jesus "suffered outside the gate" (13:12). In view of Jerusalem's topography and the statement which indicates that the place must have been at the side of a road ("those who passed by derided him," 27:39), the crucifixion must have occurred to the west, north, or northwest of the city. It was also a place of gardens and tombs (Jn 19:41). This is in the same direction that the so-called Second Wall extended in Jesus' time. From Josephus we know that this wall "took its beginning from that gate which they called 'Genath,' which belonged to the first wall; it only encompassed the northern quarter of the city, and reached as far as the tower Antonia" (*War*, V, 4, 2). It has not been possible, however, to determine the precise course this wall followed between these two points. The First Wall went eastward almost in a straight line from the gate mentioned by Josephus until it reached the Temple Mount, and westward up to what now are the Citadel and Jaffa Gate. The present north wall, built by the Turks, probably follows the line of the so-called Third Wall, erected by Herod Agrippa after the time of Jesus.

Another serious problem in determining the location of Golgotha and the sepulcher nearby is that after the capture of Jerusalem by the Romans (A.D. 70) and above all in the time of Emperor Hadrian following the second Jewish insurrection (A.D. 132–35), this site, as well as many others in the city, was razed and leveled. This was done in order to make Jerusalem a typical Roman city with the name of *Aelia Capitolina*. An old Christian tradition offered Emperor Constantine the basis for constructing on the site a basilica, which was later expanded and modified by the crusaders. This is the present

Church of the Holy Sepulcher, situated outside the line followed by the wall in Jesus' time, but now within the area encompassed by the Turkish wall. In this church tourists are shown what are claimed to be the precise locations of the crucifixion, the embalming, and the interment of Jesus, but these are probably matters of pious fiction. Nevertheless, in spite of the existing uncertainty, scholars generally agree that Golgotha and the sepulcher were probably situated in the area where the Church of the Holy Sepulcher stands today. Strong archaeological support for this conclusion comes from recent excavations of a quarry found south of the church on the site called Muristan and under the neighboring Lutheran Church of the Redeemer. Since this place was a quarry, it was undoubtedly outside the walls.

In 1842 the German traveler Otto Thenius proposed as the true Calvary a promontory situated north of the present Damascus Gate, above the so-called Grotto of Jeremiah, which had served as a quarry and showed two hollows or caves which at a distance resemble the eye sockets of a skull. His proposal apparently found no acceptance. Then in 1867 the owner of a tract of land at the foot of this promontory found a tomb carved in the rock. On one of its walls two Greek crosses painted in red were seen (one of them is still visible today). His discovery, however, did not attract much attention at the time. But in 1883 the English general Charles G. Gordon, who was visiting Jerusalem, noticed the promontory and revived this forgotten theory of Thenius with such convincing enthusiasm that an agitated controversy was stirred up. The promontory even received the name Gordon's Calvary. The tomb discovered in 1867 was then associated with it, and it also came to be considered the true "Holy Sepulcher." The Church of England became interested in the site, and so purchased, cleared, and remodeled it. The tomb came to be called the Garden Tomb. But this and other tombs in the vicinity really belong to the Byzantine period, as is evidenced by some epitaphs found in them. Both sites continue to be shown to tourists, but there is no archaeological evidence granting either of them any authenticity. In the polemic the validity of the Garden Tomb has lost out. Parrot believes that it is "necessary to say again, in the most categorical terms, that nothing was ever more certain than that the Garden Tomb is a myth. One hopes that no sensible person will ever again be misled by it."

Concerning the site under the Church of the Holy Sepulcher, his conclusion is as follows: "While it seems that in all likelihood the traditional site of Golgotha and the tomb of Jesus are to be considered as authentic, it must be added at once that very little of it is visible today under the building which covers and masks it." (IDB, II, 439; EB, II, 56–59; III, 930; GCH, 15–83; TANT, 173–74; BRA, 97)

Mt 27:35 —— *And when they had crucified him* An impressive discovery was made in 1968 in the northeastern suburb of Jerusalem called Givat ha-Mivtar. A cemetery was opened there from which 36 skeletal remains were uncovered. One of them was the first remains of a crucified man ever found anywhere—a really striking discovery. It was preserved in an ossuary and belonged to a man 5½ feet tall and between the ages of twenty-four and twenty-eight years when he was crucified. This took place sometime during the first half of the first century A.D., perhaps in the very time of Jesus. What attracted immediate and moving attention was the manner of the crucifixion. Both heels had been pierced by a single large and crude iron nail. His open arms had been nailed in the way shown in traditional crucifixion paintings, but he had not been crucified in a vertical position. His knees had been doubled up and turned sideways, and he was rather in a sitting position. It must have been an extremely painful posture. His shins, moreover, had been intentionally broken. The man's name, Johanan, was inscribed on the ossuary. There is no way of knowing the way in which Jesus was crucified, whether in this same manner or as traditionally represented. Anyway, the pathetic discovery of the skeleton of the crucified man in Givat ha-Mivtar is evidence of how cruel and inhuman crucifixion could be. (MTL, 228; BAH, 33–34)

Mt 27:60 —— *a great stone to the door of the tomb* Only two examples have been found so far of such a stone used to seal the entrance to a cave-tomb. A somewhat worn-out stone may be seen at the entrance of the tomb of Queen Helen of Adiabene, commonly called the Tombs of the Kings, in Jerusalem, north of the walled quarter. The other can be found at the entrance of Herod's family tomb near the modern King David Hotel. The stone was rolled down a sloping groove cut in the rock. This made the closing of the tomb relatively easy, but the strength of several men would be required to roll it "uphill" when opening the tomb. This explains why the women on their way to Jesus' tomb were worried about how to get the stone rolled away (Mk 16:3). (WB, V, 78; GSS, 74–76; MTL, 229)

Mt 28:13 —— *came by night and stole him away* What the Jewish dignitaries instructed the soldiers to say was not something at all difficult to believe in those days. Long before then violations of sepulchers had been common in Palestine, as also in Egypt. A decree made by Caesar Augustus against any who would damage sepulchers and remove the corpses to bury them elsewhere has been discovered in Palestine. A copy of this imperial decree was inscribed on a slab of stone which supposedly originated in Nazareth. The transgression of this decree was punishable by death. The knowledge of such a law could account for some of the excitement of the women before the empty tomb, for they too supposed that their Lord's body had been stolen. (WB, V, 79; LOC, 134)

MARK

Mk 2:26 —— *when Abiathar was high priest* This phrase does not appear in the parallel passages of Matthew 12:4 and Luke 6:4. According to 1 Samuel 21:1 and following, the high priest was not Abiathar but Ahimelech. Some important Greek manuscripts, such as Codex Washingtonius (fifth century A.D.) and Codex Bezae (sixth century A.D.), some ancient versions, and certain manuscripts from the Middle Ages do not have this phrase either, but it is supported by the manuscripts of greater authority. The appearance of this phrase in what is undoubtedly the oldest extant form of the Greek text may possibly be explained on the assumption that originally it was a marginal note written by a copyist or a reader, but from memory and wrongly, and afterward interpolated by a later copyist who thought it belonged to the original text. (WMTS, 37)

Mk 6:27 —— *the king sent a soldier of the guard* The Greek word here translated "soldier of the guard" is *spekoulator*, a loan from the Latin *speculator* (literally "observer"). In the Roman army this designation was originally given to a scout, messenger, or spy. In time the word also came to mean a royal official who served as the king's confidential assistant and bodyguard. Sometimes he was trusted with the execution of a culprit of special standing or character. Finally the word assumed the meaning "executioner." In the column erected at Rome in honor of the Emperor Marcus Aurelius, a bas-relief represents a "speculator" standing on guard at the entrance to the emperor's tent. (WB, V, 88)

Mk 6:29 —— *his disciples . . . took his body* The passage does not say where John was buried, nor does the parallel in Matthew 14:12. Likewise, the text does not indicate whether or not the disciples recovered the severed head of John and buried it with the body. An ancient tradition holds that the burial took place at Samaria. According to this tradition the body, including the head, would have been brought from the fortress at Machaerus, situated east of the Dead Sea. Two churches in Samaria, both of Byzantine origin, were dedicated to John. The first is at the site where the mosque stands today. The ruins of the second were discovered during the excavations of 1931. A Greek tradition and the narratives of medieval pilgrims speak of the place where John the Baptist's head was buried. According to other traditions it was taken as far as Constantinople or Damascus. At the Mosque of the Umayyads in Damascus a shrine with a marble dome is said to contain John's head. (SCKI, 122–27; TANT, 15–17)

Mk 7:11 —— *is Corban* In the course of the excavations carried out by Mazar in 1969 along the foot of the present southern wall of the Temple Mount, a polished fragment of pavement stone was found bearing the Hebrew inscription *qrbn* ("corban") and the incised representations of two birds. According to Mazar this stone dates from the seventh century B.C., which indicates the antiquity of the concept expressed in Mark. The general sense of the word *corban* in the Old Testament is "offering" or "donation," understood as something promised to God. The word appears only in Leviticus, Numbers, and Ezekiel. In the inscription found by Mazar the birds refer to the offering prescribed in Leviticus 12:8 (compare Lk 2:24). The same word appears also in an inscription found on an ossuary by J. T. Milik near Bir-Ayyub. Joseph A. Fitzmyer says about this, "The use of *qrbn* in the ossuary inscription is identical with that preserved in the Greek of *Mark*. . . . We have to do with a dedicatory formula in common use among the Jews of the last centuries B.C. and well into Christian times." (MTL, 108; RQ, 8 [1975], 493)

Mk 7:26 —— *Syrophoenician by birth.* In the so-called Sarcophagus of the Wailing Women from Sidon (kept in the Istanbul Museum), it is interesting to see the long and elegant vestments worn by the women of Tyre and Sidon in those times. (LOC, 56)

Mk 7:31 —— *through the region of the Decapolis.* This region is mentioned only two other times in the Gospels, and nowhere else in the rest of the New Testament. The name is Greek for "Ten Cities." Decapolis comprised a region from the southeastern half of the Sea of Galilee to Philadelphia (now called Amman) in Transjordan. Jesus visited only the portion near the Sea of Galilee. The demoniac healed by Jesus was a Gadarene or Gerasene (the manuscript evidence is mixed) from Gadara or from Gerasa (modern Jerash), two of the cities of the Decapolis. There are very important ruins at Jerash, a site farther south but apparently never visited by Jesus. The region of Decapolis was first Hellenized and later Romanized. (TANT, 61–70)

Mk 13:1 —— *Look, Teacher, what wonderful stones and what wonderful buildings!* Among the many buildings which Herod the Great built, the temple was outstanding in size and magnificence. Nothing is left of it now except stretches of the monumental wall retaining the esplanade where the temple once stood. Even these remnants rightly excite the admiration of everyone who sees them. The most famous part is the Western Wall, traditionally called the Wailing Wall, perhaps the holiest of the places sacred to Judaism. It is formed of enormous stone blocks 9 to 15 feet long and 3 to 4 feet high. One of these blocks is even 36 feet long, and there is one which weighs nearly a hundred tons and measures 21 by 6 feet. (WB, V, 95; MTL, 131–32; TANT, 126–27)

Mk 13:2 —— *There will not be left here one stone upon another* Jesus' immediate reference was to the temple buildings which were completely razed by the Romans in A.D. 70, but he may have been referring to the entire city. The historian Josephus testifies to the total destruction of Jerusalem and archaeological excavations confirm the disaster. The Romans demolished completely and then leveled off the accumulated debris, especially near the western and southern walls of the Temple Mount. The Central Valley (Tyropoeon) was filled up. The destruction was consummated when in the following century Emperor Publius Aelius Hadrian undertook to replace the Jewish Jerusalem by a typical Roman colony, which he named Aelia Capitolina in honor of himself. He built a temple to Jupiter on the very spot where the Second Temple had stood. He also built public baths, a theater, a forum, porticoes, and other buildings. Of the

Jerusalem of Jesus' time literally "not . . . one stone upon another" was left. (MTL, 232-43)

Mk 13:3 —— *he sat on the Mount of Olives opposite the temple* In the fourth century A.D., after Constantine adopted Christianity as the state religion, there was great enthusiasm to identify as many as possible of the places associated with the life of Jesus. It was then that a church called Eleona was built over a grotto where Jesus supposedly pronounced his discourse concerning the end of the age. Excavations started in 1910 uncovered scanty remains of this church, as well as of the crypt into which the grotto was converted. If, as the biblical passage seems to imply, Jesus and his disciples were looking at the temple and the whole of Jerusalem, it does not seem likely that they were sitting or standing inside of a cave. It is indeed interesting that so many "holy places" were located by tradition as being in caves, which are so abundant in the Holy Land. Perhaps the sense of mystery associated with a cave produced this tendency. The magnificent model of Jerusalem at the time of Jesus exhibited at the Holyland Hotel in modern Jerusalem gives an impressive idea of how Jerusalem must have appeared in New Testament times. (TANT, 95-97)

Mk 14:3 —— *an alabaster flask* Archaeological and literary evidence reveals that in the Hellenistic period jars for perfume, originally of alabaster, were replaced by glass jars. But these continued to be called "alabasters." They were sealed when purchased and were opened by breaking. This is why Mark very properly says that she broke the jar, a detail not recorded in Matthew 26:7, the parallel passage. (WMTS, 263-64)

Mk 14:15 —— *a large upper room* The "Upper Room" (sometimes called Cenacle, from the term employed in St. Jerome's Latin version) is believed to have been situated on the southwestern hill in Jerusalem. (This hill was called Mount Zion, although in earlier times Zion was applied to the southeastern hill, also known as the City of David.) The location of the "Upper Room" in this area is one of the oldest Christian traditions. Epiphanius (fourth century A.D.) says that when Emperor Hadrian visited the city in A.D. 130 he found on Mount Zion "the church of God, which was small, where the disciples, when they had returned after the Savior had ascended from the Mount of Olives, went to the upper room." It is almost certain that this "upper room" and the "Upper Room" and the meeting place on Pentecost (Acts 1:13) were one and the same. Very probably it was in the house of Mary, the mother of John Mark (Acts 12:12). By the second century this may well have been made into a chapel. Cyril of Jerusalem spoke in A.D. 348 of an "Upper Church," or the upper story, by then perhaps a basilica. Theodosius called it in A.D. 530 the "Holy Zion," and it is probably the basilica which appears in the Madaba Map (A.D. 560), the one mentioned by Arculf (A.D. 670) and of which he draws a sketch, and the one mentioned by Eutychius of Alexandria in the tenth century A.D. During all of this time it must certainly have suffered important modifications.

Excavations carried out there in 1899 uncovered the remains of a Byzantine church, of which a whole column is preserved. This church undoubtedly dates from the fourth century A.D. Moreover, in several tombs discovered in that area the name of this "Holy Zion" church appears. The crusaders reconstructed the church and called it the Church of Zion or the Church of St. Mary. Already at that time, on the lower floor, which seems to have been an ancient synagogue, the tomb of David was traditionally located. The Franciscans acquired the place in the fourteenth century A.D. and modified the second-floor room by adding columns and vaults of Gothic style. A small mosque came into existence nearby. The rest of the church of "Holy Zion" disappeared. What the visitor sees there today is the supposed tomb of David and the fourteenth-century A.D. Gothic room which is the traditional site of the Upper Room. Perhaps the most that can be said with any certainty is that, in view of this ancient tradition, the Upper Room was located somewhere in this area of Mount Zion. (TANT, 147–52; LOC, 109–10; IFJ, 171–73)

LUKE

Lk 1:39 —— *into the hill country, to a city of Judah* Data which might permit the exact identification of John the Baptist's birthplace are lacking. The Greek word *oreinē* ("hill country"), according to evidence from Pliny, designated the mountainous region in which Jerusalem is located. An ancient tradition, maintained until modern times, locates the home of Zechariah and Elizabeth in the modern town of Ain Karim (or Ein Karem, "Spring of the Vineyard"), some 4⅔ miles west of Jerusalem. Since the Byzantine period there have been chapels or shrines on the site. The present Church of St. John the Baptist dates from the eleventh century A.D. Another one, also very old, is the Church of the Visitation. From another (and a less probable) tradition there were in the Arab period two churches dedicated to St. John the Baptist on the Mount of Olives, one at the summit and the other at the foot. The excavations have found at Ain Karim remains of the structures from the Byzantine and medieval periods. (TANT, 3–5; IFJ, 22–25, 59)

Lk 2:2 —— *when Quirinius was governor of Syria.* There is documentary evidence that a census was taken in A.D. 6, when Quirinius was the Roman legate in Syria. But there is a problem with respect to Luke's reference, according to which Jesus would have been born during a census carried out under this imperial official. From a papyrus published by the British Museum we now know that a census was taken every fourteen years, so that toward 8 B.C., while Herod was still reigning, there was a census during which Jesus could have been born. We also know from some inscriptions that

218

about the same time Quirinius was in the Middle East. He could very well have served also as legate. (WMTS, 282)

Lk 2:7 —— *laid him in a manger* According to a tradition dating from at least the second century A.D., the place where Jesus was born is a grotto in Bethlehem, over which the present Church of the Nativity stands. Already in A.D. 135 the site was venerated, for at that time the emperor Hadrian installed there the cult of the god Adonis-Tamuz, the Phoenician patron of vegetation, in order to discourage Christians from visiting it. In the fourth century A.D. Constantine had a basilica built on the site. Its choir, which Justinian repaired in the sixth century A.D., stands precisely over the grotto. The five naves of the Constantinian basilica remain practically intact and form part of the present structure. Excavations have brought to light the general outline and the floor mosaics of Constantine's basilica. (LOC, 5–6; EB, I, 1103; TANT, 18–26)

Lk 2:38 —— *the redemption of Jerusalem.* The concept of the liberation or redemption of the Holy City from the hands of the Roman oppressors was deeply rooted in the Jewish soul of the first century A.D. Coins minted during the Jewish rebellion and armed struggle against Rome have been found which bear the inscription "The redemption of Jerusalem." The same Jewish expectation also appears in one of the hymns preserved in the scrolls of Qumran:

Your hopes, O Zion, are great indeed,
For your expectation of redemption and peace will come true. . . .
[MTL, 95]

Lk 2:42 —— *And when he was twelve years old* At this age Jesus made his first visit to the temple of Jerusalem with his father and mother. Before entering the sanctuary it was obligatory to purify oneself with water. During the excavations at the southern approach to the Temple Mount a number of ritual baths or individual pools (Hebrew *mikveh*) were found. They were used for ceremonial purification by immersion. Jesus must have complied with this requirement and used one of them or one like them, not only on this his first visit but also on successive occasions whenever as an adult he visited the temple in the company of his disciples.

As already mentioned, no remains of the Herodian temple proper have so far been found (see the comments on Mk 13:1). However, the *Jerusalem Post* in its issue of March 21, 1980, reported that several Israeli experts claimed that remains of what seemed to be part of the eastern wall of the temple building had been found as far back as 1970. According to the report, this discovery had occurred when the Supreme Mohammedan Council was conducting some excavations at a water reservoir on the Temple Mount. The place, according to this report, coincided almost exactly with the site where A. Kaufman had identified the eastern wall of the temple complex on the basis of information from ancient sources and of scientific calculations. A lively discussion followed the first announcement of this find. Some archaeologists expressed interest and encouraged Kaufman, but others were skeptical. Further excavations have been prevented by the fact that the site is sacred to the Muslims. Avigad, Dan Bahat, and Meir Ben-Dov did not believe that Kaufman had proved his case. Mazar declined to comment. The excitement about this supposed find seems now to have subsided. (MTL, 146)

Lk 3:1 ―― *and Lysanias tetrarch of Abilene*   There is a problem in harmonizing Luke's reference with the fact that the Lysanias mentioned by Josephus died in 34 B.C. But an inscription has been discovered which shows that there was another and later Lysanias of Abilene, to whom Luke could very well have referred, although exact dates concerning him are not known. (WMTS, 282)

Lk 4:17 ―― *He unrolled the scroll*   (GNB; RSV: "he opened the book.") The most important biblical scroll of Qumran is the almost complete copy of Isaiah (1QIs^a). It has fewer than a dozen small gaps and a few missing fragments on its lower edges. The reverse side preserves in perfectly visible form even the traces left by the frequent handling as it was unrolled and then rolled again as the reading proceeded. The scroll used by Jesus for his reading at the synagogue was surely very similar to this one. The Qumran Isaiah scroll, together with other Qumran manuscripts, is kept at the "Shrine of the Book" in Jerusalem.

Lk 7:5 ―― *and he built us our synagogue.*   Among the ruins of ancient Capernaum the most imposing is that of a synagogue built about A.D. 200 or early in the third century A.D. Since the custom was to build a new synagogue precisely on the site of a previous one (Maimonides stated that such was the tradition), one may assume that this synagogue was located at the same place as the one of the time of Jesus. A limited excavation in 1953–54 made under the synagogue's southeastern corner uncovered some black basalt blocks, which are probably part of the foundation of the synagogue which Jesus attended and which was possibly the one given by the friendly Roman centurion to the Jews. (TANT, 51–54; WB, V, 112)

Lk 10:34 —— *and brought him to an inn*   On the road from Jericho to Jerusalem there is a pass called by the Arabs *talat ed-damm* ("Ascent of Blood"). This is almost surely the "ascent of Adummim" (Hebrew *maaleh adummim*) of Joshua 15:7; 18:17. At this place stands a police post of modern construction, which according to tradition is the site of the "Inn of the Good Samaritan." Some tourist guides do not hesitate to refer to it as such. However, a small fort has existed in this place since the Byzantine period. The crusaders had a castle on the hill above the pass. St. Jerome explained that the pass had this name as the result of all the blood the robbers in the area had shed in their frequent assaults on travelers. St. Jerome also says that this is the place to which the Lord referred in his parable of the Good Samaritan. Even if it is impossible to identify either the exact spot where the attack described in the parable took place or the site where the inn stood, Jesus probably had such places in mind as the setting of his story. The area is desolate, barren, and eerie, and there are many caves which easily became the haunts of criminals. Moreover this area has had to be carefully guarded against since the ancient times—and even today. (TANT, 87–88; LOC, 69)

Lk 11:2 —— *When you pray, say*   The Church of the Lord's Prayer, built on the summit of the Mount of Olives and on the spot where a medieval chapel existed, marks the place where, according to a relatively late tradition, Jesus is said to have taught his disciples the Lord's Prayer. To commemorate this event, the prayer appears today inscribed in the cloister of the adjoining monastery. It is written in Aramaic, a language spoken by the Lord, and in over forty other languages. As for the place where the prayer was first pronounced, one should note that Matthew includes it in the Sermon on the Mount. (TANT, 97)

Lk 12:19 —— *eat, drink, be merry.*   In this parable the Lord was using a popular saying which was not only very common but also very ancient. In the Mesopotamian myth of Gilgamesh, whose earliest elements date back to 2000 B.C., the goddess Sabitu advises the hero, "Drink, eat, make merry." Before launching his offensive against Elam, Ashurbanipal (seventh century B.C.) consults the goddess Ishtar of Arbela, and through the soothsayer she answers, "Eat, drink, make merry." When in 333 B.C., Alexander was near Tarsus preparing for his attack on the Persian army (the battle of Isso), one of his commanders discovered a monument to the memory of Sardanapalus. In it he read, with the help of an interpreter, "Sardanapalus, the son of Anakyndaraxe, has defeated both Anchiale and Tarsus in a single day. Eat, drink, make merry. The rest is worth nothing." It is strange that the second part is found on an inscription of that nature. Maurice Vieyra, who has registered these quotations, thinks for that reason that the advice to eat, drink, and make merry may have been a comment by the interpreter about Sardanapalus, which the commander could have taken as part of the inscription. The monument has disappeared, so the inscription cannot be checked. At any rate, the story shows how ancient and common the saying was. (LTR, 63–65)

Lk 13:4 —— *the tower in Siloam*   Northeast of the pool of Siloam, but on the western edge of the Kidron Valley, can be seen a circular foundation of what must have been a tower. Some authorities suggest that these may be the remains of the tower mentioned by Jesus. Others believe that the tower may have been part of the wall which, according to Josephus, surrounded the city on the south at that time and which, he says, had a "bending above the fountain Siloam" (*War*, V, 4, 2). The present southern wall runs much farther up. (TCD, 104–7; TANT, 114)

Lk 19:1 —— *He [Jesus] entered Jericho*   The Jericho of that time was located a mile or so to the south of the Jericho of the Old Testament (Tell el-Sultan, see comment on Josh 6:20). It spread out on both sides of Wadi el-Qelt, through which the old road to Jerusalem passed. This later Jericho already existed in the Maccabean period, but it was Herod the Great who, in making it his winter capital, gave to it new and magnificent constructions, which Archelaus continued. Its ruins occupy the mounds called Tulul Abu el-Alayiq, excavated in 1950 and 1951. Remains of an Arab fortress of the ninth or tenth century A.D. were found there and also Herodian walls and ruins of a tower of the Hellenistic period. Among the

Herodian walls which existed in Jesus' day, a feature of special interest is a façade of a type of architecture called by the Romans *opus reticulatum*. It consists of small square stones put together in such a way as to give the impression of a net (*reticulum*). The Jericho of today is situated southeast of the Wadi el-Qelt. Its present location dates from the time of the crusaders. The city of Jesus' time continued in its location until the end of the reign of Agrippa I (A.D. 44). It was not again settled until the eighth century A.D. (TANT, 81–86; EB, IV, 34–45)

Lk 19:41 —— *when he drew near and saw the city he wept over it* From any point on the western slope of the Mount of Olives the view of Jerusalem is impressive. The same was true in Jesus' day. On the more direct and steeper route of descent (the main descent today is farther to the north) and as one is about to enter the Kidron Valley, there is the small and beautiful chapel called Dominus Flebit ("the Lord Wept"). It is said to be built on the spot where Jesus looked at the city and wept. The tradition about this seems to be very old, for in 1954 the ruins of a Byzantine church were found under the chapel. The main literary witnesses, however, are from the Middle Ages. (TANT, 100–1; IFJ, 163)

Lk 22:25 —— *those . . . are called benefactors.* There is literary and archaeological evidence that "benefactor" (Greek *euergetes*) was a title given to kings and other prominent persons. Antigonus (Alexander's general), Trajan, Alexander Balas, Antiocus VII Sidetes, and Gaius Stertinius Xenophon (the physician of Emperor Claudius), were among those who bore this title. An inscription in the synagogue at Nitria, which was dedicated to the king Ptolemy VII (143–116 B.C.) and his queen Cleopatra, called them "Benefactors." Ptolemy's complete official title was *Theos Éuergetes* ("Beneficent God"), but the Jews, of course, did not recognize him as a divinity. (WB, V, 130)

Lk 22:54 —— *bringing him into the high priest's house.* An old Christian tradition, dating at least from the beginning of the fourth century A.D. (from a narrative of the anonymous "Pilgrim of Burdeos") locates "the house of Caiaphas" on Mount Zion, south of the gate of the same name and on the premises of the present Armenian Monastery of St. Saviour. The 1971 excavations directed by Magen

Broshi uncovered ruins from Herod's time. Among them are two vaulted rooms, which are identified as belonging to the house of Caiaphas. Broshi believes that the Christian tradition is "historically valid." In the excavations was found a Byzantine mosaic floor measuring 13 to 16 feet long by 8 feet wide. There also is a threshold at such a distance from the mosaic that together they might indicate a building which could have been the Church of St. Peter (see comment on Mt 26:74), some 100 to 115 feet long. (AR, 25, 46–48; TANT, 153; ABB, 291)

Lk 23:7 —— *And when he learned that he belonged to Herod's jurisdiction, he sent him over to Herod* One cannot determine whether the trial of Jesus before Pilate took place in the tower of Antonia or in Herod's palace. When a Roman governor visited Jerusalem, he was usually lodged in the palace. But it is quite possible that he officially presided over affairs at the Antonia, possibly in order to be closer at hand in case disorders should break out during the festivities at the temple. At any rate, Luke states that Jesus appeared before Herod, and this must have been at the palace which this king built west of the city. This area, to the south and at the side of the Jaffa Gate, is now called the Citadel. There is no doubt about the identification of this palace. The excavations carried out by Amiran and A. Eitan in 1968–69 expanded those by C. N. Johns in 1934–48 and uncovered considerable portions of the palace's ruins, as well as remains from the previous Hasmonean and Roman-Byzantine periods. The structures built by the crusaders, the Mamelukes, and the Turks are more visible and had been previously identified. The so-called Tower of David, built by the crusaders, stands at a considerable height, on what was left of the Herodian tower of Phasael. More and more biblical and archaeological authorities are accepting the views of Bahat and Broshi about this palace: "We subscribe to the view that, after Herod Archelaus was deposed (in 6 C.E.), the palace was made the seat of the Roman procurator while in Jerusalem, and that it was also the location of the praetorium—the location of the judgment and sentencing of Jesus." The exact site of the praetorium has not been identified among the ruins of the several buildings which formed the palace. Nor can one determine the place which would have been the audience hall of Herod, in which Jesus appeared before him. But according to Luke's record Jesus must have stood somewhere among these structures which the excavations have brought to light. (JR, 52–56; TANT, 133–34; MTL, 78–80)

Lk 24:13 —— *a village named Emmaus* The identification of this place remains uncertain. According to the Greek text of this passage, based on the Bodmer Papyrus XIV (p75, of the third century A.D.), the Codex Vaticanus (fourth century A.D.), the Codex Alexandrinus (fifth century A.D.), and other witnesses, Emmaus was at a distance of 60 stadia ("about seven miles," RSV) from Jerusalem. It could thus be identified with modern el-Qubeibeh (Arabic for "Little Dome"), where the crusaders found in 1099 a Roman fortress called Castellum Emmaus. In 1852 the Franciscans found the ruins of an ancient church there. Taking for granted that this was the site of the New Testament Emmaus, they purchased the place and built there a monastery and church in 1902. The village of Quloniye has also been mentioned as possibly being the site of Emmaus. Quloniye is an adaptation of Latin *Colonia*. It is the Mozah of Joshua 18:26 and the Ammaus of Josephus where Vespasian's veterans settled after the fall of Jerusalem in A.D. 70. Since the village is only 4 miles west of Jerusalem, its location does not coincide with that of Emmaus according to the ancient Greek manuscripts mentioned previously. Other manuscripts, including Codex Sinaiticus (fourth century A.D.), read in this passage 160 stadia (about 18 miles) rather than 60 stadia. On the basis of this reading the village of Amwas (or Imwas) has been proposed as the biblical Emmaus. This village is on the ancient road from Jerusalem to Jaffa (Yafo). After A.D. 70 the Romans called it Nicopolis; the church historian Eusebius identifies this place as the biblical Emmaus. The Ecole Biblique of Jerusalem started excavations at Amwas in 1875, and completed the work in 1924–30. Ruins were found of a small crusaders' church, and beneath them the remains of both a great and a small basilica, as well as of a baptistry. As can readily be seen, the evidence for one or another identification seems to be evenly balanced, and the preference for one or the other depends largely on the authority attributed to the different forms of the Greek text. (TANT, 177–78; WB, V, 132)

JOHN

Jn 2:1 —— *a marriage at Cana in Galilee* The location of Cana is uncertain. The village called Kefr Kenna (or Kanna), a little over 4 miles northeast of Nazareth, is the site usually indicated, and it has the support of an ancient tradition. It is now believed, however, that the more probable location is Khirbet Qana, a ruin some 9 miles north of Nazareth, on the top of a hill bordering the plain of Netophah. This site has not yet been excavated, but a medieval tradition and some passages in Josephus and Eusebius seem to favor this identification. (WB, V, 138; BAW, 239–40; EB, II, 78, favors Kefr Kenna; IDB, I, 493, is for Khirbet Qana)

Jn 2:20 —— *It has taken forty-six years to build this temple* There is at present no archaeological data that confirms this length of time for the construction of the temple, but ancient literary sources do support it. Josephus states in one passage that the work was begun in 23 B.C. and in another in 20 B.C. This latter date coincides with what is said here in John, and it is supported by Talmudic references (*Sanhedrin* 41.2 and *Aboda-Zara* 8.2). The dialogue recorded by John would have occurred toward 26 B.C. The construction had continued after Herod's death, according to his plan. Even at the time of the first great Jewish revolt in A.D. 66 the work was still going on, but this revolt put a stop to it. (Josephus, *War*, I, 21, 1; *Antiquities*, XV, 11, 1; MTL, 112)

Jn 4:6 —— *Jacob's well* At the entrance to the ravine that separates Mount Ebal from Mount Gerizim there is a Greek Orthodox church, construction of which began in 1903 and which is still unfinished. A staircase, which is entered through an opening in the floor of the unroofed nave, leads down to a crypt where an old rim of a well is found. "Of all the 'Holy Places' of Palestine," writes Parrot, "none has more reason to be considered authentic than Jacob's Well." Excavations begun by the Greek Orthodox when they purchased the site uncovered the ruins of a church built there by the crusaders toward the end of the eleventh or the beginning of the twelfth century A.D. According to the story of Arculf's pilgrimage (A.D. 670), a church in the shape of a cross stood there at that time. Jacob's well (*fons Jacob*) was situated in the transept. St. Jerome's testimony is that there was a church on the site by the end of the fourth century A.D. The well is mentioned in the *Onomasticon* of Eusebius (beginning of the same century). The so-called Pilgrim of Bordeaux (A.D. 333) tells that a *balneus* (literally "bath") was filled with water from the well. The reference is probably to a baptismal font, but neither he nor Eusebius mentions a church there. The well is about 128 feet deep, and water can still be drawn from it and given to visitors to drink. "The well is deep," said the Samaritan woman to Jesus. (TANT, 36–42; LOC, 65–67)

Jn 4:20 —— *Our fathers worshiped on this mountain* The Samaritan woman referred to Mount Gerizim, especially to one of its summits, today called Tell er-Ras. At that time ruins of the Samaritan temple and its altar of sacrifices already existed. It had been destroyed by Hyrcanus in the second century B.C. Calculations made with surveying instruments confirm that these ruins could be clearly seen from Jacob's well, where Jesus and the Samaritan woman had their conversation. It is therefore very likely that when the woman mentioned the place, both she and Jesus would have turned to look up at the ruins. (BA, 38 [1975], 54–59)

Jn 5:2 —— *by the Sheep Gate a pool, . . . which has five porticoes.* North of the temple area and not far from the Lions' (or St. Stephen's) Gate stands the Church of St. Anne. It dates from the time of the Crusades. Close by and to the northwest of the church C. Schick carried out excavations in 1888 which uncovered the ruins of a basilica. This also dates from the time of the Crusades, and it was built upon the remains of a Byzantine chapel of the fifth century A.D. Under the ruins of both of these constructions are the remains of twin pools, one to the north and the other to the south. From descriptions provided by some early church fathers, the historian Eusebius, the Pilgrim of Bordeaux, as well as by other early pilgrims, there is no doubt that this is the site of the double pool where the healing of the paralytic took place. Four porticoes encircled both pools, and the fifth ran between. The best Greek manuscripts give the name of the place as Bethzatha, an Aramaic word understood by some to mean "House of the Olives." Other manuscripts call it Bethesda, a Hebrew name that might mean "House of Kindness." Still other sources give variants of the name such as Bezatha, Bezetha, and even Bethsaida. This last form may result from confusion with the name of the town north of the Sea of Galilee. In the copper scroll found with the Qumran manuscripts occurs the phrase "In *Betheshdathayim*, in the pool. . . ." Here the name bears the Hebrew dual form, which in Aramaic would be *Betheshdatha*, from which are derived both Bethesda and Bethzatha in the Greek transcription. In present-day tourist guides the name appears as the "Probatic Pool." This name is taken from the Greek *probatike* ("of the sheep"), transcribed in the Latin version (Vulgate) as *Probatica* (*piscina*). The traditional identification is practically certain, although there has been some discussion about it. Excavations at the site are going on under the direction of the White Fathers (Dominicans) of the Church of St. Anne. Those carried out since 1956 seem to indicate that the twin pools belonged to the Hasmonean period and that their use had already ceased before the time of Jesus. Another pool was built south of them (at the modern Lions' Gate). A cave situated east of the Probatic Pool is now frequently pointed out as the place of the healing of the paralytic. Waters from a nearby brook flowed into the pool. They were of a reddish color and were considered to be medicinal. However, the five porticoes and the seemingly intermittent flow of water of the scripture passage cannot be explained by reference to this cave. This is particularly so with respect to the porticoes. Nor can it explain the ancient tradition, which from very early times has continued to identify this place with more certainty than perhaps any other site associated with Jesus' life. Complete confirmation will depend on clarification as to whether or not the pools were really used at the time when the healing of the paralytic recorded by John took place. (TANT, 143–47; JR, 24; MTL, 202)

Jn 5:5 —— *ill for thirty-eight years.* In 1866 a votive offering in the shape of a foot was discovered not far from the so-called Probatic Pool. It bore the name *Pampeya Lucilia* and was offered in thankful remembrance of a healing. This votive offering indicates that sick people such as the paralytic in this passage did, in fact, come to this place seeking healing. This votive model of a foot is in the Louvre Museum. Numerous other votive offerings have been found in excavations at this site. The pool was at one time dedicated to Serapis and Asclepius, two deities of healing and medicine. (MLB, 145–46; LOC, 100)

Jn 7:14 —— *Jesus went up into the temple* Access to the temple was through four gates on the west, the so-called Huldah Gates on the south, a double gate toward the west, and a triple gate toward the east. They were openings in the wall, and by underground passages one ascended to the temple esplanade. Through the centuries, the Huldah Gates have remained visible, although they are walled up. One can also see the double gate, which is half covered where the Turkish southern wall joins the wall of the esplanade. Since access to the Royal Portico was gained through these gates, they seem to have been the main gates. The excavations begun in 1968 under the direction of Mazar uncovered at the foot of the southern wall and at the base of these gates a monumental stairway, 215 feet wide, which ascended 22 feet from a wide terrace or plaza below to the upper road at the base of the gates. This terrace or plaza could have been the place where pilgrims assembled before going up into the temple. It is highly probable that Jesus and his disciples at times used this stairway to go to the temple, especially at the time of the feasts. Mazar's excavations have clarified the mystery of the so-called Robinson's Arch. It formed part of the support of a stairway in the shape of a carpenter's square, which started from the south and led to a southwestern gate above, giving access also from that side to the Royal Portico. (JR, 27–30; MTL, 143–46)

Jn 7:37 —— *If any one thirst* Jesus was in Jerusalem on the occasion of the feast of Tabernacles (*Succoth*), shortly after the beginning of the Jewish year, toward the end of September or the beginning of October. On the last day of the feast Jesus made his momentous statement concerning "rivers of living water." What had the feast of Tabernacles to do with water? It was customary during the feast

to go in a joyous mass procession to the Gihon Spring, going out
and returning through the so-called Water Gate. A priest filled a
golden pitcher with water from the spring, and the temple singers
sang the hymn, "With joy you will draw water from the wells of
salvation" (Is 12:3). The multitude then returned carrying the symbols
of *Succoth* (branches of palm, myrtle, willow, and citron), representing the harvest. The steps which lead down to the spring show
the wear of their use through the centuries and are the same as
those used in the time of Jesus. Perhaps Jesus was standing on them
when he uttered those famous words. This probably occurred
following the ceremony at the spring, as the people were going back
up the stairs. (ABB, 290)

Jn 7:38 —— *Out of his heart shall flow rivers*   The literal expression
is "out of his belly." According to discoveries made in Ashur and
Mari it was common in the ancient Near East many centuries before
Jesus to represent goddesses holding against their bosoms pitchers
from which at times, by some ingenious device, water was made to
flow, in this way perhaps pretending to perform a miracle. It is
possible that such a concept persisted at the time of Jesus, and that
he was making use of this ancient symbolism, but giving it, of
course, a new and spiritual meaning. (WMTS, 264; TOJ, 69–70;
MLB, 10–13)

Jn 9:7 —— *the pool of Siloam*   Despite alterations suffered in the
course of the centuries, the pool where the blind man was healed
still exists. It is situated in the southeast quarter of Jerusalem. The
Arabs call it *Ain Silwan* ("Fountain of Silwan"). Hezekiah's tunnel
leads to it (see comment on 2 Kings 20:20), but the present reservoir
was excavated among the ruins of the old one, which seems to have
been surrounded by porticoes. A Byzantine basilica was built upon
it, and its ruins were uncovered in 1897. Some of its broken-off
pillars are visible in the present pool. At a later time Arabs built a
small mosque above it. People of the vicinity still come there to
draw water and wash clothes. A flight of eighteen steps leads down
to the pool. Not far from it is the Arab village of Silwan. (TANT,
114–15)

Jn 10:23 —— *the portico of Solomon.*   The temple esplanade was
encircled by porticoes (or porches) formed by two rows of columns.

The one on the east side was called the portico of Solomon. The one on the south side was called the Royal Portico. It was built like a basilica, having a sort of central nave and two aisles; each one was formed by a double row of columns with Corinthian capitals. According to Josephus, there was a total of 162 columns. This was a marketplace, since, with the exception of pious Jews such as Jesus, it was not considered as sacred as the courts and the central building of the temple. It was from here that Jesus drove out the merchants. In one section of this portico rabbis and others would discuss the law and teach the groups of people who gathered around them. It was here, no doubt, that Mary and Joseph found the twelve-year-old Jesus (Lk 2:46). The excavations directed by Mazar have produced important information about the Royal Portico, although some problems remain unresolved. Excavations at the foot of the present southern wall uncovered fragments found of friezes, cornices, capitals, and even whole columns which doubtless fell from above when the Romans razed the temple. Fragments of columns in secondary use have been found embedded in later constructions on the site. Two monolithic columns stand in the interior vestibule of the Double Gate, put in use there in Muslim times. Others were used as foundations or in the walls of Byzantine buildings, and they have turned up in the excavations. It is moving to realize that Jesus walked among these very columns when they formed part of Solomon's porticoes. (See also the comments on Acts 3:11.) From literary sources (especially Josephus) we know that these porticoes ran for about 1,500 feet along the east side of the temple, looking down to the Kidron Valley. The famous Golden Gate was probably in the same place that the present gate in the Turkish wall is located. Sultan Suleiman ordered it walled up in order that it might be opened only to let the Messiah pass through. (TANT, 116–19; MTL, 124–26)

Jn 11:38 —— *Jesus . . . came to the tomb*   In his *Onomasticon* (A.D. 330), Eusebius says that "the place of [the tomb of] Lazarus is still pointed out even until now" in Bethany. According to St. Jerome's testimony, a church had been built before the end of the fourth century A.D. in order to mark the site. Archaeological excavations have located remains of this first church, which seems to have been destroyed by an earthquake. Toward the middle of the fifth century

A.D., a second church was built. This was so altered in the twelfth century A.D. that it practically became a third church. Its crypt was connected by a passage with what was traditionally considered to be the tomb of Lazarus. The Muslims transformed this crypt into a small mosque, and the passage to the tomb was walled up. But then an entrance to the tomb was opened from the street on the north. Through this entrance visitors are admitted today. The mosque still exists under the name el-Uzeir. After the excavations referred to above (carried out from 1949 to 1955), a building called the New Church of St. Lazarus was raised on the site. It was dedicated in 1954. Portions of the ancient foundations of the previous church were used and in the interior of the new church the apses of the two oldest churches were left uncovered.

Twenty-two steps lead down to a sort of vestibule to the tomb. Two more steps then lead down to a passage which in turn leads to a chamber measuring about 7½ by 8 feet. This chamber was carved out of the rock. On each of three sides there are niches for burials. The stone which closed the tomb would have been laid horizontally over the entrance. As in other cases, in spite of the antiquity of the tradition, it cannot be said with any certainty that this is indeed the tomb of Lazarus. But even if it is not, it at least gives a more or less definite idea of the actual tomb. (TANT, 91–95)

Jn 12:36 —— *that you may become sons of light.* This same concept appears in Ephesians 5:8 and other New Testament passages, usually in implicit or explicit contrast with the "sons of darkness." This is also one of the more stressed concepts in the Qumran scrolls, especially the one which for that very reason is called *War of the Sons of Light Against the Sons of Darkness.* This pairing of opposites, like "the spirit of truth and the spirit of error" (1 Jn 4:6), which also occurs in one scroll of Qumran, reflects the dualism of Persian origin which had already been assimilated into Jewish religious thought. Like certain other expressions common to New Testament writers (especially John and Paul), these similarities are purely formal. They are manners of expression which were common among the Jews of that era, and it cannot be said that one writer imitated another or borrowed from another. Studies by biblical scholars and evidence from the documents of Qumran show clearly that similarities in literary expression can nevertheless involve substantial and often radical differences in meaning. (DDQ, 227–46; DSS, 338–45; MLD, 87–110, 119–34; LRQ, 205–7; DSSE, 124–25)

Jn 18:1 —— *he went forth . . . across the Kidron valley* If the Upper
Room was situated on Mount Zion (according to an ancient Christian
tradition; see comment on Mk 14:15), Jesus must have descended
the eastern slope of this hill toward the pool of Siloam and, skirting
it, continued toward the Kidron Valley. Alongside the Church of
St. Peter in Gallicantu goes a path that follows this route. It dates
from the Roman period. Some stone steps of this path still remain.
Down them Jesus could very well have gone with his disciples on
that memorable night. For that reason some call these steps the
Holy Thursday Stairway. (TANT, 154; LOC, 114; IFJ, 174)

Jn 19:5 —— *Behold the man!* From Josephus we know that after the
fall of Jerusalem in A.D. 70 Titus had the Antonia Tower demolished,
and that at the beginning of the second century A.D. Hadrian ordered
new demolitions in order to build his city of Aelia Capitolina.
However, a persistent tradition calls an arch bridging a street in the
north of the city the Ecce Homo Arch. This is reputed to be the
place where Pilate presented the whipped and bleeding Jesus to the
crowd and uttered his famous "Ecce homo!" ("Behold the man!").
This arch belongs to the present Convent of Our Lady of Sion.
Careful excavations under this building have shown that this famous
arch was the central one of three in the eastern gate of Aelia
Capitolina. The rest of it is embedded in the wall of the convent's
chapel. Behind the altar the northern side of the arch may be clearly
seen today. The southern arch disappears into the building on the
other side of the street. The arch was really built almost 100 years
after the occasion of Jesus' trial before Pilate. Moreover, one must
bear in mind that there is a question as to whether the trial took
place somewhere at the Antonia fortress or in Herod's palace (see
comment on Lk 23:7). This question has not been solved, and
perhaps never will be. The street of the so-called Ecce Homo Arch
is almost at the beginning of the Via Dolorosa, the route that pilgrims
follow every Holy Week, and it forms a part of it. The tradition
behind this Via assumes that the trial took place in the Antonia and
locates the praetorium near the present Lions' (or St. Stephen's)
Gate. (TANT, 162–63; IFJ, 190–91)

Jn 19:13 —— *a place called The Pavement* The Greek name is
Lithostrotos, and it is variously translated as "The Stone Pavement,"
"The Stone Platform," and "The Mosaic Pavement." As the Gospel
indicates, this place was called *Gabbatha* in Aramaic (here called

Hebrew), a word of uncertain meaning, but probably "ridge" or "elevated place." In excavations under the Convent of Our Lady of Sion (or Convent of the Sisters of Sion), situated northwest from the temple area, a stone-paved courtyard was found, measuring approximately 105 by 157 feet. In one section of it the stone slabs are grooved, with the purpose of preventing the horses' hooves from slipping. On some of the stones appear incised figures. These were no doubt used for games with which the Roman soldiers entertained themselves. Vincent, who discovered this pavement, is completely confident that it is indeed the pavement mentioned in the Gospel— the main courtyard of the Antonia Tower. This identification has been much debated, for there is no certainty as to precisely where the praetorium was located. Whenever Pilate visited Jerusalem, his most probable residence seems to have been Herod's palace, whose location in the area of the present Jaffa Gate has been fully confirmed. But it is almost certain that for this festival Pilate would have been in the Antonia Tower to be closer to the site of any emergency. According to Avi-Yonah, the most recent excavations by Israeli archaeologists in the northern area of the Temple Mount indicate that this pavement was contemporaneous with the so-called Ecce Homo Arch, which dates from the second century A.D. and which was part of Roman Aelia Capitolina. P. Benoit shares this opinion. Even if this proves to be true, it is possible and even probable that this pavement occupies the same site as the *Lithostrotos* of Jesus' time. In any case, it gives us a good idea of what that pavement was like. (JR, 24, 88; compare JAT, I, 216 ff.; TANT, 156 ff.; EB, IV, 1053–55; WB, V, 152; BAW, 226; IFJ, 194)

Jn 21:15 —— *When they had finished breakfast* A church on the shore of the Sea of Galilee, located west of the place where the Jordan River flows into it, commemorates this breakfast on the beach, Jesus' dialogue with Peter, and the miraculous catch of fish. The pious naïveté of some traditions is exemplified by the rock situated before the altar. It is called *Mensa Christi* ("Christ's Table"), and the claim is made that precisely upon this rock Jesus served the breakfast of fish and bread to his disciples. The biblical context, however, does not at all suggest that the disciples sat around a rock to eat breakfast. Even if they did, how could one rock among the many at the site be precisely identified as the one they used? No archaeological evidence whatsoever substantiates this claim.

Jn 21:24 —— *who has written these things* A number of different papyrus fragments were found in Egypt in 1920, but it was not until 1934 that a portion of the Gospel of John was identified among them. This fragment, registered as Rylands Greek Papyrus 457 with the code designation of p^{52}, is preserved in the John Rylands Library, in Manchester, England. It dates from the first half of the second century A.D. and contains 18:31–33, 37–38. The discovery and identification of this oldest copy of New Testament material known to date dealt a deathblow to the theory launched earlier by F. C. Baur and his school of textual criticism. They had maintained that John's Gospel was written not earlier than A.D. 160 and possibly even later in the second century A.D. (CHB, I, 56, 63; TNT, 38–39)

THE ACTS OF
THE APOSTLES

Acts 1:9 —— *as they were looking on, he was lifted up* The implication in verse 12 is that Jesus' ascension took place on the Mount of Olives. According to Luke 24:50 it was near Bethany, that is, not on the summit but on its eastern slope. On the basis of an early tradition a Christian lady called Poemenia ordered in A.D. 378 the building of a chapel on the site which supposedly was the precise place from which Jesus ascended to heaven. It was named Inbomon (from Greek *en bomoi*, "in the height"). Arculf (A.D. 670) described it and left a drawing of its floor plan. It was rebuilt in an octagonal form by the crusaders, and after the conquest of Palestine by Saladin, the Muslims made it into a mosque. This is the structure that is shown to tourists today. At its center there is a rock which has a peculiar indentation vaguely resembling a footprint. Tourist guides assert that this is the true footprint which Jesus left impressed in solid rock when he ascended. There is, however, a conflict in the traditions, for to the northeast of the Inbomon there is a site known as *Viri Galilei* ("Men of Galilee"), where the disciples were supposedly standing when the return of Jesus, whom they had just seen ascending, was announced to them. (TANT, 98–99; LOC, 139–40)

Acts 1:19 —— *Akeldama, that is, Field of Blood.* The name was transcribed into Greek as *Akeldamakh* from the language of the "inhabitants of Jerusalem," that is, from Aramaic. In Latin it is given as *Haceldama*. The name in Aramaic could have been *Haqal Dama*, which could also be translated as "Field of Sleep." A tradition

236

as old as at least the beginning of the fourth century A.D. (Eusebius) locates this place near the junction of the Kidron, Central (Tyropoeon), and Hinnom valleys, but somewhat more exactly on the southern slope of the Hinnom. Beside the monastery of St. Onuphrius there are ruins of a building and old tombs which indicate a cemetery, which first, according to tradition, served as a common graveyard for foreigners. (TANT, 155; LOC, 118–19; EB, III, 1003–5; IDB, I, 73–74)

Acts 2:29 —— *David . . . died . . . and his tomb is with us to this day.* On Jerusalem's southwestern hill, which is today outside the wall and which began at some early date to be called Mount Zion, a medieval memorial monument is shown to visitors as David's Tomb. (The original Mount Zion was the southeastern hill where at first the old city of Jebus and then the City of David were located.) The site is just under the room known as the Upper Room (see comment on Mk 14:15). Excavations at the site indicated that it was carved out of the rock by Jews toward the end of the first century B.C. This seems to indicate that the tradition that "David's Tomb" was there is a rather old one. If that is so, Peter would have been referring to it. Remains of Roman, Byzantine, and crusader structures have been found at this site, but its identification as the place where David was buried is doubtful. If his tomb still exists, it would be on the southeastern hill. Nevertheless, the supposed "David's Tomb" remains an important pilgrimage place for Jews until this day. (CNI, 25 [1976], 198)

Acts 3:2 —— *that gate of the temple which is called Beautiful* There are two opinions concerning the identification of the gate mentioned only in this passage. Some authorities believe it was the Nicanor Gate, made of Corinthian bronze, which according to Josephus exceeded all the others in value and which gave access from the Women's Court to the Court of Israel. But from the context which says that Peter and John were "about to go into the temple," it seems more probable the gate here called "Beautiful" was the Golden Gate, also called Shushan. This would also be in accordance with an ancient Christian tradition, which identified the gate as one situated to the east, in Solomon's portico. (See the comment on Jn 10:23.) (TANT, 129–30)

Acts 5:34 —— *Gamaliel, a teacher of the law* In the catacombs of Beth Shearim, in the section called Tomb of the Patriarchs (catacomb 14), a Hebrew and Greek inscription was found which reads, "This is the (tomb) of Rabbi Gamaliel." It probably refers to a descendant of the famous Gamaliel, who was Paul's teacher, for several of his descendants bore that name. The Beth Shearim catacombs date from the third and fourth centuries A.D. (WB, V, 162; TANT, 203 ff.)

Acts 6:2 —— *the body of the disciples* The literal translation of the Greek here is "the multitude of the disciples," and this traditional rendering is found in various versions. The Greek term *plethos* is, in turn, a translation of the Hebrew term *rabbim* (literally "many"). It has seemed strange that a "multitude" should be convened to deliberate about a matter of an election. (Compare 15:12, 30.) The use of the same word *rabbim* in the Qumran documents, where the text speaks of the form of organization and functions of the sect, provides the clue to the true, technical sense of the term. Thus, 6:2 refers either to a formal session of the assembly or to the full membership of the community. In this case it means a plenary session of the congregation. Observe that in 15:12 ("all the assembly") and again in verse 30 ("the congregation") RSV captures the real sense and makes a correct translation. (LRQ, 119–21; DSSE, 85)

Acts 6:9 —— *the synagogue of the Freedmen* In excavations on the Ophel, north of the City of David, R. Weill discovered a Greek inscription explaining that Theodotus, son of Vettenius, priest and president of the synagogue and son and grandson of synagogue presidents, was the builder of the synagogue. The inscription adds that the original synagogue on the site had been built by the parents of Theodotus, the elders, and a certain Simonides. It seems that Vettenius could have been a freedman who had been the slave of the Roman family of Vettius. Many believe, therefore, that the inscription pertains to the Synagogue of the Freedmen mentioned in this passage. (BAR-1, 238; PBE, 202–3; WB, 5, 162; BAW, 240)

Acts 7:58 —— *they cast him out of the city and stoned him* On the evident basis of an ancient tradition, the empress Eudocia erected in the fifth century A.D. a basilica to commemorate the martyrdom, which supposedly had taken place there. The ruins of this basilica were excavated in 1885. The ancient gate, which was located at the site where the present Damascus Gate stands and which in the sixth century A.D. was called the Galilean Gate, was already called St. Stephen's Gate in the seventh century A.D. But toward the ninth century A.D. a different tradition located the martyrdom of Stephen in the Kidron Valley. Hence the name of St. Stephen's Gate was given to the eastern gate, which is also called the Lions' Gate on the basis of the Turkish bas-reliefs of these beasts on both sides of the entrance. This gate was previously called the Gate of St. Mary, when people thought that the tomb of the Virgin Mary was located at the foot of the Mount of Olives and almost in front of this gate. (TANT, 174–77; IFJ, 185)

Acts 8:40 —— *till he came to Caesarea.* This city plays an important role in apostolic history. It was situated on the Mediterranean and was one of the main seaports of Palestine. Herod founded it on the site of a previous port, and it became the capital of the Roman province of Judea and the official residence of its governor. The ruins of the Roman period which have been excavated include the remains of two aqueducts, a theater, an amphitheater, and a Roman wall. In addition, ruins from the time of the crusaders and from the Turkish period have been brought to light. (TANT, 70–80)

Acts 9:11 —— *the street called Straight* When Damascus was rebuilt during the Hellenistic period, it had the shape of a rectangle, with north-south and east-west streets forming right angles at the intersections. The east-west streets were longer, and among them "the street called Straight" was the longest. Although it has undergone some modifications during the many centuries, this street still exists under the name Darb el-Mustaqim. It was at that time and continues to be the city's main thoroughfare. (WB, V, 165)

Acts 9:25 —— *and let him down through an opening in the wall* (GNB; RSV: "and let him down over the wall.") In Damascus there are still long stretches of the Roman wall of Paul's time, as well as two gates. These are the eastern gate, at the end of Straight Street, and the southern gate (called Bab Kisan) which is now closed. It shows traces of reconstruction and bears two circles with the Christian anagram composed of the Greek letters X and P. According to tradition it was through a window in this wall that the disciples lowered the apostle. (WB, V, 166)

Acts 11:26 —— *he brought him to Antioch.* Modern Antioch, which is called Antakiye and is in Turkey, is a small town in an open area surrounded by the remains of ancient walls. In Paul's day it was the third most important city in the Roman Empire. Some excavations have been made there, but much still remains to be discovered from the various periods of the city's history, beginning with the founding by Seleucus I Nicator in 301 B.C. (WB, V, 166)

Acts 12:1 —— *Herod the king* This was Herod Agrippa I (A.D. 37–44), a grandson of Herod the Great and Mariamne. In the last three years of his reign he ruled over all the Jewish regions of Palestine, after having first governed only the Roman province in the north. While excavating near the western and southern walls of the Temple Mount, Mazar found some weights dating from the fifth year of Agrippa's reign. These bear his name with the title of king in Greek, *basileus*. In 1925–27 remains of the new wall (the Third Wall) built by this Herod, were identified north of the city. This identification was much debated by archaeologists, but more recent excavations by Sarah ben-Aryeh in 1972 confirmed the identification on the basis of shards of the Herodian period found at the site. (MTL, 82–84)

Acts 12:23 —— *an angel of the Lord smote him* According to Josephus (*Antiquities*, XIX, VIII, 2) this incident occurred in the theater of Caesarea, whose ruins have been completely excavated. Possibly Herod was accustomed to sit in judgment there. Josephus tells that the king appeared dressed in robes "made wholly of silver," which gave him such a shining, imposing appearance that people acclaimed him as a god. According to this Jewish historian, at that very moment he suffered a violent pain in the abdomen. He was taken to his palace, and in five days he died. The rumor spread that he had been poisoned, but it was also reported that he had died from illness.

Acts 13:4 —— *from there they sailed to Cyprus.* In the National Museum at Beirut, Lebanon, there is a stone sarcophagus from Sidon with a ship of the first century A.D. carved on one of its sides. It is an excellent picture of the type of ships in which Paul traveled during his missionary voyages.

Acts 13:7 —— *the proconsul, Sergius Paulus* During explorations carried out between 1865 and 1877 at Soli, north of Paphos, Cyprus, an inscription was found which dates from A.D. 55 and in which the proconsul Sergius Paulus is mentioned. "It is the one reference we have to this proconsul outside the Bible and it is interesting that Luke gives us correctly his name and title" (Wright). (BAW, 252)

Acts 13:13 —— *and came to Perga in Pamphylia.* Of the cities visited by Paul in his first missionary travel, Perga is the one with the most extensive and better preserved remains. They include the acropolis, theater, stadium, palestra, some baths, and walls. The first time the apostle came there, he apparently only passed through the city and continued his journey. Upon his return, however, he preached the gospel there (see 14:25). (EB, III, 214; V, 1037–38)

Acts 13:14 —— *and came to Antioch of Pisidia.* Before and after the First World War extensive excavations were carried out in Antioch. These uncovered important ruins from the time Paul and Barnabas were there: the Square of Augustus (with the great temple of the god Men), the Square of Tiberius, the great stairway connecting these squares, and at the top of it the triumphal archways in honor of Caesar Augustus. (BAW, 253)

Acts 13:51 —— *and went to Iconium.* This is modern Konya, one of Turkey's most important cities. Emperor Claudius (A.D. 41–54) gave it the name Claudiconium, in honor of himself, and Emperor Hadrian (A.D. 117–38) made it a Roman colony. There is no archaeological information about it. (EB, IV, 60; BAW, 254)

Acts 14:6 —— *and fled to Lystra and Derbe* Identification of the site occupied by ancient Lystra was primarily based on an inscription found in 1885 by Sterrett, which established the location. The identification of Derbe has been more difficult, but a Greek inscription found on the base of a statue discovered at Kerti Hüyük and reading "The Council and people of Derbe" seems to have established this identification with relative certainty. (WMTS, 66; EB, II, 839)

Acts 16:12 —— *and from there to Philippi* The location of Philippi has been completely confirmed. Excavations there have uncovered a number of objects, including the ruins of the ancient market and of a Roman forum (see comment on verse 13). (WB, V, 176)

Acts 16:13 —— *the riverside* A great Roman highway called Via Egnatia passed through Philippi. Excavations have brought to light sections of this road, in which can be seen the ruts left by the wheels of the many wagons and chariots that rolled on it. Also excavated was an arched gateway which served as the city's western exit. The road passed through this gateway, and about a mile farther on it crossed a small river. It is without doubt the one mentioned in this passage, for there is no other river "outside the gate" of the city. Obviously, there was no synagogue in Philippi. (BAW, 258)

Acts 16:19 —— *and dragged them . . . before the rulers*   On the north side of the Roman forum excavated in Philippi there is a podium or platform with steps leading up the two sides. This is the tribunal of the magistrates before whom Paul and Silas were arraigned. It also served as a platform for orators. Although an ancient writer says that the prison (no doubt the one into which Paul and Silas were thrown after being beaten, verses 23–24), together with other public buildings, stood along the forum, the location of the prison has not been determined. (BAW, 258–60)

Acts 17:1 —— *they came to Thessalonica*   After passing through Amphipolis and Apollonia, the Via Egnatia continued through Thessalonica, the modern Salonica. Because of the many modern buildings, this city has not been excavated as it should be in order to uncover important remains of the town of Paul's days. The triple arch of its main entrance, built by the emperor Galerius, dates from the fourth century A.D. Another Roman arch, called the Varder Gate, stood at the western entrance to the city until 1876, when it was removed to make room for modern constructions. The old thoroughfare of the Via Egnatia is the modern city's main street. (BAW, 260)

Acts 17:6 —— *before the city authorities*   This is the English rendering of the original Greek term *politarchas*. In the British Museum there is an inscription from Thessalonica's western gate (see comment on verse 1) in which these officials are mentioned. Other inscriptions contain the same word, "otherwise unknown in extant Greek literature," so that "the archaeological information is a confirmation of the accuracy of Luke's narrative at this point" (Wright). (BAW, 260)

Acts 17:17 —— *he argued . . . in the market place every day*   The "market place," which was the *agora*, or public square, of Athens, has been not only excavated but also remarkably restored. To this place Paul went every day to talk with those who gathered there. The center of the city's life, according to Greek custom, and the meeting place for citizens and visitors, it was encircled by public buildings, both civil and religious. Among these was the temple of Hephaistos, which is still standing today as the best preserved building of those ancient times. This temple is at the foot and to the north of the Areopagus. (BAW, 260–63)

Acts 17:19 —— *the Areopagus*   The name means "Hill of Ares" (that is, Mars, the god of war). This hill, close to the Acropolis, is a rocky promontory rising above the city. It is one of the sites in the biblical account which have been identified with certainty. In classical times the supreme court of Athens met there. Steps carved on the rock and traces of altars and seats may still be seen on the Areopagus. (EB, I, 707; BAR-2, 370; WB, V, 179)

Acts 17:23 —— *I found also an altar*   Excavations have not so far found any remains or traces of an altar like the one Paul saw dedicated to "an unknown god," but there is evidence that Athenians did have dedicated altars to "unknown gods." One such altar was discovered among the ruins at Pergamum. The Greek inscription is mutilated, but one may clearly read, *theois ag* . . . ("To the unk . . . gods"). Also, in several places in the Roman Empire altars with Latin inscriptions have been found dedicated to unnamed gods. (WB, V, 180; BAR-2, 384, note 2)

Acts 18:1 —— *and went to Corinth.*   In addition to the ruins of the acropolis in Corinth those of the temple of Apollo are outstanding. This temple was built in the sixth century B.C. Undoubtedly Paul was acquainted with both structures, as well as with the great theater, the Odeion, and other constructions whose ruins have been excavated.

Acts 18:4 —— *And he argued in the synagogue*   On a block of white marble found on the Lechaion Road in Corinth near the entrance to the public square, there is a partially damaged inscription, which in Greek reads, . . . *GOGE EBR*. . . . In its filled-out form it would be *[SYNA]GOGE EBR[AION]*, "Synagogue of the Hebrews." No ruins of the building to which this inscription belonged have been found. From the style of the script the date of the inscription is considered to be later than Paul's time, but it is most probable that this synagogue was the successor of the one the apostle attended. (BAR-1, 187; WB, V, 181; IDB, I, 684)

Acts 18:12 —— *and brought him before the tribunal*   Among the ruins of the public square of Corinth, where Paul was forcibly made to

appear before the proconsul Gallio, there is a small platform
supported by stone blocks and with a narrow railing around the top.
Archaeologists believe this could be the remnant of the *bema*, or
tribunal, where the official chair of Gallio, acting as a judge, would
have been placed. (WB, V, 74, 182)

Acts 18:21 ——— *and he set sail from Ephesus*.   The ancient port of
Ephesus is now completely silted up, and in its place there is only
a sandy expanse that no ship can even approach. The ruins of
Ephesus are now 3 or 4 miles inland. The obliteration of the port
was no doubt due to the accumulation of mud carried by the River
Cayster which flows into it. A passage from Strabo, the Greek
geographer of the first century A.D., mentions that the port was
already having problems in Paul's day. In an effort to prevent the
silting, King Attalus had destroyed a dike at the mouth of the river.
The result was the opposite of what was intended, for the dike
simply confined the mud within the harbor. (BAR-2, 331)

Acts 19:13 ——— *I adjure you*   According to papyri discovered in Egypt
(like the so-called Magic Papyrus of Paris), this seems to have been
the usual formula employed by exorcists. (BAR-2, 350)

Acts 19:24 ——— *silver shrines of Artemis*   These were miniatures of
the temple sold to visitors as souvenirs. In the course of the centuries
all evidence of the site of this temple had been lost, although the
ruins of Ephesus were well known. By the middle of the second
half of the nineteenth century A.D., J. T. Wood, after six years of
hard work, discovered and excavated the famous temple, one of the
seven wonders of the ancient world. The ruins were buried some 20
feet deep northeast of the city, at the foot of a hill called Ayassoluk.
The temple stood upon a platform measuring about 239 feet wide
by 418 feet long. The temple itself was over 160 feet wide and 340
feet long. It had 100 columns over 55 feet high and exceeding 6 feet
in diameter at the base. Some of them were sculptured to a height
of about 20 feet. The sacred chamber was 70 feet wide and was
open to the sky. The foundation of the main altar was 20 feet square.
Behind it stood the statue of the goddess Diana (or Artemis) which
was said to have been "the sacred stone that fell from the sky"
(verse 35). This phrase may mean that the statue had been sculptured
from a large meteorite to resemble a human figure. A number of

fragments of the temple's decoration in color as well as in gold have been found. So far no silver miniatures of the goddess have been found in the excavations, but figurines made of terra-cotta and marble have been discovered. It is possible that silver miniatures of the goddess as well as of the temple were made. An inscription supposedly dating from the time of Paul mentions one Demetrius, "warden" (literally "maker") of the temple, but it is doubted that this person was the silversmith referred to in this chapter. (BAR-2, 337–38, 345–47; BAW, 255–58)

Acts 19:27 —— *and the world* The word translated "world" is *oikoumenē*, which means the whole inhabited earth of that day. Archaeology has afforded evidence that the worship of Diana-Artemis was, in fact, widely spread over the then known world. Traces of this worship have been found in more than thirty different places. In Caesarea, for example, a statue of the goddess, with only the head missing, was uncovered near the ruins of the theater. (BAR-2, 345; THL, 108)

Acts 19:28 —— *Great is Artemis* It was common to give the gods and goddesses the title of "Great." Numerous inscriptions found in Ephesus, as well as literary references of the period, indicate that this title was generally given to Diana-Artemis. (BAR-2, 350)

Acts 19:29 —— *they rushed together into the theater* The ruins of this great theater have been excavated. It had a seating capacity of some 25,000. The excavations indicate that some modifications were made in the structure after the time of Paul, but its capacity and general form were not altered. Theaters were common places for great public assemblies. (BAR-2, 351; WB, V, 185)

Acts 19:31 —— *some of the Asiarchs* The title of these officials is here a literal translation of the Greek, meaning "chiefs [or "rulers"] of Asia" (that is, the Roman province of that name). They are often mentioned in inscriptions discovered by archaeologists. The office was held for a year, but those who had served as Asiarchs retained the title, hence the plural in this passage. They were especially responsible for giving leadership to the rites of the cult rendered to the emperor. (BAR-2, 351)

Acts 19:35 —— *the city of the Ephesians is temple keeper* This was an official title bestowed upon the city of Ephesus. An inscription was found in its ruins which refers to the city as the "temple-keeper of the great Artemis." Ephesus also held the title of "temple-keeper of the imperial cult," which was also practiced in Ephesus, though not with the same importance as the cult of Artemis. (BAR-2, 348, 352)

Acts 21:8 —— *Philip the evangelist* It has been possible to identify among the ruins at Hierapolis the remains of four early Christian churches. In one of them the following inscription was found: "Eugenius the least, archdeacon who is in charge of (the church of) the holy and glorious apostle and theologian Philip." According to an old tradition, Philip spent the last part of his life at Hierapolis. (BAW, 255)

Acts 21:28 —— *he also brought Greeks into the temple* In the Jerusalem temple there was an outer court for the Gentiles, who were threatened with capital punishment if they went any closer to the sanctuary. An inscription to this effect was discovered in 1870. It is in Greek, and its translation reads, "Let no one of the Gentiles enter inside the barrier around the sanctuary and the porch; and if he trangresses he shall himself bear the blame for his ensuing death." A similar inscription, though only in fragmentary form, was found in 1935 near the Lions' (or St. Stephen's) Gate. The former is now at Istanbul, and the latter is in the Rockefeller Museum at Jerusalem. (WB, V, 188, 232; TANT, 119–20; TOJ, 83–84; MTL, 114)

Acts 21:39 —— *from Tarsus in Cilicia* Tarsus was the capital of the Roman province of Cilicia (in what is now called Asia Minor). It had been granted special privileges by Julius Caesar and Mark Anthony. Among the remains of the old city there is a Roman gate dating from Paul's time. It is now known as Paul's Gate. He no doubt passed through it many times. Tentmaking and the weaving of linen were the city's most important industries. Tarsus is mentioned in Assyrian inscriptions as early as the ninth century B.C. (WB, V, 189)

Acts 22:24 —— *commanded him to be brought into the barracks* The barracks were in the fortress of Antonia, the Roman bastion at the northwest corner of the temple precinct. Excavations have brought to light remains of its ruins, especially in the area of the Convent of Our Lady of Sion (*Ecce Homo*). (See the comments on Jn 19:5.) It was built upon a site formerly occupied Ly a fortress of Nehemiah's day, which the Persians called *Baris* (Hebrew *Birah*). This was later strengthened by the Hasmoneans and finally rebuilt by Herod as the fortress of Antonia, in honor of Mark Anthony. Several kinds of reconstructions have been proposed, but one can only be sure that it had four enormous towers and a wide inner court. (See the comment on Jn 19:13.) (WB, V, 190; BAW, 224–26; JOT, 374–81; JAT, 193–221)

Acts 25:13 —— *Agrippa the king* Herod Agrippa II (A.D. 44–66) continued the material improvements of the city in which his father had been so much engaged. The notable pavements excavated west and south of the Temple Mount by Mazar can, according to his opinion, be "definitely" attributed to this king. Josephus refers to the pavement as consisting of white stone slabs in *Antiquities*, XX, 9, 7. (MTL, 84)

Acts 27:44 —— *all escaped to land.* On the island of Malta tourists are shown the very place where, according to tradition, the shipwrecked crew and travelers reached land. The site is called St. Paul's Creek or St. Paul's Bay. It is situated on the northwest side of the island, and in view of its shape such identification is possible. The best Greek manuscripts call Malta *Melite*, but in others the name is *Melitene, Melitine, Meletene,* or *Mitilene.* Latin manuscripts give *Militina, Militena,* and *Militene.* There was another *Melite,* namely modern Mljet in the Adriatic, but it has been proved that the wind mentioned in this book blew rather toward Malta. (EB, IV, 1219; WB, V, 201)

Acts 28:15 —— *as far as the Forum of Appius* This place was on the famous Via Appia, of which important sections are still in use. Its name, as well as the name of the forum mentioned here, was in honor of the builder of the first section of this great highway, called the Queen of Roman Roads. The builder was the censor Appius Claudius the Blind (fourth century B.C.). On either side of the road old monuments of the epoch may still be seen. Paul saw them on his way to Rome. The Forum of Appius was at a distance of some 40 miles from the city.

THE LETTER OF PAUL
TO THE ROMANS

Rom 12:17 —— *Repay no one evil for evil* For this injunction Paul had the antecedent of the Sermon on the Mount (Mt 5:38–45), as well as texts of the Old Testament, such as Exodus 23:4, 5; Proverbs 24:17, 18; 25:21, 22 (from which he quotes some lines below), Leviticus 19:18, and others. In a Babylonian text written before 700 B.C., which Paul of course would not have known, there is a parallel of the same moral principle. The following advice is given:

> Unto your opponent do no evil;
> Your evildoer recompense with good;
> Unto your enemy let justice [be done].
> [ANET, 426]

Rom 16:5 —— *the church in their house.* This expression is repeated in other letters of the apostle. During the first three centuries Christians could build no visible chapels or temples, so for their worship they met in private residences. One of these domestic chapels was excavated in Dura-Europos on the River Euphrates. It was integrated into a private house, in which there was a spacious room for the *agapē* ("love feast," "brotherly meal"), an assembly hall, other rooms, and a large central court. This stucture dates from the third century A.D. (WB, V, 252)

Rom 16:23 —— *Erastus, the city treasurer* Among the ruins of Corinth a slab was found near the remains of the theater and the Odeion. It bears an inscription saying that the pavement was the work of Erastus, the *aedilis*, or commissioner of public works. He may be identified with the Erastus mentioned by Paul in this letter, and he could have been the same person mentioned in Acts 19:22 and 2 Timothy 4:20. Some authorities propose that the Erastus of Acts 19:22 was another person but that is very improbable. The fact that he is here called "treasurer" (Greek *oikonomos*) does not represent a real problem. (BAW, 265–66)

THE FIRST LETTER
OF PAUL
TO THE CORINTHIANS

1 Cor 7:22, 23 —— *is a slave of Christ. You were bought with a price* According to inscriptions in the sanctuary at Delphi, Greece, the redemption or emancipation of slaves could be achieved by purchasing them from their owners in the name of Apollo. From then on they were considered his slaves. (WMTS, 50)

1 Cor 9:25 —— *a perishable wreath* From ancient literary sources we know that the wreaths given in ancient times to the winners in the athletic contests in Greece were made of plant material and were therefore perishable. Depending on where the games were held, the wreaths were made of wild olive, laurel, pine, or even wild celery. The Isthmian wreath was originally made of pine, but from the fifth century B.C., and very probably until Paul's time, it was made of celery. Oscar Broneer says that the wreaths of celery bestowed at the Isthmian games were already withered. (BAR-2, 403–4)

1 Cor 13:12 —— *we see in a mirror dimly* The Greek phrase *en ainigmati* suggests that what is seen is puzzling reflections. Other versions translate "obscurely" or "confusedly." Paul's expression is not figurative but literal in view of what mirrors were like in his time. From the specimens recovered by archaeology, we know that the most common mirrors were made of burnished bronze. The image reflected by such a mirror would not be clear but rather blurred. Even the silver mirrors used by the wealthy produced much the same effect, since ancient burnishing methods were elementary. Glass mirrors backed with tin leaf or silvered are relatively recent. (MLB, 150–51)

THE SECOND LETTER
OF PAUL
TO THE CORINTHIANS

Cor 11:32 —— *the governor under King Aretas* This is the Greek name of the Nabataean king Harithath IV. The Nabataeans were Arabic people of the wilderness of the Negev. At one time their dominion extended as far as Damascus in Syria. Their capital was Petra in lower Transjordan. Coins have been found bearing the image of Aretas, and in Avdat, in the Negev, inscriptions have appeared with his name and the names of other Nabataean kings. (WB, V, 234)

THE LETTER OF PAUL
TO THE GALATIANS

Gal 5:1 —— *Christ has set us free; stand fast therefore*   Some Greek manuscripts add, "in the freedom wherewith Christ made us free." If this were the original reading, the apostle would have been using the legal formula for the emancipation of slaves. C. M. Cobern has called attention to a certificate of emancipation which appears in one of the so-called Oxyrhynchus papyri, which ends with the words, "I have here freed him unto this liberty wherewith I have made him free." (WMTS, 269)

THE LETTER OF PAUL TO THE EPHESIANS

Eph 2:14 —— *the dividing wall* It has been suggested that perhaps
here there is an implicit reference to the barrier in the Jerusalem
temple which separated the court of the Gentiles from the court of
the faithful Jews. A Gentile passing beyond that barrier incurred the
penalty of death. (See the comment on Acts 21:28.) (WMTS, 269)

THE LETTER OF PAUL TO THE PHILIPPIANS

Phil 1:1 —— *the bishops* RSV provides a traditional borrowing of the Greek term *episcopos*, which means "superintendent" or more exactly "overseer" (RSV margin). In the early church the word was at first used as more or less equivalent to Greek *presbuteros* ("elder," "presbyter"). This can be seen by the context in Acts 20:28. By the time the letter to the Ephesians was written, *episcopos* was already a special office in the church, along with but superior to the office of deacon. The Qumran community had a post of *mebaqer*, the Hebrew literal equivalent of *episcopos* or "superintendent." This is another of the resemblances which exist between the Qumranites and the early Christian community. Another similarity is that the Qumran supreme council consisted of twelve persons, a fact which immediately reminds one of the apostolic corps of twelve. But one cannot say that there is a direct borrowing from Qumran, for both cases had the symbolic antecedent of Israel's twelve tribes. The same is true of the "elders" in both the Christian and the Qumran organizations, as well as with the very old Israelite precedent. On the other hand, some persons have proposed the theory that there might have been Qumranite converts who joined the apostolic church, and who might have taken with them some of the forms of organization to which they were accustomed. It also has been suggested that the statement "a great many of the priests were obedient to the faith" (Acts 6:7) might refer to Qumranite converts, for some prominent members of this sect were priests. Furthermore, there was much in their doctrines which could well be considered a kind of preparation for the gospel. Although Qumran was led by priests, it also had lay members, and it is not impossible that some of them became converts to Christianity. (SNT, 143–56; LRQ, 118–20)

THE LETTER OF PAUL
TO THE COLOSSIANS

Col 1:2 —— *faithful brethren in Christ at Colossae* There is no doubt about the identification of Colossae and of Laodicea and Hierapolis, the other two cities mentioned in this letter. Numerous ruins at Colossae were in evidence up to the nineteenth century A.D. (W. J. Hamilton saw them in 1835), but the stones have since been used for buildings elsewhere. Although the other two cities have not been properly excavated, there still exist extensive ruins dating from Paul's time: theaters, baths, gymnasiums, tombs, and other buildings. (See the comment on Rev 3:14.) (BAW, 254–55)

Col 1:7 —— *Epaphras our beloved fellow servant.* This name is a contraction of *Epaphroditus* (Phil 2:25). An inscription found on the site of ancient Colossae mentions a T. Asinius Epaphroditus, "but it is most doubtful that this is the same as Epaphras" (Wright). A marble altar was found in Laodicea which is thought by some to bear the name of Epaphras. (BAW, 255)

THE FIRST LETTER
OF PAUL
TO THE THESSALONIANS

1 Thess 5:27 —— *that this letter be read to all the brethren.* "This letter" was the very first written by Paul to a church. It is dated as having been written in A.D. 50 or 51, and with it the composition of the New Testament begins. One of the manuscripts known as the Chester Beatty papyri (probably found in the Egyptian Fayum, and dating from about A.D. 200) is the oldest known collection of copies of Paul's letters grouped as a book (codex) and published, as it can readily be seen, only about 150 years after 1 Thessalonians was written. (BAW, 248)

THE SECOND LETTER
OF PAUL TO TIMOTHY

2 Tim 2:5 —— *according to the rules.* The athletes competing at Isthmia took an oath at the altar of Poseidon stating that they had followed all the rules in their training and promising that in the competitions they would abstain from cheating and engaging in foul play. The oath was made still more solemn when, as a part of the celebration, the athletes offered a sacrifice to Thesius, the founder of the games. (BAR-2, 417–18)

THE LETTER OF PAUL
TO PHILEMON

Philem 1 —— *To Philemon*   Among the ruins of Laodicea there was discovered a commemorative inscription dedicated by a freedman to a certain Marcus Sestius Philemon, no doubt an important citizen who owned slaves. One cannot be certain that this was the Philemon of Paul's letter, but the coincidence is very interesting. (BAR-2, 360)

Philem 12 —— *I am sending him back to you*   Onesimus was a fugitive slave who according to Roman law had to be returned to his owner. Normally such a slave would be brutally punished for having run away. Formerly a slave was branded with a hot iron like cattle in order to identify the person to whom he belonged. In Paul's time slaves were forced to carry around the neck a metal badge instead. One of these badges has been found with this inscription, "I have escaped, hold me, if you return me to my master (follows a name), you shall receive a *solidus* (gold coin)." (WB, V, 250)

THE LETTER OF JUDE

Jude 9 —— *Michael, contending with the devil, disputed about the body of Moses* This reference is to a Jewish tradition about the death of Moses, which was apparently preserved in the apocryphal book called the Assumption of Moses. According to Origen, Clement of Alexandria, and other ancient commentators, this passage is a direct quotation from this book. Unfortunately, this book has reached us only in an incomplete Latin version, so it is not possible to verify the quotation. The archangel Michael belongs to the postexilic development of a more elaborate angelology, which took place during the Hellenistic period. Michael in Hebrew means "Who [is] like God?" and is of considerable antiquity. It appears in the Ebla tablets, though with a different reference (but still as a personal name), in the form of *mi-ga-il*. These tablets date from the third millennium B.C. The words attributed to Michael in this book are identical with the words addressed by the Lord to Satan in Zechariah 3:2. (IDB, III, 373; EB, V, 144–45; BA, 43 [1980], 202)

Jude 14 —— *Enoch . . . prophesied, saying* Several apocryphal books were attributed to Enoch. They apparently are of Essene origin and constitute what has been called the "Enoch cycles" or, in general, the "Enoch literature." Primarily three different books are recognized, and these are designated by the language in which they appear and also by a number: First Enoch or Ethiopian Enoch, Second Enoch or Slavic Enoch, and Third Enoch or Hebrew Enoch. This last was composed in the second century A.D. The quotation in Jude corresponds to 1 Enoch 1:9. This book was originally written in Hebrew or Aramaic, probably in the first century B.C. The original has been lost, but it was edited by Christian Jews who reshaped and enlarged it. Fragments of this book turned up in Qumran Cave 1, and eight fragmentary copies of it in Aramaic were found in Cave 4. It was evidently one of the favorite apocryphal books of the Qumran community. (ABB, 322; EB, III, 36–37; IDB, II, 103–5)

THE REVELATION
TO JOHN

(THE APOCALYPSE)

Rev 1:9 —— *the island called Patmos*   As in so many other cases, a "Grotto of the Revelation," inside the Monastery of the Apocalypse, is shown as the traditional site of the revelation to John. Even the precise spots are marked where John was supposed to have rested his head and to have knelt to pray. There is also a Monastery of St. John the Theologian, with supposed relics from apostolic times. These are of course doubtful identifications, but despite the dubious authenticity of such details, the island itself is a biblical and historical reality of unquestionable value. (BA, 37 [1974], 69)

Rev 2:8 —— *the church in Smyrna*   Izmir is the present name of Smyrna, to which the second of seven letters to the churches in 1:20–3:22 was addressed. No Christian ruins from apostolic times have been found there. A present-day traveler, Otto F. A. Meinardus, writes, "Except for a few small remnants of a Byzantine church, no substantial archaeological remains testify to the church which was to receive the crown of life (2.10)." (BA, 37 [1974], 76)

Rev 2:12 —— *the church in Pergamum*   Archaeological investigations begun at Pergamum during the last quarter of the nineteenth century A.D. and continued for some fifty years by German archaeological missions uncovered magnificent ruins of the Roman epoch. The most important include a sumptuous altar to Zeus, a theater, an amphitheater, a circus, the temple of Athena, and the sanctuary of Aesculapius. Christian ruins found there date only from the Byzantine period. These include four churches. One of them, called the Red Basilica and traditionally associated with John, the author of Revelation, was built upon the ruins of an ancient temple of Serapis. Only some marble fragments of another church can be seen today. All the traces of still another church have now disappeared. Everything indicates that Pergamum was a flourishing city in the first century A.D. It consisted of three great sections: the "Upper City," the "Lower and Middle City," and the "Roman City." Pergamum was a religious rather than a commercial center. Not only was it a center for the worship of several pagan deities, but it was an important place for the cult of the emperor. Some authorities believe that is why the letter to the church in Pergamum calls it the place "where Satan's throne is" (verse 13). Its modern name is Bergama. (EB, V, 1033–36; IDB, III, 733–35; BA, 37 [1974], 78)

Rev 2:18 —— *the church in Thyatira* As in the case of Pergamum, only scant remains of Christian churches from the Byzantine period exist today, mainly consisting of marble fragments, and the foundations of the large apse of a church called St. Basil the Great. Since 1922, because of the Turkish-Greek war when Christians in the town were massacred or expelled, there has been no Christian community at this place, now called Akhisar. (BA, 37 [1974], 76–78)

Rev 3:1 —— *the church in Sardis* An archaeological expedition of Princeton University in 1910 discovered only Byzantine ruins in Sartmustafa, a small village on the site of this ancient capital of Lydia. Included in the ruins is a small church from the end of the fourth or the beginning of the fifth century A.D. Dating was possible because of a hoard of coins found at the place. Two apses were uncovered and an altar was found in place. This is one of the earliest Christian altars known. The ruins were near the Temple of Artemis. More recently a fourth-century A.D. basilica with three aisles and two apses was discovered near the road leading to this temple. The remains of a second-century A.D. synagogue have also been uncovered. It was probably built on the same site as the synagogue of the time of the first Christians in the community. (BA, 3 [1940], 79–80)

Rev 3:7 —— *the church in Philadelphia* The only ancient Christian ruins left in this town, now called Alasheir, are those of a red brick basilica called the Church of St. John. It dates perhaps from the eleventh century A.D. Remains of the frescoes which decorated it can still be seen on its walls. Until 1922 five Greek Orthodox churches existed in the city, but these were destroyed by the Turks after their victorious war against Greece. (BA, 37 [1974], 81)

Rev 3:12 —— *I will make him a pillar . . . and I will write on him*   In the ruins of the synagogue at Capernaum there are two pillars with dedicatory inscriptions (one in Greek and the other in Aramaic), which indicate that the custom of writing on the columns of buildings was quite common. The monumental columns of the Egyptian temples were, of course, covered with hieroglyphic inscriptions. Also, inscriptions in the synagogues bearing the names of patrons or donors were common. One pillar in the synagogue at Capernaum, for instance, has these words in Greek: "Herod, the son of Makimos, and his descendants." (WB, V, 274; ABB, 331)

Rev 3:14 —— *the church in Laodicea*   This place has remained uninhabited since the twelfth century A.D. Between the modern towns of Eskihisar and Goncale the only remnants of Roman and Byzantine times are an amphitheater, a gymnasium, and a monumental fountain. An early Christian church may have existed near this fountain and another probably stood next to the so-called Syrian Gate. But in the excavations conducted by the University of Laval, in Canada, in 1961–63, only a few marble slabs were found. These bear the symbol of the cross and date from the Byzantine period. (BA, 37 [1974], 82)

Rev 3:16 —— *because you are lukewarm*   In the ruins of Laodicea the remains of the city's potable water-supply system have been found. These include the ruins of an old water tower, some terracotta pipes, and an aqueduct. The water probably came from hot springs in the area, and for this reason it reached the city lukewarm— "neither cold nor hot." (BAW, 255)

Rev 16:16 —— *Armageddon.*   It is said here that this name is Hebrew, though the Hebrew name is really *har Megiddo* ("mount of Megiddo"). It was there that the famous battle of Barak and Deborah against the Canaanites was fought. Owing to its geographical position at the entrance to the hilly region of Judea, it was the site of several great and decisive battles. For this reason the author of this book makes it the symbolic place for the decisive conflict at the end of the age. The place has been the object of great and important excavations, as already indicated in other parts of this volume.

Rev 17:9 —— *seven mountains on which the woman is seated* In a coin of the emperor Vespasian the city of Rome is represented as a woman seated on its seven hills: Palatine, Capitoline, Esquiline, Aventine, Quirinal, Caelian, and Viminal. (WMTS, 270)

Rev. 21:10 —— *the holy city Jerusalem coming down out of heaven* The theme of the heavenly Jerusalem occurs in rabbinic literature: "Jerusalem of the Height" or "Jerusalem on High." It is also a favorite symbol of early Christianity, as in this book. It is depicted in the celebrated synagogue excavated at Dura-Europos on the Euphrates, dating from the beginning of the third century A.D. The walls of this synagogue were covered with frescoes. It may also be seen reconstructed at the Damascus Museum. Apparently in the earliest phase of construction it was a house of prayer for Jewish Christians built on the pattern of a synagogue but hidden, as a chapel of a private residence. (ABB, 333)

A SELECTED ADDITIONAL
BIBLIOGRAPHY

Albright, W. F., and J. L. Kelso. *The Excavation of Bethel*. Cambridge, Mass.: American Schools of Oriental Research, 1968.

Archaeology. Jerusalem: Israel Pocket Library, Keter, 1974.

Avigad, N. *Archaeological Discoveries in the Jewish Quarter of Jerusalem*. Jerusalem: Israel Exploration Society and Israel Museum, 1976.

Avi-Yonah, M., ed. *Jerusalem*. Jerusalem: Israeli Publishing Institute, 1960.

Biran, A., ed. *Temples and High Places in Biblical Times*. Jerusalem: Hebrew Union College–Jewish Institute of Religion, 1981.

Boraas, R. S., and L. T. Geraty. *Heshbon 1976*. Berrien Springs, Mich.: Andrews University Press, 1978.

Caiger, S. L. *Bible and Spade: An Introduction to Biblical Archaeology*. London: Oxford University Press, 1951.

Corswant, W. *A Dictionary of Life in Bible Times*. New York: Oxford University Press, 1960.

Freedman, D. N., ed. *Preliminary Excavation Reports: Bâb ed-Dhrā, Sardis, Meiron, Tell el-Hesi, Carthage (Punic)*. Cambridge, Mass.: American Schools of Oriental Research, 1978.

Fritsch, C. T., ed. *The Joint Expedition to Caesarea Maritima*. Missoula, Mont.: Scholars Press, 1975.

Horgan, M. P. *Pesharim: Qumran Interpretations of Biblical Books*. Washington, D.C.: Catholic Biblical Association, 1979.

Jerusalem City Museum. *Finds from the Archaeological Excavations Near the Temple Mount*. Jerusalem: Israel Exploration Society, n.d.

Kelso, J. L., ed. *Excavations at New Testament Jericho and Khirbet en-Nitla*. New Haven: American Schools of Oriental Research, 1955.

Kollek, T., and M. Pearlman. *Jerusalem*. Jerusalem: Steimatzky, 1968.

Lapp, P. W., and N. L. Lapp. *Discoveries in the Wadi ed-Daliyeh*. Cambridge, Mass.: American Schools of Oriental Research, 1974.

Mackowski, R. M. *Jerusalem, City of Jesus*. Grand Rapids, Mich.: Eerdmans, 1980.

Marsino, F. *Jerusalem, Rock of Ages*. New York: Harcourt Brace Jovanovich, 1969.

Matthiae, P. *Ebla: An Empire Rediscovered*. Garden City, N.Y.: Doubleday, 1981.

Rendel-Short, A. *Modern Discovery and the Bible*. London: Inter-Varsity, 1942.

Yadin, Yigael. *Masada*. New York: Random House, 1966.

INDEX

Aaron, 36
Abdi-Tirshi, 64
Abdu-Heba, 15, 62
Abel, 6
Abiathar, 213
Abigail, 81
Abijah, 105
Abishar, 28
Abner, 84
Abraham, 9–20
Abu, month of, 187
Abu Dis, 204
Abu Matar, 19
Abu Simbel, 31
Acropolis, Hazor, 93
Adad, 176
Adadah, 68
Adadnirari III, 104, 157
Adam, 6, 59
Adar, 118
Adiabene, xviii
Admah, 12
Adon, 117–18
Adonai, 35
Adonizedek, 62
Adoption tablets, 16
Aelia Capitolina, 90, 215
Aenon, 198
Aetheria, 203

Agora, Athens, 242
Ahab, 96–101
Aharoni, Yohanan, xx, 20,
    45, 47–48, 50–51, 63,
    106, 115–16, 119
Ahasuerus, 136
Ahatmilku, 157
Ahaz, 108, 112, 123
Ahiqar, The Words of,
    146–47, 151, 153, 167
Ahmose, 69
Ahura-mazda, 136
Ai, 61, 63
Ain Karim, 218
Ain Lifta, 67
Ain Silwan, 230
Akeldama, 236
Akkad, 128
Akki, 33
Alabaster, 216
Alalakh, 101
Al-al-gar, 6
Albright, W. F., xv, xvii,
    xix, xxiv, 7, 11–12, 15,
    18–20, 58, 62–63, 69,
    75–76, 113, 119, 143,
    157
Aleppo, xix
Alexander the Great, 12, 222

Alexandria, 131
Almah, 161
Alt, Albrecht, 66
Altars, 45
A-lu-lim, 6
Amarna. *See* Tell el-Amarna
Amasis, 88
Amaziah, 105
Amen-em-opet, 29, 149
Amen-hotep II, 144
Amen-hotep III, 88
Amen-hotep IV, 143
American Schools of Oriental
    Research, xviii
Amestris, 136
Amiran, Ruth, xx, 125, 224
Ammon, 123, 131
Amon, 32
Amorites, 14, 29, 62
Amoz, 159
Amrit, 100
Amwas, 225
Anak, 50
Anakim, 13
Anat, 164
Anath, 20, 43
Anathoth, 167
Ani, 153
Ankhmahor, 17
Anonymous of Piacenza,
    197, 202
Antigonus, Mattathias, 44
Antioch, 239
Antioch of Pisidia, 241
Antiochus IV Epiphanes, 206
Antonia (fortress), 131, 195,
    224, 234, 246
Anubis, 25
Anum, 8
Aphek, 117
Apiru, 16, 23–24, 70
Apollo, 116, 243, 250
Apostolic Constitutions, 127
Appius Claudius the Blind,
    247
Apsu, 3
Aqaba, Gulf of, 12, 37, 94,
    96
Aqhat, 83
Arabia, 96
Arad, 47–48, 50–51,
    89–90, 92, 167
Aram, 10
Aramaic, 129
Arameans, 10, 14, 22
Araunah, 87
Arch of Titus, Rome, 44
Arculf, 217, 227, 236
Areopagus, Athens, 243
Aretas, 251
Arioch, 13
Arish, el-, 37
Aristeas, Letter of, 129, 131
Ark of the Covenant, 69, 79,
    89, 98, 168
Armageddon, 264
Aroer, 68
Arriyuk, 13
Arslan Tash, 103
Artaxerxes II, 134
Artemis, 244–45
Asa, 99

Asahel, 84
Asaph, 111
Ashayahu, 81
Ashdod, 68, 191
Asherah, 43, 55
Ashkelon, 117–18, 171–72
Ashna, 108
Ashtaroth, 72, 82
Ashtart,72
Ashur, 3, 230
Ashurbanipal, 109, 126,
    130, 177–78, 185, 187,
    222
Ashurnazirpal, 135
Asiarchs, 245
Assumption of Moses, 260
Assyria, 11, 56, 107–10,
    117
Astarte, 43, 107
Athens, 242–43
Atrahasis Epic, 7
Atum, 31, 154
Avaris, 27, 32
Avigad, Nahman, xx, 16,
    114, 117, 119, 125,
    163, 173, 220
Avi-Yonah, M., xx, 234
Azariah, 105–6
Azariyeh, el-, 204
Azekah, 169
Aztecs, 7

Baal, 3, 20, 43, 72, 100,
    144, 164
Baal-hadad, 142, 164
Baal Zaphon, 172

Baal-zephon, 38–39
Baana ben Ahilud, 94
Baasha, 99, 157
Bab edh-Dhra, 12
Babel, 9
Babylon, 8–9, 118, 120, 128
Babylonian Chronicle,
    116–18
Babylonians, 26, 117
Babylonian Talmud, 79
Bahat, Dan, 220
Balaam, 52
Balatah, 12
Banu-Simal, 23, 29
Banu-Yamin, 23, 29
Baptism, 198–99
Bar Adon, P., xx, 68
Bar Ama, 103
Baramki, D. C., 196
Bar Kokhba, 145, 209
Baruch, 170
Bata, 25
Bedouins, 12
Beer-sheba, 19, 45, 51, 62,
    68, 111, 115–16, 123,
    182–83
Behistun, 191
Bel, 128, 165
Bela, 12
Belshazzar, 161, 180
Bema, 244
Ben Aryeh, Sarah, 240
Ben-Dov, Meir, 220
Benefactor (title), 223
Ben-hadad I, 98
Ben-hadad II, 100, 105

Beni Hasan, 12
Benjamin, 23–24, 28, 59, 61
Benoit, P., 234
Berekhyahu, 170
Berossus, 162
Bethany, 203
Bethany (beyond the Jordan),
    198
Bethel, 61–63, 97
Beth-haccherem, 106
Beth-horon, 124
Bethlehem, 23–24, 219
Bethphage, 203
Beth-shan (Beth-shean), xix,
    42, 54, 82, 90, 124
Beth Shearim, 238
Beth-shemesh, 86
Bethzatha, 228
Biran, Avraham, xx, 68, 75,
    98
Bir Ayub, 67
Biridiya, 72
Birthstool, 32
Bishops, 254
Bit-Lahmi, 24
Black Obelisk, 104
Bliss, F. J., xviii, 63
Boaz, 77, 91
Boghazkoi, 19
Boomerangs, 178
Braslavi, J., 85
Broshi, Magen, xx
Burrows, Millar, xvi,
    xxii–xxiii, 15, 106,
    129, 159

Caesarea, 196, 208, 239,
    245
Cain, 6
Calah, 121
Caligula, 206
Cambyses, 88
Cana, 226
Canaan, xix, 8, 11, 14, 16,
    22–23, 28, 36, 42,
    57–58, 62, 64, 66, 72
Canaanites, 28
Capernaum, 202, 220
Capitals, of pillars, 91
Captivity, Symbol of, 188
Carchemish, 117
Carmel, 66
Cazelles, H., 14
Chaldeans, 10, 177
Chalice of Antioch, 206
Chariots, 27
Chemosh, 102
Cherubim, 43, 78, 179
Chester Beatty Papyri, 26,
    257
Chorazin, 205
Church of All Nations, 207
Church of St. Anne, 227–28
Church of St. Gabriel, 197
Church of St. John, 263
Church of St. Joseph, 197
Church of St. Peter in
    Gallicantu, 208, 233
Church of the Annunciation,
    197
Church of the Holy
    Sepulcher, 210

Church of Zion, 217
Circumcision, 17
City of David, xviii, 88
City of Salt, 68
Claudius, 241
Clement of Alexandria, 260
Clermont-Ganneau, Charles,
   xviii
Coburn, C. M., 252
Code of Eshnunna, 41
Code of Hammurabi, 17,
   40–41, 46, 77
Cohen, Rudolph, 68
Colossae, 256
Conder, C. R., xviii
Constantine, 13
Convent of Our Lady of
   Sion, 233–34, 246
Corban, 214
Corinth, 243, 248
Cornfeld, G., 95
Covenant, 7–8, 16, 18
Crowfoot, J., 133
Crucifixion, 210–11
Cuneiform, xviii–xix, 43, 79
Cymmerians, 178
Cyprus, 240
Cyril of Jerusalem, 217
Cyrus, 91, 128–29, 161

Dagon, 43
Dahood, Mitchell, 36
Damascus, 17, 103, 105,
   108, 239
Damascus Gate, Jerusalem,
   114, 238

Dan, 64, 75, 77, 86, 97
Danel, 13, 83
Daniel, 176, 205
Danites, 75
Darius, 122, 135–36, 162,
   180, 191
David, 63, 81, 85, 121
David's Tomb, 237
Dead Sea, 5, 12, 18, 141
Debir, 63, 118
Deborah, 73, 264
Decapolis, 215
Deir Alla, 52
Delphi, 250
Demetrius, 245
Department of Antiquities
   and Museums of Israel,
   xviii
Department of Antiquities of
   Jordan, xviii
Derbe, 241
Desolating sacrilege, 205
Deutsche-Evangelische
   Institut für
   Altertumskunde des
   Heiligen Landes, xviii
Deutsche Orient-
   Gesellschaft, xviii
De Vaux, Roland, xix, xxii,
   14, 157
Dever, William G., 94
Dialogue About Human
   Misery, A, 155
Diana (Artemis), 244–45
Didascalia, 127
Disciples, 238

Dome of the Rock, 90
Dominus Flebit (chapel), 223
Dothan, Moshe, 68
Dothan, T., xx, 182
Dreams, 25–26
Drioton, E., 149
Dumuzi, 6
Dunayevsky, I., 156
Duncan, J. G., 132
Dung Gate, City of David,
　132
Dura-Europos, 248, 265
Dur-Sharrukin, 161

Eanna Tower, Erech, 8
Eannatum, 73
Earthquake, at Hazor, 182
Ebal, Mount, 8, 226
Eber, 14
Ebla, xix, 3, 5, 7, 9–10, 15,
　17, 22, 35, 80, 260
Ecce Homo Arch Jerusalem,
　233
Ecclesiasticus, 114
Ecole Biblique de Jérusalem,
　xviii–xix
Edom, 51
Eglon, 63
Egypt, 11–12, 16, 23,
　25–28, 30, 43, 71–72,
　82, 97, 117
Egyptian language, 14, 43
Ehrlich, A. B., 33
Eitan, A., 224
Ekron, 109, 190
El, 16, 43, 55, 143, 188

Elah, 81
Elam, 172, 178
Elath, 96, 105
El-berith, 74
El-elyon, 16
Elephantine, 26, 129, 132,
　134, 146
Eliakim, 111, 117–18
Eliezer, 16
Elijah, 34, 67, 102
Ellasar, 13
El-Shaddai, 35
Embalming, 29
Emim, 13
Emmaus, 225
Engedi, 81, 141, 156
Enkimdu, 6
En-man-lu-Anna, 6
Ennead, 154
Enoch, 260
En-rogel, 67
Enuma Elish, 3–4
Epaphras, 256
Ephesus, 244
Ephraim, 24
Ephrath(ah), 24
Ephron, 19
Epic of Gilgamesh, The, 7,
　154, 221
Epiphanius, 204, 208
Er, 24
Erastus, 248
Erech, 8
Esagil, 9
Esarhaddon, 126
Esau, 20

Esdraelon, Plain of, 82, 196
Essenes, 188
Esther, 136–37
E-temen-an-ki, 9
Etham, 38
Ethiopia, 135
Et Tell, 61
Eudocia, 238
Euphrates, 10, 14
Eusebius, 69, 200, 204, 226,
    228
  Onomasticon, 207, 227,
    231
Eutychius of Alexandria,
    203, 217
Evil-merodach, 120
Execration Texts, 15, 63, 70
Exodus, 65
Eye, tomb of, 144
Ezekiel, 14
Ezion-geber, xix, 37, 94, 96,
    105, 108
Ezra, 134

Famine, in Egypt, 26
Fara, 7
Feast of Tabernacles, 229
Feifa, 12
Finegan, Jack, 203
Fisher, C. S., xix
Fish Gate, Jerusalem, 114
Fitzgerald, G. M., xix
Fitzmyer, Joseph A., 214
Flood, 6–7
Forum of Appius, Rome,
    247

Frankincense, 196
Freud, Sigmund, 26

Gadd, C. J., 116
Gadd Chronicle, 187
Galerius, 242
Gamaliel, 238
Gamla, 200
Gapn, 164
Garber, P. L., 89
Garden of the Steles,
    Ismailia, 32
Garden of Uzza, Jerusalem,
    124
Garstang, J., xix, 60, 64
Gates, City, 86
Gath, 84
Gaza, 37
Gebal, 79, 120
Gebel el-Rumeidi, 13
Gedaliah, 119
Gehman, Henry S., 165
Genesis Apocryphon, 5, 15
Gerar, 19
Gerizim, Mount, 8, 226–27
Geshem, 132
Gethsemane, 206
Gezer, xix, 54, 58, 60,
    92–94
Gezer Calendar, 54, 183
Gibeah, 76, 80
Gibeon, 83, 124
Gideon, 59
Gihon, 5
Gihon Spring, 15, 84, 113,
    125, 133, 230

Gilgal, 69
Gittaim, 84
Givat ha-Mivtar, 211
Glueck, Nelson, xix, xxi,
　　18, 51, 54, 68, 94–95,
　　105, 108
Goedicke, Hans, 39–40
Gog, 178
Gold, 196
Golden Gate, Jerusalem,
　　204, 231, 237
Golgotha, 209
Goliath, 81
Gomer, 178
Gomorrah, 12–13, 18
Good Samaritan, 221
Gordon, Cyrus H., 10, 106
Gordon's Calvary, 210
Goshen, 27, 32
Gozan, 81, 83, 175
Greece, Xerxes' attack on,
　　135
Gulf of Aqaba, 12, 37, 94,
　　96
Gulf of Suez, 38
Guthe, H., xviii
Guy, P. L. O., 96

Habiru (Hapiru), 14
Hadad, 43, 108, 143
Hadadezer, 100
Hadrian, 13, 219
Hagar, 17
Hamilton, W. J., 256
Hammath, 69
Hammurabi, 8, 64

Code of, 17, 40–41, 46,
　　77
Hamor, 23
Hanazir, 12
Hapiru (Habiru), 14
Haran, 9–11
Harem el-Halil, 20
Harithath IV, 251
Harlan, J. Penrose, 18
Harris Papyrus 500. See
　　Song of the Harper
Hasavyahu, 42
Hatshepsut, 34, 40
Hatti, 118
Hazael, 103–4
Hazor, xvii, xix, xxiv, 49,
　　51, 53–54, 58, 63–66,
　　73, 89, 91–92, 94, 100,
　　106–7, 145, 156, 182
Heber, 14
Hebrews, 14, 36, 41
Hebrew University of
　　Jerusalem, xviii
Hebron, 13, 20, 49–51, 58
Heights of the Friend, 13
Helen, queen of Adiabene,
　　xviii
Hepatoscopy, 177
Hermon, 16
Hermopolis, 154, 167
Herod, 90, 131, 211, 224
Herod Agrippa I, 240
Herod Agrippa II, 247
Herodium, 196, 200
Herodotus, xx, 9, 29, 88
Herod the Great, 100, 129,

195, 215, 222
Hetepheres, 157
Hezekiah, 67, 84, 109–12,
  114, 116, 124–25, 133,
  190
Hezion, 98
Hierapolis, 246
Hilkiah, 111
Hilquiyahu, 124
Hittites, 10, 19, 80
Holy of Holies, 47, 51, 53,
  89–90
Holy Place, 47, 51, 89–90
Hophra, 172
Hor, 37
Horeb, 34
Hormah, 50
Horus, 37, 96
Hoshayahu, 119, 164
Hoshea, 107
Howland, E. G., 89
Huldah Gates, Jerusalem,
  229
Hyksos, 11, 27, 32, 49–50,
  65, 69–70
Hymn to the Aton, The, 143
Hyrcanus, John, 12

Ibni-Adad, 64
Ibsha, 52
Iconium, 241
Inanna, 6, 8
India, 135
*Instruction of Amen-em-opet,
  The,* 141, 146–51
*Instruction of the Vizier

Ptah-hotep, The,* 30,
  155
Iraq el-Amir, 132
Iron, 80
Isaac, 19–21
Isaiah, 111–12
Ishmael, 17
Ish-ra-il, 22
Ishtar, 167
  See also Astarte
Ismailia, 32
Israel, 22, 28, 36, 51
Israelites, 32, 39, 79
Isthmian Games, 250, 258
Ivory, 96, 101, 182
Iyaneq, 50
Iyqa-ammu, 15
Izbeth Sarte, 54

Jaazaniah, 119–20, 139–40
Jabin, 64–65, 73
Jachin, 91
Jacob, 12, 14, 17, 20–22,
  28, 71
Jacob's well, 227
Jebus, 59
Jebusites, 62, 84–85, 87
Jefferson, Thomas, xv
Jehoahaz, 105, 117
Jehoiachin, 118, 120
Jehoiakim, 117–18
Jehozeriah, 124
Jehu, 102, 104
Jerahmeel, 170
Jeremiah, 69, 117, 171

Jericho, xvii, xix, 54,
59–60, 222
Jeroboam I, 97–98
Jeroboam II, 98–99, 104–5
Jerome, 69, 79, 216, 221,
231
Jerusalem, xvii, xix, 14–16,
44, 47, 49, 58–59, 62,
68, 85, 92, 109–10,
114, 116, 118–19, 123,
125–26, 129, 132–34,
157, 219, 265
Jezebel, 100
Joab, 84–85
Joah, 111
Joash, 86
Johanan, 133–34
Johns, C. N., 224
John the Baptist, 214, 218
Jones, Felix, 185
Joppa, 69–70, 184
Jordan River, 58–59, 198
Jordan Valley, 12
Joseph, 24–27, 30–31
Josephus, xviii, 15, 67, 129,
131, 200, 215, 226,
231, 240, 247
Joshua ben Josedech, 129
Joshua ben Nun, 58, 71, 116
Josiah, 81, 115–17
Jotham, 108
Jubilee, 15
Judah, 118, 122, 126, 130
Judas, 236
Jupiter (planet), 115
Jupiter, temple of,

Jerusalem, 215
Jupiter Capitolinus, 186

Kabara, 145
Kadashmanenlil, 88
Kadesh, 142
Kalakh, 136
Kaplan, J., xx
Karatepe, 16
Karnak, 31–32, 37, 123
Kathar, 43
Katirat, 161
Kaufman, A., 220
Kelim-ninu, 17
Kelso, J. L., 196
Kenites, 6, 35, 47
Kenyon, Kathleen, xix, 14,
60–61, 84–85, 92, 99,
101, 116, 119, 126,
132, 202
Keren-happuch, 103
Kerti Hüyük, 241
Khafaja, 61
Khirbet, xvi
Khirbet Ararah, 68
Khirbet-Beit-Lei, 165
Khirbet el-Karmil, 66
Khirbet Nimrah, 13
Khirbet Rabud, 63
Khirbet Seilun, 69, 168
Khirbet Sibtha, 13
Khirbet Tibnah, 71
Khnum, 26
Khnum-hotep III, 28
Khorsabad, 109, 177, 184
Khu-Sebek, 70

Kidron Valley, 168, 233
Kiriath-arba, 19, 50
Kiriath-sepher, xix, 63
Kish, 3, 7
Kitchener, H. H., xviii
Kjaer, Hans, 98
Kochavi, Moshe, 63
Koheleth, 155
Krahmalkov, Charles R., 40
Kue, 97
Kulisi, 72
Kuntillet Ajrud, 172
Kurpazak, 20

Laban, 21–22
Labayu, 70
Lachish, 46, 54, 58, 62–63,
    80, 86, 110, 118–19,
    121, 124, 169
  Letters, 118, 164, 170–71
Lamentation over the
    Destruction of Ur, 174
Laodicea, 256, 259, 264
Lapp, Paul W., 12
Larsa, 8
Law, 41
  Assyrian, 41–42, 47
  Hebrew, 46–47
  of talion, 41
Lazarus, 232
Leah, 17, 20
Legend of King Keret, The,
    56, 73, 141, 143
Leijjun, 21
Leviathan, 143, 164
Levirate, 56

Levites, 59
Lions' Gate, Jerusalem, 239,
    246
Lithostrotos, 233
Lord's Prayer, 201–2, 221
Lullu, 4, 17
Lysanias of Abilene, 220
Lystra, 241

Macalister, R. A. S., xix,
    54, 85, 94, 132, 183
Maccabees, 129
Machpelah, 20
Madaba Map, 13, 198, 217
Magic Papyrus of Paris, 244
Mahaneh-dan, 75
Mahd adh Dhahab, 96
Maimonides, 42
Makhtesh, 190
Mallowan, M. E. L., 135, 185
Malta, 247
Mamre, 13, 50
Manasseh, 114, 117, 124,
    126–27
Manger, and birth of Jesus,
    219
Maqaam el-Halil, 16
Marduk, 128, 162, 176
Marduka, 137
Mari, xxiv, 10–11, 13,
    23–24, 28, 63, 90, 105,
    230
Marquet-Krause, J., 61
Mars (planet), 115
Masada, 57, 90, 143, 196,
    200

Maspero, Gaston, 25
Matthiae, Paolo, 35
Mazar, Benjamin, xviii–xix,
　48, 85–86, 124–26,
　132, 156, 166, 168,
　179, 195, 214, 220,
　229, 231, 240, 247
Medes, 117
Mediterranean, 38–39
Meek, T. J., 41, 77
Megiddo, xvii, 7, 45, 54,
　60, 64, 72, 86, 90–94,
　96–97, 100, 105, 111,
　117, 124, 145, 188
Meinardus, Otto F. A., 262
Mekal, 42
Melchizedek, 15
Melkart, 91, 100, 178
Menahem, 106
Menahem of Samaria, 106
Mendenhall, G. E., 7
Menorah, 44
Menzaleh, Lake, 39
Meremoth, 48
Merenptah. See Merneptah
Merneptah, 22–23, 36, 62,
　67–68
Merodach-baladan, 112
Merom, 64
Mesad, 42
Mesha, 102
Meshed-a-Teir, 16
Meshel, Zeev, 172
Mesopotamia, 8, 10, 16–17,
　43
Messiah, legend of entrance

into temple at
　Jerusalem, 204
Michael, (archangel), 260
Midian, 34
Migdol, 38
Milik, J. T., 214
Millo, 85–86
Minet el-Beida, 164
Mirrors, 250
Mishnah, 156
Mitinti, 110
Mizbeah, 48
Mizpah, 99
Moab, xviii, 51–52, 102
Moabites, 52
Monastery of St. John the
　Theologian, 262
Monotheism, 8, 145
Mordecai, 137
Moriah, Mount, 85
Moses, 8, 33–34, 36, 43,
　48, 260
Moses' seat, 205
Mot, 164
Mount of Olives, 114, 124,
　216, 221, 223, 236
Mummu Tiamat, 3
Murashu Archives, 168
Musri, 97
Mutawali, 165
Myrrh, 196

Naaman, 108
Nabal, 81
Nabataeans, 251
Nablus, 145

Nabonidus, 128, 161, 180
  Chronicle, 161–62
Nabopolassar, 187
Naboth, 101
Nahor, 9
Nash Papyrus, 40, 53
Nashwi, 21
Nativity, site of Jesus', 219
Naville, E., 32
Nazareth, 196
Neapolis, 12
Nebo, 128, 165
Nebuchadnezzar
  (Nebuchadrezzar), 63,
  117–18, 120, 171–72
Neco, 116–17
Negev, xix, 47, 54, 92
Negev, A., xx
Nehebu-kau, 154
Nehemiah, 132–34, 247
Nemi, 154
Nemit, 154
Nephtoah, Waters of, 67
Netjer-er-khet, 26
Netzer, Ehud, 196
Nikkal, 161
Nile River, 26, 38, 144, 154
Nimrod, 8
Nimrud, 157, 184
Nineveh, 3, 7, 110, 117,
  126, 144–45, 183–85,
  187
Ninhursag, 4
Nintu, 4
Nippur, 6, 138, 169, 174
Nir David, 145

Noah, 7
Noth, Martin, 63
Numeira, 12–13
Nuzi, 16–17, 20–22, 78

Odeion, Corinth, 243, 248
Omri, 99–100, 102, 157
Onan, 24
Onesimus, 259
Ophel, 85–86, 132–33
Ophir, 95–96, 121
Origen, 23, 260
Orthostats, 81, 83
Oryx, 12
Osnappar, 129
Ostraca, xvii
Ovis laticaudata, 79
Oxyrhynchus papyri, 252

Paleo-Hebraic script, 43
Palestine, 12, 58
Palestine Exploration Fund,
  xviii
Palmyra, 48
Pampeya Lucilia, 229
Pantheism, 129
Papyrus Anastasi I, 70
Parker, R. A., xix, 84, 125
Parrot, André, xvii, xxiv,
  10, 14, 104, 184–85,
  227
Pashhur, 48, 168
Paternoster, 202
Patmos, 262
Patriarchal Age, 20
Patriarchs, 17, 21, 34

Paul, 241–47
Pekah, 107
Penates, 21
Perga, 241
Pergamum, 243, 262
Persepolis, 135–36
Pesher, 188
*Pessimistic Dialogue
Between Master and
Servant, A,* 142, 146,
152
Peter, 202
Petrie, Flinders, xviii, 32, 63
Pettinato, Giovanni, 4, 35
Philadelphia, Lydia, 263
Philip (evangelist), 246
Philippi, 241–42
Philistines, 36–37, 39, 69,
75, 78–80, 82, 98, 168
Phoenicia, 94
Phoenician language, 43
Pi-ha-hiroth, 38–39
Pilate, 208, 224, 233–34
Pilgrim of Bordeaux, 208,
227–28
Pim, 79
Pithom, 31–32
Plague, 189
Pliny, 218
Plutarch, xx
Poemenia, 236
Pompeii, 202
Portico of Solomon, 231
Potiphar, 25
Potsherds, xvii, 19, 92, 121
Prayer of Manasseh, 127

Pritchard, James B., 196
Proto-Sinaitic Inscriptions,
43
Psusennes II, 88
Ptolemy II Philadelphus, 131
Pul, 106

Qainu, 133
Qarqar, 100–1
Qayits, 183
Qedar, 132
Qoseir, 40
Quarantal, 199
Qubbat el-Rahil, 23
Qubeibeh, el-, 225
Queen of Heaven (Ishtar),
167
Quirinius, 218
Quloniye, 225
Qumran, xviii–xix, 5, 15,
49, 59, 68–69, 78, 80,
112, 142, 159, 181,
186–88, 190, 197,
199–200, 219–20, 228,
232, 238, 254, 261

Raamses, 31–32, 38
Rabmag, 110
Rabsaris, 110
Rabshakeh, 110
Rachel, 17, 21, 23–24
Rachel's Tomb, 23–24
Rahab, 59
Rainey, A. F., 115–16, 119
Ramah, 24, 99
Ramat Rahel, 106

Rameses, 32
Ramet el-Khalil, 13
Ramses II, 25, 31–32, 34,
    36–37, 50, 52, 70, 74,
    101
Ramses III, 79
Rapha, 13
Ras el-Safsafa, 34
Ras esh-Shiyah, 204
Ras Shamra, xviii–xix, 15,
    42–43, 79, 87, 106,
    143, 161, 164, 178, 183
Rast, W. E., 12–13
Rebecca, 20
Red Sea, 5, 38
Rehoboam, 63, 123
Reisner, G. A., xix
Rekh-mi-Re, 32
Renan, Ernest, 89
Rephaim, 13
Resheph, 43, 189
Retebeh, er-, 32
Reubenites, 121
Rimmon, 108
Rim-Sin, 8
Robinson, Edward, xvii,
    68–69
Robinson's Arch, Jerusalem,
    229
Rock of the Agony, 207
Rome, 265
Rothenberg, Beno, 95
Rowe, A., xix
Rylands Papyrus, 235

Sabitu, 222

Sacrilege, desolating, 205
Safadi, 19
Safi, 12–13
Safsafa, 34
St. Basil the Great, 263
St. Stephen's Gate,
    Jerusalem, 238–39, 246
Salem, 15
Samaria, xix, 12, 86, 91, 96,
    99, 100–2, 108–9,
    131–32, 157, 182
Samson, 74–75
Sanballat, 131–32
San el-Hagar, 50
Santorini, 39
Saqqara, 117, 154, 171
Sarah, 17, 20
Sarcophagi, 30, 88
Sardis, 263
Sargon I, 139
Sargon II, 108–9, 190–91
Sargon of Agade, 33, 35
Saul, 76, 79–80, 82
Saulcy, Louis, xviii
Scarabs, 36, 68
Schaub, T., 12–13
Schick, C., 227
Schumacher, G., xviii, 105
Scrolls, xviii–xix
Seals, 5, 36, 68, 72, 81,
    108, 111, 114, 117–20,
    124, 159
Sea of Galilee, xxiii, 12, 234
Sea of Reeds, 5, 37–39
Sea Peoples, 79
Sebaste, 100

Secacah, 68
Sehetep-ib-Re, 153
Sekmem, 70
Sela, 105
Sela, es-, 105
Sellin, E., xix, 14, 23, 74
Semadar, 107, 156
Semites, 12, 27–28, 57
Semitic inscriptions, 43
Sennacherib, 109–10, 116,
    119, 124, 144, 170
Sen-usert III, 70
Sepulchers, 210, 212
Serabit el-Hadem, 43
Seraiah, 173
Seraphim, 160
Serbal, 34
Sergius Paulus, 240
Sermon on the Mount, 248
Shalem, 15
Shalmaneser III, 72, 100,
    103
Shalmaneser IV, 103
Shalmaneser V, 108
Shamash, 116, 192
Sharuhen, 69
Shebaniah, 105
Shebna (Shebnah), 111, 163
Shechem, xix, 11, 15, 23,
    70–71, 74, 97
Sheep Gate, Jerusalem, 227
Shem, 14
Shema, 53, 105
Shennima, 17
Sheshong, 123
Sheth, 52

Shiloh, 15, 69, 98, 168
Shinar, 60
Shishak, 69, 98, 123
Shofar, 93
Shoshu, 52
Shulman, 43
Shur, 37–39
Shutu, 52
Siamon, 88
Signets, 24–25, 27
    See also Seals
Siheil, 26
Sillibel, 110
Siloam, 113–14, 125, 165,
    222, 230
    Pool, 67
Simeon, 69
Simons, J., 61, 84, 114
Sinai, 34, 37–38, 43
Si-nuhe, 53
Sirbonis Lake, 38
Sit Shamshi, 55, 102
Skmimi, 70
Slavery, 259
Smith, Eli, xvii
Smith, George, 3
Smyrna, 262
Sodom, 12–13, 18
Soli, 240
Solomon, xix, 65, 72, 79,
    86, 88–90, 92–95, 97,
    123, 129, 133, 140,
    152, 155, 157
Song of the Harper, 70,
    153–54
Song of the Sea, 40

Starkey, J. L., 62, 169
Stele of the Vultures, 73
Stele of the Year 400, 50
Steles, 21, 23, 36, 42, 53,
    74, 98, 100, 102, 109
Stephens, F. J., 192
The Story of Si-nuhe, 53
Strabo, 244
Strata, xvii
Succoth, 32, 38, 230
Suez, 36–37
    Gulf of, 38
Sukenek, E. L., xix
Sumer, 7, 128
Sumerian Job, 138
Sumerian King List, 6
Sumerian literature, 6
Susa, 55, 135–36, 188
Synagogue of the Freedmen,
    238
Synagogues, 200, 220, 243,
    264
Syria-Palestine, 118
Syrophoenician, 214

Taanach, xix, 14, 60, 124
Tabe-el, 160
Tabernacle, 43–44, 69, 89
Tabgha, xxiii, 203
Tablets, xviii–xix, 79
Tabrimmon, 98
Talmud, 226
Tanin, 143
Tanis, 32, 36, 60
Tarsus, 246
Tartan, 110

Tekoa, 182
Tell Abu Harmal, 41
Tell Abu Hureira, 19
Tell Arad, 51
Tell Batash, 74
Tell Beersheba, 20
Tell Beit Mirsim, 63, 118
Tell Dan, 177
Tell Daphna, 171
Tell ed-Duweir, 62, 110-11
Tell el-Amarna, 13, 15, 24,
    58, 62, 64, 70, 72, 88,
    121, 144
Tell el-Damiya, 59
Tell el-Farah, 69, 99, 157
Tell el-Ful, 75, 80
Tell el-Hesi, 63
Tell el-Husn, 82
Tell el-Jurn, 156
Tell el-Kheleifeh, 94, 105
Tell el-Maskhutah, 32, 132
Tell el-Muhmar, 117
Tell el-Qedah, 64
Tell el-San, 32
Tell el-Sultan, 222
Tell en-Nasbeh, 99, 119
Tell er-Ras, 227
Tell er-Retebeh, 32
Tell es-Sultan, xvii, 60
Tell Halaf, 81, 160
Tell Masos, 50
Tell Qasileh, 75, 121, 181
Tell Ras abu Hamid, 84
Tell Ras el-Kharubeh, 167
Tell Tainat, 89–90
Tell Umm Hamad, 59

Tells, xvi, xvii, 55, 66
Temileh, 51
Temple, of Jerusalem, 51,
     88–89, 91, 116,
     125–26, 129, 131, 195,
     199, 204–5, 215, 219,
     229, 237, 246, 253
     Herod's, 44
Temple Mount, xviii, xx
Temples, Canaanite, 123
Ten Commandments, 40, 53
Terah, 10
Thebes, Egypt, 24, 26, 28,
     36, 40, 111, 187
Thenius, Otto, 210
Thera, 39
Thessalonica, 242
Thomas of Malhenda, 95
Thoth, 70
Thummim, 44
Thutmose I, 34
Thutmose II, 34
Thutmose III, 31, 69
Thutmose IV, 101
Thyatira, 263
Tiamat, 176
Tibni, 99
Tiglath-Pileser III, 65, 106,
     108, 165
Timnah, 6, 54, 74–75,
     94–95
Timnath-heres, 71
Timnath-serah, 71
Tirhakah, 111
Tirzah, xix, 99, 157
Titus, 44, 207

Titus, Arch of, Rome, 44
Tobiah, 131–32
Tomb of Pharaoh's
     Daughter, 91
Tomb of the Kings, xviii,
     211
Tower of Babel, 8
Tree of Life, 5
Trever, John C., 159
Tsah, 167
Tubal-cain, 6
Tufnell, Olga, 119
Tulul Abu el-Alayiq, 222
Tupkitilla, 20
Tut-ankh-amen, 27, 29, 144,
     160, 178
Twenty-four Priestly
     Courses, 197
Twisting Serpent, 143
Twitchell, Karl, 96
Tyre, 89, 126, 144, 178
Tyropoeon Valley, xviii,
     126–27, 133, 190

Ugar, 164
Ugarit, xviii, 7, 10, 42–43,
     90, 112, 142
Ugaritic literature, 3, 19–20,
     43, 56, 73, 83, 106
Umm el-Bayyara, 105
Unis, 154
Upper Room, Jerusalem,
     208, 216–17
Ur, 7–11, 174
Urim, 44
Uruk, 8, 10

Ushishkin, David, 119
Uzziah, 67, 108, 124
Uzziyau, 105

Valley Gate, Jerusalem, 133
Van Beek, G. W., xxi
Venus (planet), 115
Vespasian, 265
Via Dolorosa, 131, 233
Vieyra, Maurice, 222
Vincent, L. H., xix, 20,
    84–85, 234
Vizier, to pharaoh, 27

Wadi Daliyeh, 131
Wadi el-Charrar, 198
Wadi esh-Sheira, 19
Wadi Tumilat, 32
Warka, 8
Warka Cylinder, 130
*War of the Sons of Light
    Against the Sons of
    Darkness,* 49, 59, 200,
    232
Warren, Charles, xviii, 84,
    86
Water Gate, Jerusalem, 133
Watzinger, Carl, 90
Weights and measures, 46
Weill, R., 238
Weld-Blundell prism, 7
Western Wall, Jerusalem,
    125, 195, 215
Wheeler, Mortimer, xv
Wood, J. T., 244

Woolley, Leonard, 10
Wright, G. Ernest, xix,
    xxi–xxii, 32, 50, 52,
    62–63, 74, 93, 97, 119,
    126
Wullu, 21

Xenophon, xx
Xerxes, 135–37

Yaa, 53
Yadin, Yigael, xix, xxiv,
    64–66, 73, 92–94,
    106–7, 115–16, 141,
    143, 156, 169, 182
Yahweh, 34–35, 47–48, 90,
    92, 98, 111, 141–43,
    165
Yam, 3, 143
Yaosh, 119
Yebel Musa, 34
Yebel Serbal, 34
Yehozarah, 111
Yehud, 122, 130
Yemen, 23
Yirmeyah, 171

Zabul, 43
Zalmunna, 74
Zarethan, 59
Zebah, 74
Zeboiim, 12
Zebul, 43
Zedekiah, 118, 171–72
Zenjirli, 126
Zephaniah, 114

Zerubbabel, 90, 129
Zeus, 205
Ziggurats, 8–9, 179
Zimri-lim, 24, 28
Zion, 159, 186
Zion, Mount, 124–25
Zoan, 49–50
Zoar, 12–13
Zu, 44

GONZALO BÁEZ-CAMARGO was born in Oaxaca City, Mexico, in 1899 of a Methodist family. He taught at the Methodist Mexican Institute in Puebla and was executive secretary of the National Evangelical Council of Mexico, Henry M. Luce Visiting Professor at Union Theological Seminary in New York, a translator, special consultant, and research associate in the United Bible Societies, contributor and columnist of *Excelsior*, Mexico's leading newspaper, and prolific author for publishers all over the world. He died in 1983 in Mexico.